THE SWORD OF HIS MOUTH

THE SOCIETY OF BIBLICAL LITERATURE

SEMEIA SUPPLEMENTS

Edited by

William A. Beardslee

Number 1

THE SWORD OF HIS MOUTH

by

Robert C. Tannehill

THE SWORD OF HIS MOUTH
*Forceful and Imaginative Language
in Synoptic Sayings*

by

Robert C. Tannehill

FORTRESS PRESS
Philadelphia, Pennsylvania

SCHOLARS PRESS
Missoula, Montana

Library of Congress Catalog Card Number:75-18948
ISBN: 0-8006-1501-8

First Fortress Press Edition 1975
Second Printing 1981

Printed in the United States of America   1-1501

CONTENTS

To my Father and Mother

in honor of forty-five years of service

in the Christian ministry

and in gratitude for clearing a space

for wisdom's growth.

For God's word is living and powerful, sharper than any two-edged sword, cutting apart soul and spirit, joints and marrow, and dividing in judgment the reflections and thoughts of the heart.

Hebrews 4:12

. . . from his mouth projected a sharp two-edged sword.

Revelation 1:16

ABBREVIATIONS

Bib	Biblica
BZ	Biblische Zeitschrift
CBQ	Catholic Biblical Quarterly
Int	Interpretation
JBL	Journal of Biblical Literature
JRel	Journal of Religion
NT	Novum Testamentum
NTS	New Testament Studies
TDNT	Theological Dictionary of the New Testament
ThR	Theologische Rundschau
VT	Vetus Testamentum
VTSup	Supplements to Vetus Testamentum
ZNW	Zeitschrift für die Neutestamentliche Wissenschaft
ZThK	Zeitschrift für Theologie und Kirche

Works are cited by the name of the author only or, if reference will be made to more than one work by an author, by author and publication date. For full information see the list of Works Consulted at the end of this volume.

INTRODUCTION

It is my conviction that Biblical scholarship has overlooked the significance of forceful and imaginative language in the synoptic sayings. This is not due to a lack of material with which to work or to the obscurity of the basic data. The data are present for all to see and are occasionally noted, but they seem unimportant. There has been no context of understanding which suggests that the investigation of this material might be worth while. It seems to be "mere rhetoric," which is either unimportant or a hindrance in the search for truth.

Such a view is short-sighted and misleading. How a statement or command is made, the mode of language used, is important. Forceful and imaginative language has a role in human life which other language cannot fulfill, a role which is especially significant for the religious dimension of life. The scholar ignores this when he seeks only the informational content of a text, a content which can be expressed in plain speech. This prevents him from seeing clearly the value of the text, the human good which it might serve. It also prevents him from understanding the text as a meaningful whole, in which form and content unite in significant human utterance. The purpose of a human utterance is seldom restricted to conveying information. If the scholar is concerned only with informational content, he will often not be able to understand fully the speaker's purpose, nor the significance of his strategy of communication, nor the type of response sought from the hearer. Without an accurate understanding of these matters, it is impossible to reach accurate conclusions on the value of an utterance either for the original hearers or for men today.

Biblical scholarship can do better than this. Insights from the field of literature, and from the work of philosophers and theologians concerned with language, provide a new context of understanding which suggests new approaches to Biblical texts. Such approaches are already showing their fruitfulness in certain

1

areas of Biblical study. My own work has been stimulated by
recent research on the parable, particularly that of Robert W.
Funk (1966:123-222), Dan O. Via, Jr. (1967), and John Dominic
Crossan (1973b). These scholars have shown that the parable is a
special mode of language whose powers should not be ignored.
However, I have come to believe that some of the characteristics
which these scholars attribute to the parable, or to metaphor,
apply more broadly to other types of forceful and imaginative
language in the Gospels. Preliminary support for this conviction is
provided by Amos Wilder, whose pioneering work shows the
fruitfulness of a broad interest in the many "modes and genres" of
New Testament language, and by William Beardslee, who has
shown that the intensified proverb, like the parable, is able to jolt
the hearer out of familiar continuities into a new judgment about
existence.

My work is concerned both with developing a context of
understanding which suggests the importance of the data to be
studied and with demonstrating the fruitfulness of this context for
the concrete task of text interpretation. Part I of this book is a
brief summary of my present context of understanding, developed
from the study of certain works of literary theory, philosophy, and
theology, which suggests that investigation of forceful and
imaginative language in the Gospels will be worth while.
Although incomplete and inadequate in many respects, it points
to important possibilities. Part II deals generally with some
important features of synoptic sayings. Part III demonstrates that
the views advanced in the preceding parts can be applied in
detailed study of synoptic texts. It shows that there are features of
the texts which require an appreciation of forceful and
imaginative language and that appreciative investigation of these
features results in deeper understanding of the texts.

The features of texts to which I refer are found not among
things which appear important (they are important because they
are relevant to questions which have already been asked) but
among things which appear unimportant. The questions to which
they give rise may also seem naive and unilluminating. Why do

texts which, on the whole, are very concise nevertheless contain a good deal of repetition? For instance, when we are commanded to not be anxious in Matt 6:25-33, why does the text refer first to the birds and then to the flowers when basically the same thing is said in the one case as in the other? Why are some texts so specific and extreme? Why, for example, are we given instructions in Matt 5:39b-41 concerning a slap on the right cheek, loss of a tunic through court action, and conscription for forced service, instructions which appear both very limited in scope and unreasonable? Why do many texts contain a contrast, often an extreme contrast? In Matt 7:3-5 why are we accused of having a log in the eye, in contrast to the speck in our brother's eye? This language is hardly calculated to gain the acceptance of reasonable men! As we examine such texts, we will find, time after time, that the text is very carefully formed but that this form contributes little to conceptual precision or to the argument and evidence which result in rational acceptance. Perhaps the text is shaped to another purpose. We must use the form of such texts as a clue to the function which they properly perform, just as we might infer the function of a tool from its shape.

While this study is especially concerned with formal features of texts, it will not investigate these in isolation from content. This would actually demonstrate the unimportance of the formal features, for it would suggest that they do not affect content. I wish to show that the formal features to be noted cause the text as a whole to grow in significance and enable it to perform important functions. The significance of a formal feature depends on how it contributes to a particular text. Therefore I will make no attempt to catalogue formal devices but will study a number of texts in sufficient depth to demonstrate the importance of forceful and imaginative language in those particular texts. Sensitivity to the way in which form and content interact in each case is required, for each text will have aspects which are unique. Nevertheless, we will discover that the study of one text will suggest ways that we can approach other texts, so that the argument of the book will be cumulative and will also be suggestive for understanding Biblical passages not discussed here.

I will point out some, of the features shared by different texts during the course of this study. I will also suggest that the "focal instance" and the "antithetical aphorism" are significant classes of texts within the synoptic tradition. However, I make no attempt to classify all texts according to genre or literary type. The study of genre is important and can probably be carried further than has been done in this book. However, we must not forget the difference between the genre of a text, i.e., its typical aspects, and the text itself. Even when a text clearly belongs to a particular genre, it is always something more specific than its genre. It uses generic features in a particular way. The discussion of genre is most illuminating when we are able to understand the function of generic elements in a particular text. Traditional genres are useful because they arouse a set of expectations in the hearer or reader, which may either be fulfilled or thwarted by a surprising twist. The function of the generic elements in a particular text can only be determined by looking closely at that particular text. The more specific and clear the genre, the more effectively it can be used / 1 /. Yet much of the language of the New Testament, and much of our language, does not fit into specific and clear genres but only into general ones, which arouse only vague and general expectations. Therefore genre is not always the most fruitful area of investigation in studying a text.

While discussion of parallels to features of synoptic sayings in other literature would be illuminating, I do not attempt this here, beyond some references to modern literary studies. The absence of references to parallels outside the New Testament does not mean that the formal features are unique to the Gospels. If there is anything unique, it is more likely to be found in the total text, consisting of meanings molded by formal pattern.

I will concentrate on the synoptic sayings tradition, i.e., the material in the first three Gospels which has been transmitted as words of Jesus either without individual narrative setting or in a short narrative scene in which a saying of Jesus is central. Furthermore, I have excluded the parables from consideration, for the importance of literary form in the parables has already been shown by some recent studies (see above, p. 2). From the synoptic sayings I have chosen texts suited to showing the significance of forceful and imaginative language. One cannot assume that this mode of language is as important in all synoptic sayings as it is in the selected texts. However, similar formal characteristics are found in many texts not discussed, so the approach used here should prove fruitful for other texts as well. Since it seemed best to begin with the simplest literary forms, I have concentrated on isolated small units of tradition. Investigation of the relation of these units to their immediate context and their place within the larger structure of a Gospel is also important and will bring out aspects of literary form not adequately considered here.

In studying synoptic sayings I am not primarily concerned with the history of traditions. In many cases I simply study the text as it stands in one of the Gospels. When I do distinguish between an earlier text and later additions or modifications, it is because an important feature of forceful and imaginative language appears more clearly in the earlier version. I am concerned with the literary qualities of texts rather than their age or origin, and I see no simple relation between the two. The argument that the poetic form of some synoptic material is evidence that these are authentic words of the historical Jesus /2/ appears dubious to me. While poetic form may help to preserve an utterance from change, it does not prove that it originated with Jesus. Poetic characteristics such as parallelism, antithesis, and metaphor are widespread in the Gospels and are not confined to the sayings of Jesus. Indeed, in some parts of the tradition there may have been a development toward such forms rather than away from them, and so they are not necessarily evidence for a primitive stage of the tradition /3/. Furthermore, I will not attempt to reconstruct an Aramaic text and comment on its poetic features (see Black: 160-85, and Jeremias, 1971:3-29). The forceful and imaginative language clearly present in the Greek text is sufficient to keep us busy for some time if we know how to ask the right questions.

While the concerns of this study are primarily literary rather than historical, the literary and the historical cannot be isolated from each other. Discourse, especially oral discourse, presupposes a situation which may be quite important to its interpretation (see Lapointe). Furthermore, features of the situation may be reflected in the discourse itself. For instance, the antithetical form of some synoptic material may reflect conflict in the historical situation. It may also reflect a decision to adopt a position outside the prevailing perspective in the historical situation, thus creating conflict. In such cases the conflict is already present in the form of the text and can be considered as a literary phenomenon, but knowledge of the historical situation from other sources can enrich our understanding of the nature of the conflict and of what the speaker is doing through his utterance. Just as historical study can provide a guide and check to literary interpretation, so literary interpretation can play a similar role for historical study. Historical inferences drawn from texts should be made on the basis of sound understanding of their literary qualities. The arguments of historical criticism for a stage of the text earlier than that found in the Gospels are often dependent on some incoherence in the text. The discovery that the offending feature is, after all, a coherent part of the text, e.g., part of a significant tension which gives the text power and depth, may sometimes make such arguments doubtful (cf., e.g., p. 129 below). It is possible that both the literary and the developmental explanations of the text may be true, but the historical critic will have to consider whether his explanation is still necessary.

While I do not want to belittle historical research, the predominant orientation of Biblical scholarship toward the search for historical information seems to me to involve an unfortunate narrowing of the scholar's task. There are texts whose primary purpose is to convey information, but this purpose is not characteristic of Gospel texts, especially not of synoptic sayings. As their form shows, these texts are shaped for a different function. When the scholar uses these texts as sources of information about historical events, persons, or views which lie behind them, he is forcing concerns which are subordinate in the text into a dominant position. This may be legitimate, for there are many purposes which a text may serve. However, it means that the scholar and the text are working at cross-purposes, and the information must be extracted in spite of the stubborn efforts of the text to speak in its own way. In order to remind ourselves of this, it is helpful to distinguish between using a text as a source of information and interpreting a text. One can properly claim to interpret a text only if he takes account of the intention embodied in the text. The interpreter must allow the text to speak in its own way. He must recognize and respect the particular kind of event which is intended to take place between text and reader and clarify the nature of that event for others. The fact that we so often use texts as sources of information suggests that we unconsciously assume that language is primarily an instrument for conveying information and making assertions, an instrument which reaches its perfection in academic discourse, following strict rules of logic. An awareness of other possibilities of language opens an approach to synoptic sayings which may enable us to respect the other purposes embodied in our texts.

The predominance of the search for information about matters behind the text appears also in that branch of New Testament scholarship which would seem to be most closely related to my project. Form criticism is also concerned with the form of texts and seeks to relate this to their function. However, in the classical statements of New Testament form criticism, both form and function are conceived in a narrow way for the sake of the search for what is behind the text. Martin Dibelius and Rudolf Bultmann understood the task of form criticism to be the reconstruction of the origin and history of the small units of tradition and distinguished this from an aesthetic concern with form (see Dibelius, 1929:187-88, and Bultmann: 4). Following the lead of Dibelius and Bultmann, form criticism has been interested in formal characteristics of texts insofar as these can be related to a type of speech used by representatives of a group in particular social situations. Bultmann recognized that there are some formal

features of texts which are not helpful in this regard because their
occurrence cannot be correlated with the literary types and social
settings in which form criticism is interested. Therefore he
distinguished between "constitutive" and "ornamental" motifs
and placed "simile, metaphor, paradox, hyperbole, parallelism,
antithesis and the like" in the latter class (70). This shows
Bultmann's limited interest in form. While form may be important
in helping to trace the history of the tradition, there is little
awareness that form is an integral aspect of a text which must be
considered if its full significance is to be understood. At various
points in the work of Dibelius and Bultmann the assumption
appears that the form and content of a text can be separated
without loss. This assumption appears in the fact that Bultmann
regards the important aspects of literary form listed above as
"ornamental." It appears also in Dibelius' view that the paradigms
do nothing more than illustrate the theological assertions central
to the preaching of the early church (n.d.:24-6), i.e., they merely
support thoughts which can be adequately expressed in sermons
apart from the paradigms /4/.

   Not only has form criticism had a limited interest in form; it has
also limited exploration of the function of texts and text types by
its sociological perspective. It has sought to explain how a text
functioned within the institutions or patterns of life of a group.
While this may be illuminating, the question of function can be
pushed further. The possible functions of forceful and imaginative
language in human life should be explored. Furthermore, social
institutions themselves have a function. They are the expressions
of a culture, and a culture is a patterning of human existence, an
interpretation of what it means to be a man and a people. Thus
social institutions are relatively fixed expressions of an underlying
interpretation of existence. Language is one of the primary means
by which man interprets existence. When we appeal to a social
institution to explain a linguistic utterance, we are appealing from
one form of man's interpretive activity to another, and we do not
necessarily reach a level more basic than the utterance (for a
similar view, see Erhardt Güttgemanns, 1970:256). Language can

not only repeat the past, institutionalized interpretations of a culture but can also challenge the past and gesture toward something new. Such language may occur within an institutional context and use some of its modes of expression, but its function is not just an institutional one. It assumes the deeper function of interpreting reality afresh and revealing its mystery. Certain aspects of a text's form may indicate an intention to play this role.

Traditional form criticism seeks to understand a text on the basis of its origin. This is important, but it does not complete the task of understanding. It is also important to understand what a text is fitted for, what significant human purpose it is shaped to fulfill. Presumably this will be related to its original purpose, but the primary evidence must come from the text itself and must be examined with an awareness of the various powers of language and literature. It is especially important that explanation of a text from its origin or social setting not be used as a way of ending discussion. For instance, Bultmann's appeal to "elements of style typical of popular story telling" to explain repetition in the parables (191) should not be allowed to bring the interpreter's task to an end. One can still ask why "popular story telling" again and again found this feature of style to be useful and why it is useful in the particular parables where it is found. Determining the background of a formal feature does not complete the task of understanding how it contributes to the text as discourse significant for man.

The task before us will be clearer if I summarize the points of difference between it and the form criticism of Dibelius and Bultmann: 1) While form criticism has been concerned with features of texts which help to establish a literary type and its social-historical setting, all formal features which give special qualities to a text, particularly features which increase its power to challenge the will and awaken the imagination, are relevant to the following study. Features which Bultmann dismissed as "ornamental" will be quite important. 2) While Dibelius and Bultmann assumed that form could be separated from content, I will attempt to show that in the texts studied the form is an integral part of the text and contributes in important ways to its significance. 3) Form criticism has sought to relate the form of a text to its function within the institutions of a group. In the following study the function of certain modes of language will be explored beyond the limits of this sociological perspective. 4) The form of a text is not only a clue to its origin in the past life of a group but also a clue to the text's potential for the future. Interpretation must not stop when it has determined the origin of a text; it must go on to show, if it can, its significance as human discourse and how its literary form contributes to this. I am seeking insights and methods which make it possible to do this in a disciplined way.

NOTES

/1/   Wolfgang Richter (133-34) points out that *Gattungen* comprise different planes of abstraction and that the planes of least abstraction are most important.

/2/   C. F. Burney makes a contribution to the study of repetitive pattern in the Gospels, but he was primarily interested in poetry because he regarded it as a guarantee of the tradition's accuracy.

/3/   The extensive use of repetitive patterns in Matthew, not only in the small units of tradition but also in the larger compositions which are the result of redaction, indicates this. Charles H. Lohr suggests how extensive these are. However, I am not sure that these patterns are specifically "oral." We must also take account of the formation of new material by analogy, to which Rudolf Bultmann points (85-86). Heinz Schürmann argues that certain linguistic features were recognized as characteristic of "the language of Christ" in the tradition and so spread to material where they were not originally found. This may also apply to some of the formal characteristics which we will study.

/4/   On the other hand, Klaus Koch's (153ff., 197ff.) discussion of saga and legend as each an "expression of a particular way of thinking" seems to point away from this separation of form and content.

I. THE SIGNIFICANCE OF FORCEFUL AND IMAGINATIVE LANGUAGE

1. *Literary Art and Synoptic Sayings*

The interpreter's assumptions as to what is important appear in the way in which he interprets his texts. Frequently Biblical interpretation involves a translation of the text into clear assertions about historical facts or clear theological propositions. Ideally these assertions and propositions are stated in logical form and use words that can be exactly defined. If the text does not seem to lend itself to this type of translation, the interpreter may give up the effort to understand and turn to cataloguing assorted facts about the text. Or he may point out the text's inadequacies, with a sense of his own superiority.

Such translation of the content of a text into logical statements with clear definition may have a place in interpretation, but we should be aware of the limits of this procedure. There are other types of language which have their own values, of which interpretation must take account. In studying the language of literary art and, to some extent, of religion, Philip Wheelwright (1968) speaks of a "depth" or "expressive" language with characteristics quite different than the language of the scholar's translation. The rules of logic are violated; the importance of clear definition is ignored. Yet the gifted writer does not produce nonsense but something rich with meaning. Wheelwright specifies the characteristics of this language by comparing it to the language of logic and exact definition, which he calls "steno-language." The exact definitions of steno-language contrast with the "soft focus" of the poet's words, which have blurred edges, for they carry a connotative fringe which is difficult to specify fully (1968:86-8). Furthermore, the depth symbol tends to be a "plurisign," which carries "more than one legitimate reference," so that "its full meaning involves a tension between two or more directions of semantic stress" (1968:81). Paradox also involves tension, bringing together two assertions which logically conflict

11

(on paradox see 1968:96-100). Metaphor, too, gains its power from the "semantic tensiŏn" which results from joining heterogeneous elements (1968:102). The importance of tension in a number of these characteristic features of depth language leads Wheelwright to speak elsewhere of "tensive language" (1962:45-69). We will discover that various forms of tension are common within the synoptic texts which we will examine, and the importance which Wheelwright attributes to this feature should cause us to consider the significance of such tension carefully.

The characteristics of depth language mentioned above, as well as others discussed by Wheelwright, are not signs of sickness in language, in spite of their marked contrast with the ideals of logic and clear definition. Nor does depth language cease to be referential when it departs from these ideals. It is precisely because, as T. E. Hulme remarked, "plain speech is essentially inaccurate" (quoted by Wheelwright, 1968:86) that the poet adopts a different strategy. While steno-language enables man to communicate with precision and efficiency, and so is valuable for man's practical and technical affairs, it depends on abstraction, the tacit agreement to ignore those realities and meanings not pertinent to the task at hand and not easily shared. The poet wants to capture more of the rich complexity and individuality of his subject matter. He is not content to speak, in plain speech, of a tree. He wants to convey something of the unique presence of *this* tree. According to Wheelwright, man lives on the "threshold of otherness." Man's awareness of an other involves an awareness of "a certain *such*ness, never adequately captured and expressed by ordinary word usage," and yet, because of poetry, not totally incommunicable (1968:21-4; italics in original). Man also has a sense of an "upward threshold," that is, a "sense of a reality 'higher' — i.e., intrinsically worthier and more real — than himself" (1968:26). Depth language is also able to communicate something of this important aspect of human experience.

Because he believes that depth language is referential, Wheelwright also believes that the characteristics of depth language are a significant clue to the nature of the reality to which it refers. In *Metaphor and Reality* he provides a preliminary sketch of an ontology based on poetic language. The living reality of which such language speaks is permeated with a sense of presence; it is tensive; it is characterized not by sharp dividing lines but by coalescence and interpenetration between subject and object, particular and universal; and it is perspectival, for it can only be glimpsed in part and from varying viewpoints, while ultimate reality remains hidden (153-73). Depth language seeks to convey this reality accurately.

Wheelwright and others (see, e.g., Whalley) are able to argue with some persuasiveness against the assumption that the language of logic and clear definition is the language of reality and the poet's language merely the expression of subjective feelings. Feelings are involved in poetry, but they may arise from the reality which the poet encounters, for reality discloses itself to him as valuable independent of its practical usefulness. This reality therefore calls for his sympathy and love (For an argument that reality consists of events of relationship, of which feeling and value are integral parts, see Whalley: 27-45, 64-76, 96.). The language of logic and clear definition has greater efficiency and precision, but it abstracts from the rich significance of man's encounters with reality. The reality encountered is not allowed to be fully present, and important dimensions of its meaning for man are ignored. Depth language seeks to respond more adequately to the richness of reality.

In this search "tensive language" is an important part of the poet's strategy. It is appropriate not only because man's existence is itself a "pervasive living tension" (Wheelwright, 1962:45-8), but also because the language with which the poet must begin is shaped to the practical concerns of daily living and regularly throws a blanket of superficial familiarity over the reality which the poet wants to explore. Ordinary language used in ordinary ways reveals only the superficialities of ordinary experience. The poet is less like the sculptor who begins with clay or stone than like the sculptor who works with car bumpers to produce something the maker of car bumpers never intended. If he is to escape the tyranny of the superficial, the poet must combine words in strange ways. He must engage in meaningful distortion of his raw material. He must place his work in tension with the old perspective which obscures our vision. His words will show this tension. In the synoptic sayings also we will find reflections in form and language of the necessary fight with the old perspective in order to found the new.

Wheelwright tends to focus on isolated features of poetic language rather than on the poem as a whole. The emphasis of some literary critics on the poem as an organic unity is a valuable supplement (see, e.g., Krieger, 1963:20). They would argue that the words in a poem do not refer directly and atomistically to things outside the poem. Individual words are subjected to the controlling context of the poem as a whole. The meaning of each part is determined by its place within the whole, as words interact with words. To be sure, context is important even in ordinary discourse, for words tend to be equivocal apart from context. However, the pressure of the context in a poem tends to be more intense and complex and to produce not the univocal meanings of ordinary discourse but a rich complexity of meaning. Furthermore, contextual meanings are produced not only according to the patterns of ordinary grammar but through modification of these patterns and the addition of others. Therefore the poem is more than an example of the general language system; it is a system which is unique. Thus the poet loosens words from their ordinary meanings by subjecting them to the pressure of the poem, and his poem is "a pattern of resolved stresses," "an equilibrium of forces" (Brooks: 203, 207), which must be read as a unified whole. To remove or change any part upsets the equilibrium. One corollary of this view is that there can be no fully adequate paraphrase of a poem, for in a paraphrase words and ideas are removed from the controlling context of the poem and the equilibrium is disturbed.

It is the poem itself which determines what is a proper reading of the poem, rather than any statement by the author of what he intended to do or by the reader of how the poem affects him. The poem is a delicate "aesthetic control of the reader" (Krieger, 1963:107), and every reading of the poem should be evaluated and corrected by appeal to this control. Thus the interpreter is directed to the poem in its complex unity as his primary datum. Statements about the author's intention and the reader's response will be relevant only if they can be supported from the poem itself.

Murray Krieger has investigated how a poem can both be an organic unity, its words closed off from direct reference to the outside world, and also be meaningful for human existence. In *A Window to Criticism* he deals with this question in terms of the metaphors of window and mirror. He indicates that the language of poems functions in three ways: "(1) as window to the world, (2) as an enclosed set of endlessly faceted mirrors ever multiplying its maze of reflections but finally shut up within itself, and (3) as this same set of mirrors that miraculously becomes window again" (3). The first of these allows the reader to approach the poem. It is only because the words seem to function in the same way as in ordinary discourse that we have any access to the poem at all. However, at this level we are only dealing with the "raw materials" of poetry and not with the poem itself. The second function of poetic language, represented by the mirrors, corresponds to the emphasis on the poem as organic unity, each part gaining its significance through interaction with the rest of the poem. At a third stage in reading the poem it is again a window to the world. However, this is not the same as stage one. At stage three it is the poem in its mirrored complexity which serves as window, not the separate parts of the poem functioning in their normal way. Therefore something different now appears in the window.

Krieger develops this into an allegory which shows how a poem may both involve withdrawal from the ordinary world and its language and bring about a change in the reader's perception of the world. A wanderer comes upon a glass house filled with interesting objects. At first he peers into the house from the outside, but then, attracted by the objects, he enters. The objects are replicas of things in the outside world, but made with craft and subtlety. As he examines them, he glances out through the window-walls, comparing them with things in the "real" world outside. However, as he becomes more and more fascinated, he ceases to glance out the windows. When he finally does look up, he sees with amazement that the windows have been transformed into mirrors and the objects in the house can be seen in multiple reflections, intriguingly bathed with varied lights. Now the traveler's attention is wholly drawn to these objects and they no longer appear to be mere replicas of what is outside the house. Then another transformation takes place. The mirrors become windows again, but what the traveler sees through them is not what he saw before. The objects of the familiar world outside have taken on some of the features of the objects in the house. They now appear as replicas of the fascinating objects in the house, and this continues to be so even when the traveler leaves the house. To be sure, many of the things outside are only shabby imitations, but in order to make the world a fit place to live, the traveler begins to refashion it after the vision which he had in the glass house (1964:67-9).

This allegory makes clear that a poem may be the medium of a new vision of the world which enables the reader to live in a new way. It performs this important function *as poetry*, not because of certain ideas which may be extracted from the poem. Indeed, concentration on the ideas of the poem rather than on the poem itself will weaken the poem's power to awaken new vision, for abstract ideas do not have the same power to fascinate nor to involve all levels of our being (intellect, sense experience, memory, feelings, etc.), and they are usually easier to integrate into our familiar ways of thinking without disturbing challenge. The interplay between a poem and one's vision of reality will concern us later when we begin to examine some of the synoptic sayings, for we must ask whether the literary qualities of these sayings indicate that they are fitted for a similar function. The previous discussion also suggests that we should look closely at the form of synoptic sayings to see how part interacts with part, modifying and enriching meaning, and how tension between parts twists words away from their surface meanings and points to something deeper. It suggests that we must respect the unity of our texts, regarding each as an equilibrium of forces which is disturbed when any part is examined without attention to the whole.

The views discussed above were developed through reflection on the language of literary art, especially poetry. In spite of the fact that C. F. Burney spoke of "the poetry of Our Lord" (in his book by that title), referring to some of the same texts that we will study, it is not certain that we can properly speak of the synoptic sayings as poetry. It is difficult to determine where poetry ends and prose begins, but there are some important differences between the synoptic sayings and the texts on which a scholar like Krieger bases his conclusions. I must explore some of these differences and explain why the preceding discussion of literary art is nevertheless relevant to our task.

A poem, according to Krieger, is an "aesthetic object." It is something which we value for its own sake and which engages our "intransitive rapt attention" (1963:129, quoting Eliseo Vivas). When a poem is engaged as an aesthetic object, meanings and values "must be seen as lying immanently within the object rather than as transcending the object and thereby leading the spectator back to the world" (1963:129). Krieger significantly modifies this point by insisting that in the end the aesthetic object does become a window to the world, but he would insist that the poem does this properly only when it is also an aesthetic object. This aesthetic dimension is weaker in synoptic sayings than in fine poetry /1/. While these sayings often play with words, this play is not developed to a degree which invites rapt enjoyment of the art of words. Nor are we allowed to leave our world behind in the experience of an object which is valuable in itself. The sayings do not invite contemplation of themselves as objects of value but require us to contemplate our lives. They address themselves to the will of the hearer and demand that he understand and act. It is especially this strong appeal to the will which distinguishes these sayings from aesthetic objects. This would suggest that they fall within the sphere of rhetoric rather than poetry. This must give us pause, for some literary theorists see a sharp contrast between poetry and rhetoric. Krieger, for instance, indicates that his critical tradition "makes its criterion for poetic failure the work's falling into 'mere rhetoric' " (1967:165). He admits that he is operating with a "card-stacked definition" of rhetoric. In this definition two features stand out. Rhetoric refers to language used to persuade, and so "related to decision and action," while "poetry is related to contemplation and . . . free play." Rhetoric also implies that such persuasive language operates in the normal, limited way rather than freeing words from their everyday limitations as poetry does. It attempts to persuade "concerning a propositional claim that can be referred to independently of the discourse" rather than being the necessary medium for a deeper vision of life (1967:166). However, Krieger recognizes the need for "a new and far subtler, far more flexible and even poetic, definition of rhetoric" (1967:176). This hint leads me to suggest that the two aspects of rhetoric mentioned above, its concern with decision and action, on the one hand, and its failure to transcend the propositions of ordinary language, on the other, need not go together. If there is language which demands decision and action and yet is able to break through the limits of ordinary language, making new action possible by conveying a new vision, we would have what we might call a "depth rhetoric," language which does not invite aesthetic enjoyment and yet has a kinship with poetry. This, I believe, is what we find in many synoptic sayings.

It is doubtful that a clear line can be drawn between rhetoric and literary art /2/. The strategies of language traditionally discussed in rhetoric play a major role within literary art; indeed, literature could scarcely be literature without them /3/. Furthermore, some literary critics suggest that "rhetorical criticism" is an appropriate approach to a literary work. Edward P. J. Corbett sketches the role of such criticism (see pp. xi-xxviii). It is concerned with the "interactions between the work, the author, and the audience," and so is particularly appropriate to "those forms of literature which . . . 'have designs on an audience' " (xxii). Rhetorical criticism does not fall under W. K. Wimsatt's strictures against the "Affective Fallacy" because it does not proceed from the subjective effects of the work on the critic or others but "focuses on the text itself" and from there "works *outward* . . . to considerations of the author and the audience" (xvii-xx; italics in original). The critic can "protect himself against impressionism and subjectivism by confining his analysis as much as possible to those elements in the work which are capable of producing an effect of a certain kind on an audience," i.e., "by concentrating on the response as it is potentially contained in the work" (xxi-xxii) /4/. This approach to literature is quite similar to my approach to synoptic sayings in the third part of this study /5./ It is appropriate to these sayings because they do have "designs on an audience." The fact that it is also appropriate to certain literary works suggests that this aspect of our texts does not remove them completely from the world of literary art.

It is difficult to maintain a clear distinction between texts which have "designs on an audience" and those which are aesthetic objects, especially if we agree with Krieger that an aesthetic object may change the way in which we view the world. Furthermore, this distinction must be supplemented by another of equal importance, that between texts which appeal to what an audience already is, to its prejudices, in an effort to persuade, and other texts which, though trying to move an audience, can only accomplish their purpose if they are able to transform the audience deeply. Texts of the latter type may seem to lie on the borderline between rhetoric and poetry. They may appeal to us directly for decision and action, and yet, if they succeed, it is because they have been able to touch the depths from which our personal visions of life arise, an ability which we associate with poetry. It is on this borderline that some of the synoptic sayings are to be found. Indeed, this may be more than a borderline between two other areas. It may be a place large enough to merit attention for its own sake as one of the important possibilities of language.

The organic unity of poetry corresponds to a characteristic of the synoptic tradition. There are several indications of this: 1) It has been recognized for some time that the synoptic Gospels are groupings of small units of material which could circulate separately. It has been possible to identify these small units and distinguish them from later additions because they are unified internally and thereby marked off externally from other material. 2) We will find as we study synoptic texts that the internal relations between parts of the text are of great importance in interpretation. The meaning of the parts becomes clear only as we view them within the whole text as an interlocking unity, which speaks in a deeper and more forceful way than a simple statement.

However, the synoptic sayings seem to lack the complexity which many modern critics expect of good literature. If a writer is to move beyond everyday language, where meanings have worn thin and insight is blocked by stereotypes, he must keep his words from falling prey to easy and shallow interpretation. A poem's disciplined complexity can help to move the reader beyond what he knows and expects. In contrast, the synoptic sayings seem simple and clear. However, the following factors suggest that this judgment may be too hasty: 1) This judgment may in part be due to the assumption that we are dealing with the language of logic and clear definition. If more careful study indicates that the sayings have characteristics of "depth" language, this will show that they are not as simple as they seem. 2) Many of these sayings are clearly attempting to move the hearer to decision and action. However, this clear pressure does not lead to a simple and easy response by the hearer, for what is demanded often contradicts his customary patterns of life. Instead, the distance between the speaker's demand and the hearer's life is emphasized, producing a tension which prevents simple and easy response. 3) In the following studies of synoptic texts we will concentrate on the small units of tradition and will not give adequate attention to their settings. This limitation is justified only by the necessity of beginning with a detailed examination of a manageable body of material. Groupings of small units have their own literary value. The interaction of a text with other texts may greatly increase its complexity and depth. If we were to investigate the relation of a text to its immediate context, to the major literary units within a Gospel, to the Gospel as a whole, and to the whole Bible as a major literary unit, we might discover that in each case the text is part of a larger pattern through which it gains additional nuances and its meaning is reinforced or modified.

The organic unity of our small texts gives to them a gem-like hardness. The interpretation of a Gospel requires us to catch the glint of each little gem while perceiving the small and large patterns of the necklace into which these gems are set, adding a new dimension of beauty /6/. The unity of a small text does not prevent it from interacting with other texts and becoming part of a larger whole, but it does require that such interaction be on the text's own terms. The text must be allowed to be the unique thing which it is; it must be allowed to say its own word sharply. Then we may also hear an answering word from another text — perhaps affirming, perhaps qualifying or contradicting — and find new depth of meaning in the unity-in-tension of the two.

2. Revelation and Imagination

I have mentioned some important characteristics of the language of literary art, the language of the imagination, and have noted that this language may lead the reader to a new vision of himself and his world. Since we are dealing with texts which are explicitly religious, it is also appropriate to consider their mode of language from a theological perspective. This is important because there are some theologians who suggest that forceful and imaginative language has even greater significance than I have so far indicated. The work of Ray L. Hart is particularly helpful, for he has developed in some detail an understanding of man and revelation in which the imagination and imaginative language have a central place. I will begin by summarizing selected aspects of Hart's book.

Revelation, according to Hart, is God's call to man to be man, to become human. Therefore he develops his thought on revelation in conjunction with a regional ontology of man. Ontological thinking about man finds its beginning point in man's

will, by which Hart does not mean the power to make conscious
decisions but an ordering principle in the self which is prior to
perception and thought, influencing both. The imagination is the
will's "mental mode" (116), the medium by which the will interacts
with the world. As such, it has a major role "in the constitution
and expansion of human being" (124), and is the medium of
revelatory knowledge. Revelation, as God's call to man to be man,
is mediated through the imagination, which, as the will's mental
mode, makes possible the modification of the will, the principle of
order at the center of man's being.

The significance of imagination in the constitution of the self
becomes clearer when we consider its role in memory and
intention. Memory, like perception, is selective, an indication that
the will is at work. The memory retains those things which we
endow with significance. The contents of memory exist as
complex memory images, which are the products of the active
imagination. Memory is an essential dimension of the ongoing
self, for "the past is a fund of possibilities bearing upon our
emergent being" (190). However, this fund of possibilities is often
restricted because the imagination becomes passive in the face of
its own previous work. "We exist, for the most part, in the power
of a *custom*arily finished past and so are in bondage to a future
that is only more of the same" (214; italics in original). The
meaning of the past is not fixed once for all but it appears to be
fixed when the imagination no longer works actively in the well of
memory. When this happens, much of the power of the past to
contribute to present being is lost. This loss of power appears
within the Christian tradition when it hardens into fixed meanings
which represent appropriations of this tradition in the past. How
can the imagination be awakened when it has fallen asleep? Hart
speaks of the event of "imaginative shock" in which the
imagination again becomes active. He asserts that "imagination is
put in shock only by language spoken in its own tongue" (216-17).
It is imaginative language which is able to meet the imagination on
its own level, awaken it, and turn it against its own past products.
This means that the power of the Christ-event for the expansion of

human being is released only as we return to the imaginative language which most richly embodies that event and acknowledge it for what it is by responding imaginatively.

Not only memory but also intention is an essential aspect of human being. "To be a self is to be ordered by the will toward a certain direction . . . ; it is to be both a 'something' in every present moment and a *policy* for being something that transcends the present moment in intention" (143; italics in original). Hart distinguishes two forms of intention, the intention of the specific project and the intention of dominant direction. We are conscious of our specific projects, but behind these lie our intentions of dominant direction. These are not the plans and ideals which we think about, but the basic "policy for being something" which we know only indirectly (cf. 148-51). Imagination is involved in both types of intention but most deeply in the intentions of dominant direction. Discursive language is unable to contact and capture the deep workings of the imagination in these basic intentions, but, just as with memory, the shock induced by imaginative language can awaken the imagination to envision a new world toward which the self may be directed. This points again to the importance of language which speaks to the imagination.

Imagination is not only a cognitive but "an ontic power," for it "engages those levels of being in which our creativity is involved, which require human *response* for the maturation of their kind and act of being" (136; italics in original). The relation between being and knowing is a "hermeneutical spiral" which involves an expansion not only of the knowing mind but of the given itself (61-62), for "there are orders of being in which the very *is-ness* of some things depends upon (among other factors) our participation in them" (195; italics in original). This is clearest in the case of the work of art, which is what it is only as it engages our answering imagination. Hart distinguishes between the art object and the work of art. The art object is a potency which in itself is incomplete. It becomes the work of art only as it calls forth the imagination of the perceiver. The work of art, then, is dependent not merely on the imagination of the artist but also on the answering imagination of the beholder or hearer. This does not mean that there is no guidance or control, no right or wrong, in this response, for the art object properly evokes the imagination along particular lines. It contains "lineaments of provocation" which exert "a unique pressure on the tendency of its actual completion in imagination" (260). Revelation also involves the imaginative interaction of revelation's given and receiving man. In revelation man's unique being before God "is presented and actualizable . . . in a way that is formally analogous to the presence and actualization of a work of art" (255). It is not actualized apart from man's answering imagination, but this is provoked and led by that which is prior to it. The given in revelation cannot be simply identified with a previous cognitive fixation of the tradition, which may be passively received. Rather the symbolic tradition, like the art object, has the power to awaken the answering imagination of contemporary man and illumine present being. It is not surprising that this understanding of revelation leads Hart to give preference to imaginative discourse in sifting the Christian tradition for its revelatory potential (cf. 275).

Hart's account of the imagination's role in revelation gives impetus to the careful study of imaginative language in the Bible. More specifically, his account of the imagination's role in memory and intention, central aspects of the self, and of the importance of imaginative language in awakening the imagination to turn against the hardened products of its own past work, suggests that the forceful and imaginative language of the Gospels is shaped to a fundamental purpose which must be respected by the interpreter.

The preceding train of thought may be extended by briefly considering the importance of forceful and imaginative language for ethical action. This is relevant to our task because many of the synoptic texts which we will examine contain commands.

The work of H. Richard Niebuhr provides a suggestive starting point. Niebuhr sought to develop an ethics of responsibility, in which moral action is understood as response to action upon us (1963). Of course, we speak of moral action, as distinct from mechanical reaction, only when "it is response to *interpreted* action upon us" (1963:61; italics in original). Thus the question of how we interpret action upon us becomes central. According to Niebuhr, such interpretation "is not simply an affair of our conscious, and rational, mind but also of the deep memories that are buried within us, of feelings and intuitions that are only partly under our immediate control" (1963:63). Man is more a symbolic than a rational animal. He "is a being who grasps and shapes reality . . . with the aid of great images, metaphors, and analogies" (1963:161). Therefore Niebuhr is concerned with the major symbols by which man interprets situations and responds, especially those symbols which are central to Christian faith.

We can see how the Bible, as the source of many of these major symbols, plays an important role in the moral decisions of the Christian. Furthermore, I would like to suggest that the function of some of the synoptic commandments becomes clearer if we develop Niebuhr's ideas further in the following way: The deep-lying symbols by which we interpret and respond do not form a simple and homogeneous world within any one of us. We carry with us a complex mass of competing symbols. Much will depend on what symbol is dominant as we interpret a particular situation. Biblical texts can be significant not only in contributing to the basic images by which life is structured but also in activating certain of these images in relation to certain types of situations. Since it is through the world of images that we interpret action upon us and respond, imaginative language, language with the power to stir this world of images and to selectively bring it into play, has special significance. In our response to situations much depends on what stands out as important. This is a result of the interpretive image which dominates our understanding of the situation. Forceful and imaginative language may affect our perception of the situation by bringing a new image into play or activating symbols which were recessive, thereby combating perceptions based on other images. We tend to see situations in fixed terms because they have been attached to certain images to the exclusion of others. The text with imaginative power can help us to see situations differently by providing or awakening an alternative image, thereby changing what seems important and unimportant. Thus an imaginative text can act as an *illuminator* of a situation, awakening the moral imagination to envision the situation in a new way. From this new perception, new action may result (for application and further explanation of these assertions, see pp. 74-76 below).

The same thing may be said by picturing man as decision maker in the following way: He responds to the action upon him as seems appropriate to the picture of the situation which appears in the lens through which he looks, a lens which brings some things into sharp focus while other things blur and appear only as background. This lens is always present, but its shape can change, with a resulting change in the features of the situation which stand out in sharp focus. Imaginative language is important in ethical decisions because it is able to act upon the images which make up this lens and thereby change our perception of the situation and our judgment of the action appropriate to it.

Such imaginative language, even when used to make commands, is not to be confused with legal rules. A legal rule is content to regulate external behavior while a text as illuminator inserts itself in the world of images through which we perceive the world. The legal rule permits obedience to be measured by conduct, while the text as illuminator puts insight before conduct and may permit various expressions of that insight in conduct. The legal rule demands legal clarity and so requires literal language; the text as illuminator requires language with imaginative force (see further pp. 72-76 below). In what follows I will argue that the form of many synoptic commands equips them for the latter function rather than the former.

I hope that the reader has come to share with me an interest in the possibility that features of texts which have consciously or unconsciously been dismissed as "merely rhetorical," i.e., unimportant decoration for theological ideas or historical facts, are important after all. They may be indications of a desire to speak with sufficient imaginative force to touch those fundamental images, those prerational visions of self and world, which determine how we think and what we are. Such force, in spite of some clear tendencies toward hyperbole in the Gospels, is not just a matter of shouting loudly and going to extremes. By a variety of means the Gospels speak with strong personal impact, challenging fundamental assumptions, thereby requiring the imagination to awake from its slumbers and interpret the world anew. That is why it is appropriate to speak of *forceful* and *imaginative* language. Our visions of self and world can be sinful or redemptive, false and crippling or a guide to fullness of life. False and crippling visions often hold us in bondage because we cannot imagine anything else. The event which rescues us from these "evil imaginations of the heart" (see H. Richard Niebuhr's use of this phrase [1941:99ff.]) grants to the imagination a new way of seeing which leads to new depth and richness in the personal and communal life of man. For it to be effective, this event must be expressed in a form which enables it to challenge the evil imaginations on their own ground and create something to replace them. This is the appropriate function of forceful and imaginative language.

We can now understand what is lost when we reduce the sayings of Jesus to "plain speech." Plain speech is good for communication within established interpretations of the world but it bypasses the imagination and so has little power to change these fundamental interpretations. Therefore it has little power to change men. The communication of plain speech will be accepted as an "idea" and placed in the pigeonhole where it will least disturb our basic vision of self and world. Or it will be accepted as a rule of behavior without affecting the basic orientation of the self. This will happen if the discourse permits it, for our basic visions show that they are basic by secretly determining our evaluation of everything else. Plain speech does permit this and so permits acceptance on the intellectual level, without any corresponding change in the self, or acceptance as a rule of behavior, without any change in the self's goals. Both are ways in which we protect our old selves against the threat of change. By these means we become hypocrites, usually without being aware of it, and the words of religion cease to be redemptive. We have even learned to treat forceful and imaginative language in this way. But this language resists us, and a little attention will bring this resistance to light. Our study of the form of synoptic sayings is a way of uncovering this resistance, which makes these words both dangerous and important.

3. *Formal Analysis*

The attempt to discover imaginative force in sayings which we have read again and again without the slightest disturbance to our sleeping imaginations may seem a dubious enterprise. If our situation is to change, we must find reasons to question the assumption, engendered by a false familiarity, that we are dealing with platitudes and prosaic instructions. Careful formal analysis can help us to find those reasons. Some explanation of the role of formal analysis in the following studies of texts may be helpful.

The previous references to imaginative language may suggest to some readers an uncontrolled subjectivism in interpretation. Such language arouses the imagination, and doesn't this lead us to wild subjectivity? However, the reader will discover that the interpretations which follow are strongly analytical and contain a considerable amount of detailed argument. Indeed, they may seem too cool and complex, for while there are suggestions of ways in which the texts may challenge us, these are brief and come only after detailed analysis of the text. Thus another question may be raised, the question of whether there is a conflict between the purpose of this language and the method of interpretation which is being used.

To these questions the following reply can be made: Certain formal features of the texts are the public signs that we are dealing with a distinctive mode of language. Biblical scholarship will begin to take this mode of language into account only if convinced that there are observable data with a significance which has been ignored. Formal analysis is a way of pointing to the data so that the question of significance can be raised. Furthermore, imaginative language is not an invitation to uncontrolled subjectivism. An imaginative utterance invites an imaginative response, but not by forgoing discipline and control. A poem is a highly refined system of controls on the answering imagination of the reader. This system of controls is necessary if the poem is to lead us beyond the superficial levels on which our imaginations normally function. Formal analysis can protect us against superficial responses to imaginative utterance by examining in detail this system of controls. This should shield us both against the assumption that we are merely dealing with prosaic instructions and against superficial appropriation in which the text triggers our undisciplined thoughts and emotions, which then overwhelm the text. The discipline of close reading of the text is an attempt to discern the text's own discipline, which may be able to release our thoughts and emotions from their superficiality and blindness.

This formal analysis will be conducted in discursive language, the language of the academic world. Thus there will be a clear difference between the language of the text and the language of interpretation. However, discursive thought can be self-critical. It can recognize what is other than itself, acknowledging its own limits. This makes it useful for our task. To be sure, all analysis tends to rob a text of its unity and compactness. Disassembling the text leads to clarity of the parts, but the text thereby loses the intense and tensive interaction of its parts so important to its imaginative force. Therefore the parts of the text must regain their unity. In the final stage of interpretation the whole text must confront the whole man in the struggle for meaning. Whatever richness of detail the analysis has uncovered must be returned to the complex unity of the text so that the text may be apprehended as a meaningful whole. This is itself an imaginative act. It is the event to which interpretation should lead, but the interpretation is not itself the event. The artful language which can awaken the imagination reveals its full power only in the vibrant unity of the text. At the end of the interpretation, then, the reader must return to the text. In the analysis we will attempt to discern the "lineaments of provocation" in the text and thus set the "answering imagination" on the right track. We will follow these "lineaments of provocation" to the point of making suggestions as to the area of engagement between text and reader, the place where the text calls for the reader's response. At this point my work will stop, for something must be left to you, the reader.

I am arguing that the form of many synoptic sayings indicates that they wish to challenge the reader at a deep level. Therefore I have attempted to carry the interpretations far enough to suggest how these texts challenge us. Some readers may feel that at this point I become "homiletical." However, this is not something tacked on for the pious. The text itself wishes to preach, to call forth faith and obedience. We will miss the significance of the text's forceful and imaginative language if we do not recognize this. If we do not begin to "feel the bite" of the text, we cannot really appreciate why the text is shaped as it is.

Formal analysis which separates form from content is a process of abstraction which reduces living utterance to formal types. If it becomes the goal of investigation, it is an example of the attempt to reduce forceful and imaginative language to something else. Instead, we must catch form in action. We must ask why this particular matter comes to expression in this form. This is different in each text. Therefore the major part of this book will consist of studies of individual texts, one by one.

The language of our texts does not exclude rigorous analysis in interpretation; neither does it exclude rigorous thought on the subject matter of the text. If the text does not do this thinking for us, this does not mean that either the text or the thinking is unimportant. Religion without thought becomes blind and debased; hence the importance of theology. But thought must start from somewhere. It must find a perspective from which to think. Usually thought becomes vital only when an old perspective is challenged and a new one begins to emerge. It is at this point that forceful and imaginative language is important, for it can grant this new perspective from which to think. Such insight does not come merely by putting old thought through its accustomed paces. It arises when there is a challenge to the basic concerns from which thought sprang, a shift in our field of care, with the appearance of a new concern which stimulates thought. It is forceful and imaginative language which inserts itself in the world of our basic concerns and so can give us this new starting point. Thought must be rigorous and hard-headed. It must include the kind of arguments and evidence appropriate to its subject matter. However, this does not lessen the importance of the language which grants us something to think. Paul Ricoeur expresses a similar point by his dictum, "The symbol gives rise to thought" (1967b: especially 19ff. and 347ff.) /7/. For Ricoeur's philosophical program this means that philosophy cannot be presuppositionless but must begin with a meditation on the full, rich language of symbol and myth. Then, through a hermeneutics of symbols, it must promote their meaning "in the full responsibility of autonomous thought" (1967b:350). It is not only for the philosopher that depth language gives rise to thought. Within the world of everyday affairs the man who hears the forceful challenge of the text, or is caught by its seductive strangeness, begins to think, for the new vision granted by the text seeks expression in the multifarious world of daily thought and action.

Appendix: Linguistics and the Search for "Deep Structure"

Noam Chomsky, in his efforts to exhibit language as a system of rules which, once mastered, are used over and over to form and interpret new sentences, distinguishes between the "deep structure" and the "surface structure" of sentences. The variety of surface structures in sentences conceals deep structures which are simpler and much more regular, and there are regular rules of transformation which link these deep and surface structures. Furthermore, the semantic interpretation of a sentence is dependent solely on the lexical items and on the grammatical relations present in the deep structure. The transformations do not introduce new meaning (see 1966:33, and 1965:16, 132, 136). Thus the complexities of language can be reduced to "kernel" sentences which consist solely of "simple, declarative, active sentences" (1957:80) or to more abstract structures behind these simple sentences.

There is currently a good deal of interest in applying linguistic principles to the analysis of literary texts. Much of this interest is guided by the theory that principles which have proved useful in the study of language as sentences may also apply to larger units of language. A text, or a text-type, may also have a deep structure which determines its formation as meaningful discourse and its interpretation. If so, it would be important for interpretation to exhibit this underlying structure and system of rules. This leads to a search for structure behind the surface structure of the text. Two varieties of this search which are already making an impact on Biblical studies and theology are the structuralism influenced by Claude Lévi-Strauss, which tends to reduce a text to a system of contrasts not apparent on the surface /8/, and the effort of Erhardt Güttgemanns to refashion Biblical interpretation and theology on a linguistic basis (see 1971, and Güttgemanns' articles in *Linguistica Biblica*). Güttgemanns takes over some of the categories of Chomsky.

While insights from linguistics show promise for the analysis of Biblical texts, it will take some time to develop proper methods. This is not only because the application to Biblical texts is new but also because text linguistics as a whole is in process of rapid development. In the meantime caution is necessary, particularly with regard to claims made for the "deep structure" or "base" of a text. There are at least three factors which should lead us to be cautious at this point:

(1) Speaking of "deep structure" may enable the scholar to point out important similarities between apparently different sentences of texts, but it is doubtful that the meaning of so-called "surface structures" is completely reducible to "deep structures." While reduction of a poem to Chomsky's "kernel sentences" might teach us something about it, its meaning (if it is a good poem) would certainly be impoverished. The various syntactic forms which Chomsky classifies as "surface structure" are necessary to

the poem's meaning, for they promote delicate interactions and modifications of its words. The rich and subtle meanings which result must not be excluded from the meaning of poetry. Something similar is true of stories. Benjamin N. Colby has pointed out that any complete description of narrative structure must take account of "highlighting structure," features of the narrative such as contrast, use of initial and final position, and repetition which focus attention on particular aspects of the narrative (186-90). Departure from the surface structure of the text may change these highlighting effects, thereby changing the balance of emphasis and to some extent the meaning. In light of this it is important that Chomsky has recently modified his position, recognizing that both surface structure and deep structure can contribute to the meaning of a sentence (1970:70ff.). For instance, the focus and presupposition of a sentence are determined by the intonation center of the surface structure, and there are other indications that the previous theory needs to be modified.

(2) One should also be cautious about assuming that "deep structures" have some sort of ontological status in the natural language or in the mind. Fritz Hermanns has recently argued that so-called "descriptions" of deep structures are actually translations into artificial languages, useful because they enable the linguist to compare the natural language with an artificial language which is simple and regular, but not a disclosure of the underlying reality of language. He quotes with approval Wittgenstein, who, in his later thought, recognized the value of setting up objects of comparison but was sceptical of arriving at a single, final analysis of our language (75; see Wittgenstein: sect. 91, 130).

(3) The possibility of viewing human speech as a structured system is based upon the decision to exclude what is individual in speech and incidental to the system. Ferdinand de Saussure, whose emphasis on the systematic structure of language has been very influential in modern linguistics, distinguished between language (*langue*) and speaking (*parole*) (7-23). Speaking refers to

the actual combinations of sounds produced by a particular speaker at a particular time and includes all features that are merely individual and momentary. Language, on the other hand, is the social system which enables us to interpret what we hear by specifying the significance of certain features. The terms "competence" and "performance" are often substituted for "language" and "speaking," but the decision to separate these two aspects continues to be fundamental in modern linguistics.

Paul Ricoeur has devoted considerable thought to the consequences of this decision. He points out that the following characteristics of the event of speaking are lost if we think only of language as a system: speaking is an *act* involving *free choice*, producing combinations which are *new*. Furthermore, it is in the act of speaking that language has both reference to the world and a subject who speaks (1969a:87-88). In contrast, the study of language as system is based upon a fundamental "decision to keep within the enclosure of the universe of signs. By virtue of this decision the system of signs no longer has an outside, but only an inside" (1967a:17) /9/. However, the fact that language transcends itself is basic to its significance. The language system, which in itself is only a potential, exists in order that it may be activated by a speaking subject in referring to a world. This is indicated by the peculiar function of certain words in the system, such as the word "I." "The meaning of I is formed only at the moment when the person speaking appropriates its sense to designate himself." This pronoun "lies there in my language like a ready tool for use in converting this language into communication through my appropriation of this empty sign" (1967a:25). This insight is relevant to the interpretation of texts also. The task of interpretation leads beyond structural explanation, in which the text is viewed as a language system, to the state of appropriation, in which the text regains reference to an external world, the world of the reader. This actualization of the text is similar to the act of speaking in which the language system is personally appropriated to speak of a world (1970:188-200).

Ricoeur not only makes us aware of the limits of the approach to language as structure or system but also helps clarify the issue of whether exact analysis by linguists dispels the mystery of literature which many have treasured. He approaches this issue through his study of the symbol. The symbol, like other language, is subject to exact linguistic description as part of a language system which is viewed as closed. However, symbolism may be understood not only by what constitutes it but also by what it wishes to say. It is hermeneutics which is concerned with language as saying. This entails both a strength and a weakness.

The strength and the weakness of hermeneutics is always there; the weakness because, taking language where it escapes from itself, hermeneutics also takes it when it escapes from a scientific treatment, which begins only with the postulate of the cloture of the signifying universe . . . . But this weakness is its strength, because the place where language escapes from itself and us is also the place where language comes to itself: it is the place where language is *saying* (1969b:68; italics in original).

When hermeneutics encounters the calculated ambiguity of symbolism, it will ask, "*In order to say what?*" (1969b:78; italics in original). It is interested in symbolism because "it reveals, by its structure of double-sense, the ambiguity of being: 'Being speaks in many ways' "(1969b:68). Thus one can agree with the linguist that

there is no mystery in language; the most poetic symbolism, the most sacred, operates with the same semic variables as does the most banal word in the dictionary. But there is a mystery of language: it is that language says, says something, says something about being. If there is an enigma of symbolism, it resides completely on the plane of manifestation, where being's equivocality comes to be said in the equivocality of discourse (1969b:79, with a slight change in the translation) /10/.

Ricoeur helps us to see, then, that scientific study does not dissipate the mystery *of* language nor detract from the special importance of symbolism and other aspects of literary art for revealing mystery.

While the arguments above do not exclude the possibility of studying "deep structures" of texts, this course will not be attempted in the following. Important features of forceful and imaginative language would be lost if we were to concentrate on analysis at a level of high abstraction. This also means that our methods will be less esoteric than some mentioned above.

NOTES

/1/   This holds for the parables also, in spite of Dan Via's assertion that they are aesthetic objects (1967, especially ch. 3).

/2/   The tendency to contrast the two is relatively recent. Walter J. Ong points out that "rhetoric, . . . for all practical purposes, from antiquity until the eighteenth century, included poetic. . . . Poetry enjoyed no particular status as an independent academic discipline whereas rhetoric enjoyed enormous academic prestige, so that any use of words for effects other than the strictly logical was thought of as formally governed by rhetoric" (6).

/3/   According to Northrop Frye, "If the direct union of grammar and logic is characteristic of non-literary verbal structures, literature may be described as the rhetorical organization of grammar and logic. Most of the features characteristic of literary form, such as rhyme, alliteration, metre, antithetical balance, the use of exempla, are also rhetorical schemata" (245).

/4/   H. R. Jauss, noting a neglect of the audience in recent literary theory, has announced a program of study which will focus on the "reception and impact" of literary works. This is a program of much broader scope than Corbett's rhetorical criticism, for it is concerned with literary history as a complex series of encounters between a new work and the given horizon of expectations at a particular time, resulting in "horizon change."

/5/   This suggests the title "rhetorical criticism" for our task, in spite of the bad connotations which the word rhetoric has developed. See the use of this phrase by James Muilenburg (1969:8ff.) and the title of Amos Wilder's book *Early Christian Rhetoric: The Language of the Gospel.*

/6/   This statement is necessary to balance Erhardt Güttgemanns' rightful emphasis on the Gospel as a literary form which is more than the sum of its parts (1970:184-88 and *passim*).

/7/   H. Richard Niebuhr had a similar understanding of the relation between the revelatory image and reason (see 1941:109).

/8/   Some discussions of structuralist interpretation of the New Testament and examples of this approach: Roland Barthes, Louis Marin, Jean Delorme, Robert A. Spivey, Richard Jacobson, and Dan O. Via, Jr (1974).

/9/   To be sure, linguists analyze the communication event, but in such analysis "sender," "receiver," etc., appear as functions of the language system.

/10/   The French text of this article may be found in *Le conflit des interprétations* (64-79).

II. PATTERN AND TENSION IN SYNOPTIC SAYINGS

As we turn now to the synoptic Gospels, we will find in the sayings to be examined that the speaker frequently appeals to some aspect of the experience or tradition of his hearers in the effort to move his hearers to new understanding and insight. Since speaker and hearer are separated by a broad chasm, a bridge is needed. Therefore the speaker introduces a point of comparison, which, whether viewed positively or negatively, becomes the means of communication across this chasm. The speaker speaks to the hearer by means of something which both share, urging the hearer to consider his own situation and behavior in light of this point of comparison. The point of comparison provides the fulcrum by which the speaker hopes to move the hearer to a new position. Thus we find in the texts to be studied later that there is reference to birds and flowers in Matt 6:25-33; to the hypocrites in Matt 6:2-6, 16-18; to the Gentile rulers in Mark 10:42-44; to a speck in the eye in Matt 7:3-5; to Noah and Lot in Luke 17:26-30; and to predicting the weather in Luke 12:54-56. We will want to examine how the speaker uses this point of comparison in these texts.

We will also discover that repetitive pattern and tension are common features of the texts which we will examine. It will be helpful to discuss these features at some length before we begin to study individual texts.

We are not always aware of the extensive use of repetitive patterns in the synoptic Gospels, for it seldom impresses us as *just* repetition, which would be boring. However, close examination shows that such patterns are widespread and sometimes carefully developed. They range from repetition of words or short phrases and use of similar phrases with a rhythmic beat to couplet parallelism and even to parallelism of quite elaborate structures which T. W. Manson did not hesitate to call "strophes" (cf. 1955:54-56). Why are such repetitive patterns so important in the synoptic tradition? The basic informational content of the text could be conveyed in simpler form. Why are repetitive patterns preferred?

Here we encounter a major indication that the language of the Gospels wishes to do more than convey information and ideas. Some other interest is at work; some other function is being fulfilled. In seeking to understand this function, it is helpful to recall that repetitive patterns have been developed into a fine art in poetry. Meter, rhyme, and alliteration are all repetitive patterns, and if these are not used, other patterns are usually developed to help make the poem a poem. According to Northrop Frye, "some principle of recurrence seems to be fundamental to all works of art" (77), and the application of this to poetry is supported by other scholars /1/. The repetitive patterns of sound and thought in poetry may be extremely subtle and complex or they may be quite simple, as in the first three lines of T. S. Eliot's "Ash-Wednesday":

> Because I do not hope to turn again
> Because I do not hope
> Because I do not hope to turn

This seems to be repetition at its most primitive, the rhythm of the incantation, for only the length of the line varies. Yet this slight variation invites us to turn the phrase over in our minds, to see it with different points of emphasis and from different angles. Although no idea has been expressed that was not already in the first line, the phrase begins to expand in meaning and continues to expand in the more varied repetition of the phrase in the rest of the poem. In other words, the phrase becomes poetry through this repetition with subtle variation.

One of the simplest forms of repetition is the immediate repetition of a word. This occurs in poetry but also in ordinary speech, as when the scholar's reply to a request to stop writing and do something useful is a resounding "No, no!" rather than a simple "No." The basic information in the first answer is also contained in the second, but the repeated "No" conveys the message more emphatically. It indicates the importance of the matter to the speaker and the emotional force behind the decision. As Heinrich Lausberg says,

Repetition is useful for forcefulness, which most of the time has an affective stress . . . . The sameness of the repetition implies an affective surcharge: the first occurrence of the word has the normal semantic function of supplying information . . . , the second occurrence of the same word presupposes the information-function of the first occurrence and goes beyond it with an affective-enforcing function. (310-11)

The simple observation that repetition adds force and feeling to the words is already significant for understanding the mode of language in which such repetition is found. It indicates that this language deals with areas where thought is not separate from feeling and where more than ordinary force is necessary if the hearer is to respond rightly.

In poetry we find repetitive patterns which are much more complex than the simple example above. We find a complex interaction of rhythmic pattern, sound pattern (rhyme, alliteration, assonance), and patterns of meaning which subtly modify each other. Certain words stand out because of their place in the rhythmic pattern; they are modified through interaction with other words which have phonic similarities, and they grow in meaning through repetition in several contexts or through entering into relations with synonyms and antonyms. The importance of such patterns in poetry suggests that we should investigate the major forms of repetitive pattern in synoptic sayings.

C. F. Burney, in his discussion of Jesus' sayings as poetry, concentrates on parallelism, rhythm, and rhyme, all of which are repetitive patterns /2/. While one could criticize Burney's exclusive attention to these features, his work did call attention to the importance of repetitive patterns in the Gospel tradition. He was correct that parallelism is an important formal characteristic of the language of the Gospels. We find the parallelism of short paired lines which is so common in Old Testament poetry. However, there is a tendency toward parallelism of more complex structures (cf., e.g., Matt 6:2-6, 16-18). Furthermore, there is less use of traditional word pairs (see Gevirtz), for the parallel constructions commonly repeat the *same* words, except for a few significant changes (cf., e.g., Mark 8:35, Luke 17:26-29), and sometimes form an extended series, using a number of synonyms or referring to a number of similar situations, rather than being confined to a pair of lines (cf., e.g., Luke 6:37-38a).

Wherever we find parallel structures, a process of "coupling" takes place between words which correspond within them. We no longer hear the words separately but in their interaction with each other. One such coupling tends to suggest other couplings, so that even when the parallelism is not complete, similarities and contrasts which may exist between other words are "foregrounded" (see Levin). Such repetitive patterns encourage us to turn a thought over in our minds. Generally words slip past us too quickly. We absorb their conventional meaning and then pass on to something else. Poetry must slow us down and make us listen more carefully, so that we realize that there is more to these words than we thought. The simple device of saying things twice involves a retardation of the forward movement of thought which gives place to deeper meaning, including the felt meanings which are important to our total humanness. The coupling of elements in parallelism also causes words to blend and modify each other. Synonyms are not simply synonyms. They differ in subtle ways, and the parallel lines contain significant variations, thereby bringing out different aspects of a thought, helping it to grow in importance and richness of meaning /3/. This gives the words a softer focus /4/ and may loosen words from their literal sense, especially when a word is coupled with another word which is not literally equivalent. Furthermore, a repetitive pattern embracing a series of particulars can point us beyond the literal sense of the words by suggesting that a series is open ended, that the pattern extends to many situations which have not been named (see below, pp. 69-70). There is a connection between repetitive pattern and a sense of "more," for repetitive pattern suggests a rhythm, and when a rhythm is established we anticipate its continuance. When various elements are set within a repetitive pattern, we also experience an expansion of meaning within the pattern. We find it connected not only to *this* but also to *that*, which leads us to expect it capable of more expansion.

Proper emphasis is crucial in a text which, like a poem, is an equilibrium of stresses. Repetition emphasizes, thus allowing a text to disclose its own points of emphasis and so providing a key to the proper interpretation of the text /5/.

Repetitive pattern also gives to a text unity and particularity. The pattern makes clear what belongs to the text and what does not, for it makes the text stand out as something unique, something unified in itself and distinct from all words that do not fit this pattern. In a great poem it is very difficult to change anything without doing damage. In most of the material in the Gospels the patterns are not that complex and demanding. However, something of the same result is achieved: the text presents itself strongly in its uniqueness. This is important, for artful language must have the strength to stand up against our preconceived world. Only then do we listen carefully, so that the text gives rise to new thought. This goal may be furthered by patterns which, in themselves, are quite artificial, such as rhyme and meter. Such patterns serve to loosen language from the patterns of everyday, setting up a competing "logic" or sense of rightness for the words of the poem, which can coax us away from everyday logic and persuade us to allow the text to have its own way long enough to lead us to new insight.

Repetitive pattern also makes it possible to arouse expectancy, which may be used in various ways. This is especially clear when we have a threefold repetition of a pattern. It is no accident that threefold repetition is common not only in the Gospels but also in nursery tales (recall the three little pigs, the three bears, etc.) /6/. Two instances are sufficient to establish a pattern firmly. We then approach the third instance with a definite expectation that it will conform to this pattern. To be sure, we may suspect that the pattern will be twisted in the third instance (the third little pig triumphs over the wolf), but there is an element of suspense in this anticipation, which is the result of the pattern established by the first two instances. The pattern of expectation may function in several ways, then. It points forward to the third instance, and the third instance may simply be a forceful example of this same pattern. In that case, it becomes the climax, for we approach it with the feelings and meanings gathered from the two previous instances (see, e.g., Mark 14:66-72). However, the third instance may contain an important difference. Then the difference stands out strongly. The first two instances serve as a foil for the third, our attention being attracted by the variation in the pattern. Contrast within a pattern is a way in which a skillful speaker points to what is crucial, for the contrast can be limited to a single dimension of entities which are otherwise similar. Therefore the crucial concern is not obscured by irrelevant differences /7/. Here also the third instance gains in meaning and force through the pattern established by the first two. Our attention is concentrated on a single, sharp antithesis. Antithetical elements are mutually interpretive. We understand the significance of our loss in the light of another's gain. It is the fact that they are part of a common pattern that causes this interaction of meaning between the contrasting elements /8/ and forces us to face the resulting tension (cf. below on Luke 12:54-56, 9:58). Antithesis is also common when there are only two instances of a pattern. This is possible because the repeated elements of the pattern make clear that the differences are to be understood as antithetical. However, the threefold pattern makes possible the firm establishment of expectancy, which results in a more forceful contrast, with special emphasis on the climactic third instance.

Earlier I asserted that even simple repetition adds something, for the thought is presented with emphasis and with emotional overtones. However, much depends on how repetitive pattern combines with other features of language. Repetition does not always have a poetic effect. Everything depends on *what* is emphasized through repetition. Repetition also occurs in very unpoetic lists. Such lists reduce words to their informative function. They become digits supplying one bit of information necessary to complete a series. This is illustrated by some of the

Biblical genealogies. They are certainly repetitive, but not poetic. The extensive repetition causes the repeated elements to fade from consciousness, so that our attention focuses solely on the changing names. These names fall into an easily recognized class, that of ancestors in genealogical order. This teaches us several things about the effect of repetition. First, while repetition of a pattern a few times may enforce that pattern, lengthy repetition causes it to fade from consciousness in favor of any varying elements. Second, if the varying elements consist only of members of a common class, the effect is not poetic. This is especially true if the text strives to be exhaustive rather than suggestive in its enumeration. However, if the repetitive pattern is the matrix of imaginative language, the pattern can heighten the imaginative power of such language. We will pay special attention to such cases in our study of synoptic sayings.

In the discussion of particular passages which follows I will try to show that careful use of repetitive pattern can give material which is prosaic, or, at best, mildly poetic, potency for "resonance" (cf. Whalley: 148). By resonance I mean that the imaginative power of such material is sufficiently amplified and enriched that it challenges our preconceived perceptions of the world, activates our imaginations through the "sympathetic vibrations" awakened in the deeper layers of the self, and so opens us to new ways of perceiving, feeling, and acting. Resonance means an increase in both richness and intensity. The responsive reader becomes aware that the text has wide-ranging implications, that it is touching upon deep areas of experience which concern him profoundly, and that these words have the power to reorder his life. This may appear in the reader's realization that the text invites and rewards meditation. It may also appear in the realization that these words are dangerous, that the solid earth is beginning to shift beneath our feet and we had better look for shelter. When the text achieves such resonance with the reader, there is a sense of heightened awareness, of the questionableness of the common, of the unimportance of what we thought was important and the presence of a deeper reality.

Burney detected not only parallelism but also rhythm and rhyme in the Gospels. In many cases his views on rhythm and rhyme cannot be justified on the basis of the Greek text. Since we have excluded reconstruction of a hypothetical Aramaic text, these cases will not be considered. We do occasionally find rhyme in our Greek text (cf., e.g., Matt 5:4, 6-9; 6:9c-10b). However, it is not common and, when it does occur, it seems to be the incidental result of parallelism and grammatical inflection. Therefore, rhyme will receive little attention in our discussion. There are passages of the Greek text, however, in which rhythm plays a significant role. In these passages we do not find a pattern of accent nor of long and short syllables. Instead we find a rhythm of small sense units in which a major word and its adjuncts rhythmically balance other such units. As Burney saw (102-03), this kind of rhythm is closely related to parallelism. In fact it seems to be a secondary result of parallelism. In Biblical parallelism the line is grammatically complete and expresses a complete thought. The parallel lines commonly subdivide in corresponding ways into smaller sense units. These small units within the line may vary in length. They are determined by two factors: by the pressure which parallelism exerts toward grouping units within the lines so that the lines correspond and by natural grammatical groupings within the sentence. Because in parallelism the small grammatical units within adjacent lines tend to balance one another, it is natural to bring out this balance by reading them rhythmically. This is especially true since the small units are natural sense units, so that the rhythm reinforces the meaning /9/. Matt 7:7-8//Luke 11:9-10 is a clear example:

αἰτεῖτε Ask,	καὶ δοθήσεται ὑμῖν and it will be given you;
ζητεῖτε seek,	καὶ εὑρήσετε and you will find;
κρούετε knock,	καὶ ἀνοιγήσεται ὑμῖν and it will be opened to you.

πᾶς γὰρ ὁ αἰτῶν   λαμβάνει
For every one who asks   receives,

καὶ ὁ ζητῶν   εὑρίσκει
and he who seeks   finds,

καὶ τῷ κρούοντι   ἀνοιγήσεται
and to him who knocks   it will be opened.

Each of the small units above we may designate a "foot" in this type of rhythm. We have here, then, a rhythmic pattern of two feet per line. In spite of the fact that the number of syllables and accents in each foot varies, the division of each sentence into two elements is so clearly marked and the parallelism is so strong that it is difficult not to read this rhythmically. The parallelism makes clear what corresponds to what, and the voice naturally emphasizes this correspondence by making the units rhythmically similar. In English it is natural to put one strong accent in each of the small units above, with the accent falling on the most important word (here the verb in every case).

That the rhythm of such texts was appreciated is clearest in cases where the parallelism is less strict, but rhythmical balance is still maintained. In these cases also the rhythm is dependent on the overall parallelism. The rhythm serves to support this parallelism, for a sense of balance between the lines is preserved while allowing more flexibility of expression. For instance, in Luke 6:29-30 there is variation in both the order and the nature of the parts, and yet the basic parallelism is maintained, in part because there is rhythmical balance between the three lines of four feet each.

τῷ τύπτοντί σε   ἐπὶ τὴν σιαγόνα
To him who strikes you   on the cheek

πάρεχε   καὶ τὴν ἄλλην
offer   the other also;

καὶ ἀπὸ τοῦ αἴροντός   σου τὸ ἱμάτιον
and from him who takes away   your cloak

καὶ τὸν χιτῶνα	μὴ κωλύσῃς
the tunic also	do not withhold.

παντὶ αἰτοῦντί σε	δίδου
To everyone who asks you	give;

καὶ ἀπὸ τοῦ αἴροντος τὰ σὰ	μὴ ἀπαίτει
and from him who takes away your goods /10/	do not ask again.

We have here a series of four parallel commands. The last two are only half as long as the first two, yet a rhythmical balance is maintained, for taken together they balance the longer commands. Matt 6:19-20 is another rhythmical passage.

μὴ θησαυρίζετε ὑμῖν	θησαυροὺς	ἐπὶ τῆς γῆς
Do not lay up for yourselves	treasures	on earth,

ὅπου σὴς	καὶ βρῶσις	ἀφανίζει
where moth	and rust	consume

καὶ ὅπου κλέπται	διορύσσουσιν	καὶ κλέπτουσιν
and where robbers	break in	and rob,

θησαυρίζετε δὲ ὑμῖν	θησαυροὺς	ἐν οὐρανῷ
but lay up for yourselves	treasures	in heaven,

ὅπου οὔτε σὴς	οὔτε βρῶσις	ἀφανίζει
where neither moth	nor rust	consumes

καὶ ὅπου κλέπται	οὐ διορύσσουσιν οὐδὲ κλέπτουσιν
and where robbers	do not break in nor rob.

Vs. 21, which follows, seems to contain two lines of two feet each, which changes the rhythmic pattern and sets it off somewhat from vss. 19-20. The concern for rhythm in vss. 19-20 is shown by the fact that the last verb of each verse is superfluous as far as the meaning goes. When robbers break in we know what they do. We don't need to be told that they rob. Nor would the overall parallelism of the two verses be damaged if these verbs were omitted. However, they do serve to fill out the rhythm /11/.

Other passages could be cited, but the examples given above are sufficient to illustrate a type of rhythm which develops, perhaps secondarily, when there is no concern to count syllables or accents but a strong sense of parallelism, as well as a strong sense of what words are important and of how they group into sense units. The line consists of a major syntactical unit and the foot of a minor syntactical unit, so that a noun, a verb, a participle, etc., form the core of a foot and the conjunctions, articles, prepositions, and generally the personal pronouns attach themselves to these more important words. This leaves some uncertainties in determining how the words of a line should be grouped, but we are dealing with rhythm which is an outgrowth of parallelism and for which there probably were no detailed or strict rules. We are least likely to go astray in rhythmical analysis if we look both at the natural syntactical units, consisting of an important word or an important word and its adjuncts, and at the way in which parts of parallel lines balance one another, suggesting certain divisions within the lines.

We should not force a rhythmic pattern on texts where its presence is doubtful. In many passages where a sharp-eyed scholar might detect rhythm the sense of rhythmic recurrence is not strong enough to make the effort worth while. In a sense, all parallelism is rhythmic, for in it we find a pattern of recurrence. But many of the parallel units which we will examine are too large and complex to sustain a sense of rhythmic beat. Too much takes place between occurrence and recurrence. When we encounter short lines with similar parts, however, the rhythm is unmistakable, for the parallel sense units return fast enough and often enough to give a strong sense of recurrence. This is the case especially in Matt 7:7-8 above. Such rhythm has the same effect as the rhythmic beat of music. It involves us more fully in the experience of hearing. We respond not only with the mind but also with the feelings and the body. Thus the rhythm suggests that a more than intellectual response is appropriate. It invites the whole man to step into its meaning /12/.

Rhythm can also be a way in which a text asserts its own unity

and particularity, marking itself off from all language which does
not conform to its rhythm, and so claiming the right to be heard as
a unique utterance rather than as an example of what we all know
and say. This claim is important to the work of art, for it gives it
power to resist our tendency to reduce it to a commonplace (cf. p.
43 above). However, many synoptic passages which have other
features of poetic form show no overall rhythmic pattern. In these
cases rhythm does not contribute to the text's unity, but it may
have another function. A special purpose may be served by
making a *part* of the text markedly rhythmic. This may reinforce a
contrast between the rhythmic portion and the rest of the text.
Furthermore, a rhythm, once established, should continue, we
feel. If it does not, we are surprised and left ill at ease. Or we
anticipate its end and await it with suspense, feeling the end more
sharply because of this.

In the parable of the two houses (Matt 7:24-27) we find an
example of this use of rhythm. The parable is basically antithetical
in form. The key features in the antithesis, i.e., the different
foundations of the two houses and the corresponding difference in
their power to resist the storm, stand out sharply because they are
embedded in a pattern of parallelism. This is true of both versions
of the parable, though there is less literal repetition in Luke (cf.
Luke 6:47-49). Nevertheless, there is a significant difference
between the two versions, for Luke places more emphasis on the
human activity of building while Matthew emphasizes the threats
to the structure. The latter is accomplished through a rhythmic
series of similar short clauses. Matthew's version contains a
stylistic contrast. Each half of the antithesis is introduced by a
fairly lengthy sentence with relative clauses, or relative clause and
participles (7:24, 26). However, when the story comes to the storm
which threatens the house, not only do we find graphic detail
which is not present in Luke but also the style changes to a
rhythmic series of short clauses connected by "and" (7:25, 27).
This stylistic change makes the rhythmic series stand out more
clearly. We are encouraged to see vss. 25 and 27 as a rhythmic
series by the similarity in meaning of the clauses (referring to

aspects of a storm), the consistent pattern of word order (the verb is always first, emphasizing the action), and the similarity in length of clauses. The shortness of these clauses contrasts sharply with the preceding verse, and, since the clauses are so short and the pattern returns quickly, we feel a rhythmic beat. This is clearest in the first three clauses ("And the rain fell, and the floods came, and the winds blew"), for each consists of the same grammatical elements in the same order. Once established, the rhythm tends to persist, carrying over to the following clause, which is also a line of two rhythmic feet with the verb as the first major word (vs. 25: καὶ προσέπεσαν / τῇ οἰκίᾳ ἐκείνῃ, "and beat upon/that house"). However, what follows (vs. 25: καὶ οὐκ ἔπεσεν, "and it fell not"; vs. 27: καὶ ἔπεσεν, "and it fell") is clearly shorter, consisting of only one major word in the Greek, and cuts off the rhythm. This makes these words stand out and, especially in vs. 27, strengthens the meaning, suggesting a sudden and dramatic collapse, a suggestion made explicit by the last clause of vs. 27.

Here the rhythm of the clauses enforces the meaning, seeking to carry that meaning below the level of the general and objective into the feeling-filled world of the personal. We are not merely told about stormy weather; we feel the blows of the elements in the threatening rhythm of the clauses. We are not merely told that a house fell; we feel it collapse in the collapse of the rhythm. Since the hearer knows that these words are not merely about houses but speak parabolically of *him*, this rhythm is able to awaken an answering vibration in our deep-lying fears and desires (further examples of the use of rhythm in parts of texts are discussed below, pp. 119-21, 146-47).

Repetition without variety would be boring. It is repetitive pattern combined with significant variation which gives richness and interest to language. If this variation within the pattern embraces contrasting elements, the language will gain in force, for the one element will stand out sharply against the other. The tension which is thereby introduced into language is the result of both pattern and contrast. There is no tension between aspects of our world which are separate and unrelated. However, pattern can unify the apparently unrelated. What previously seemed separate now appears in relation, a relation which is odd in the light of prevailing assumptions, and so full of tension. Or what previously seemed separate now appears in relation, making us sharply aware of a conflict. This unity-in-difference is necessary to produce tension. Disparate things must be pushed together under the pressure of the unifying pattern. This is one of the principal reasons for the careful patterning which we find in many synoptic sayings.

The synoptic Gospels contain a large amount of such "tensive" language (for Philip Wheelwright's use of this term, see above, p. 12). In many cases it would be possible to convey the basic information in the passage quite simply without adding a contrast; nevertheless, contrast appears. Evidently it is important for the purpose which this language seeks to serve. Many synoptic stories, including the parables, contrast two figures or groups, or one figure and a series of others. In the little stories which Bultmann calls "controversy dialogues" not only Jesus' views but also the contrasting views of critics are given expression. Many sayings stand in striking contrast to prevailing assumptions and desires, and rather than minimizing this in order to gain acceptance, they emphasize the conflict. Bold antithesis is common.

In the texts selected for study the following types of tensive language seem particularly important: First, antithesis appears in a number of specific forms. The "antithetical aphorism" presents a sharp antithesis in concise form through use of the positive and negative of the same words, or words which are opposites, in the two halves of the saying (see below, pp. 88-101). More extensive texts are also antithetically structured, some heightening the contrast by first establishing a pattern of two similar members and then introducing the third, contrasting member (cf. Luke 9:58, 12:54-56), others heightening the contrast to the point of hyperbole and caricature and deliberately excluding the normal range of behavior between the two extremes (cf. Matt 6:2-6, 16-18; 7:3-5).

Second, metaphor is a major form of tensive language, for in metaphor we assert something to be what it literally is not. As Wheelwright pointed out, true metaphor has a high degree of "semantic tension" (see above, p. 12). To be sure, much that may loosely be called metaphor is only slightly tensive, tending toward stereotyped phrases and mild comparison. Within the synoptic Gospels, also, there is great variety in the tensive quality of metaphors. In some cases we encounter metaphors with a high degree of tension, sufficient to give force to the whole passage (cf. Matt 19:12). More characteristic of the synoptic tradition is the use of metaphor or simile /13/ which, in itself, is not very forceful, either because it is traditional or rather obvious, but significantly increasing the metaphorical force through the way the metaphor or simile interacts with other aspects of the passage. Thus in Matt 6:25-33 the comparison of man's life to that of birds and flowers, mildly poetic at best, becomes forceful through combination with contrast, repetition, and strong diction. In other cases metaphors are developed in defiance of their normal meaning (Luke 6:38), in hyperbolic antithesis (Matt 7:3-5), or in direct contrast with the same words used in the literal sense (Mark 3:31-35, Luke 9:60, Matt 19:12), in each case adding greatly to the tensive power of the metaphor.

We also find other forms of tension. The "focal instance" (cf. pp. 67-77 below) is not metaphorical, since it is an example of the field of meaning to which it refers. However, it is a very specific and extreme example, which gives it the power of imaginative shock often associated with metaphor. Many of the little stories of Jesus' encounters with others contain dramatic tension, presenting conflict between persons and a surprising development in a vivid scene (cf. Mark 3:31-35, 12:13-17). Thus through antithesis, metaphor, and in other ways, synoptic texts tend to be strongly tensive. They are carefully formed to heighten tension and are quite willing to sacrifice other values, such as clarity and reasonableness, to this end. Why is this so important in the synoptic sayings tradition?

At this point we must recall what was said in section I about the

importance of forceful and imaginative language in awakening
the imagination to restructure the prerational configuration of
memories, meanings, and goals out of which we live. The features
of language being discussed are an important aspect of forceful
and imaginative language. More specifically, the tension in
synoptic sayings is a reflection of the fact that they seek to
challenge men who already live in a structured personal world.
New structure can arise only by attacking the old. Everything
important to us has its place within our personal world, and the
structures of this world are the means by which we interpret
experience. We unconsciously fit whatever we experience into
these structures, so experience does not ordinarily challenge them.
These interpretive structures have a ravenous appetite, seeking to
digest all that we encounter. If speech is to induce "imaginative
shock," effectively challenging the old structures and suggesting
new visions, it must resist such digestion. It must stick in the
throat. Forceful and imaginative language can do its work only if
it does not fit into our ordinary interpretive structures. The result
is tension, which often finds its formal reflection within a text.
This helps us to understand the frequent use of antithesis in the
Gospels. In antithesis the prevailing perspective is allowed
expression so that it can be challenged, and the new perspective
appears over against it. Thus the hearer is prevented from
subsuming the new perspective under the old. It is this clash of
perspectives which is revelatory. Otherwise, the new cannot assert
its newness; it is merely an additional item for the prevailing
perspective to digest. In some sayings which are not formally
antithetical other signs of tension appear: striking metaphor or
extremeness. Reasonable ideas are not sufficient, for the speaker
seeks to challenge the reasoning which arises from the prevailing
perspective.

The tension of the saying carries with it a demand for decision, a
decision in which the hearer has much at stake. The text seeks to
block the well-marked path along which the hearer is moving so
that it may point to another one — a faint trace leading into an
uncharted wilderness. The hearer must decide. Thus the tension in

the text awakens an answering tension in the hearer, the tension of having to make a decision. This decision lies at a deeper level than the technical and practical decisions of ordinary life. The language of rational argument and the unimaginative commands of daily life are also concerned with decision, but they do not reach the same depth. Rational argument, for instance, ignores the will's involvement in a world of feeling-laden images. This is possible so long as the decision in question is merely the implementation of established structures of the personal world. However, these feeling-laden images cannot be ignored in decisions which involve the nature of the self and his world. Furthermore, arguments themselves presuppose structures of meaning and become less and less decisive the more deeply we question these structures. Technical and practical decisions are relatively easy, provided we have enough information. The texts we will study try to make decision hard. They block the easy path, and the path to which they point is difficult. Indeed, they *cannot* appeal for easy acceptance because easy acceptance always takes place *within* the prevailing structures of interpretation. These texts do not seek easy acceptance but change. They must frustrate easy acceptance so that change can take place / 14/. Thus the tension in the text is necessary to its purpose. This tension enables the text to resist being digested by the prevailing patterns of interpretation and instead to challenge these patterns. The tension enables the text to speak with the necessary depth, to address the self on the level of basic structures of his personal world rather than on the level of technical decisions, thereby awakening an answering tension within the self, which can lead to change. When the interpreter allows the decision to become an easy one, he is betraying the text, having misunderstood the purpose of its forceful form.

Pattern and tension are major ways in which these little sayings gain the imaginative force necessary for their task. Through pattern the text gains unity and particularity. Pattern heightens the interaction of the parts, enforcing, contrasting, and enriching. The patterns of these sayings contribute especially to tension, which is strong and pervasive. This tension is the formal reflection of the text's desire to challenge prevailing structures of the personal world and to grant a new vision of some region of existence. Of course, whether this takes place depends not only on the text but on ourselves. If the text has its weapons, we have our armor. We are not inclined to allow tampering with the depths of our personal existence. One of our best defenses is to read these texts as if they were a different sort of language, moral instructions, perhaps, which only involve outward behavior. In that case the forceful language of the text will appear to be mere rhetorical decoration. Even if the text does penetrate our armor with a new image of self and world, the struggle is not over. The tension remains, for this new image of self and world is based on a reality beyond ourselves, beyond our world, and we are continually tempted to make something more manageable the basis of our lives. Thus the form of the text does not guarantee its success. There remains a mystery as to why the text wins out on some occasions and not on others. However, the form of the text does make clearer the goal for which the speaker is striving and so helps the interpreter to see the speaker's criteria for success or failure.

Within the synoptic Gospels the "Kingdom of God" is the symbolic name for the reality beyond ourselves which is the cause and justification of this tension. The Kingdom of God is the (often uncited) basis for the challenge to the old perspective and is the reality which grants us a right to the new vision to which the sayings point. These sayings show us how things look from the viewpoint of the Kingdom. Furthermore, because they resist our attempts to digest them within the perspective of the old world, these sayings preserve the Kingdom's newness, its reality as *God's* Kingdom, which cannot be assimilated to the old world. We must not suppose that we know what the Kingdom of God is apart from the indirect and tensive language of the sayings, parables, and stories in the Gospels. Apart from them the Kingdom of God becomes a cipher in an ideology; it becomes a disguised version of the old kingdom of the world. However, through the forceful and imaginative language of the Gospels this symbol may show its transforming power and become the bearer of a reality by which we can live. Thus God's Kingdom is the basis for the new vision of the sayings, but these sayings themselves, along with the parables and stories of the Gospels, are the gate through which we must pass if we are to discover the reality which is their basis.

NOTES

/1/ For instance, the *Encyclopedia of Poetry and Poetics*, ed. Alex Preminger (699), speaks of repetition as "a basic unifying device in all poetry." T. W. Manson (1955:53-54) makes a similar remark: "This principle of recurrence with variation whether of ideas or sounds, is what distinguishes poetry from prose, which, on the other hand, is characterised by its linear structure."

/2/ Burney's work has been continued by Matthew Black (143-85) and by Joachim Jeremias (1971:14-29). Black discusses alliteration, assonance, and paronomasia, as well as parallelism; Jeremias focuses on antithetic parallelism and rhythm. Both rely heavily on their translations of the sayings into Aramaic; neither goes far in discussing the significance of poetic form.

/3/ Cf. James Muilenburg (1953:98): Synonymous parallelism "is in reality very seldom precisely synonymous. The parallel line does not simply repeat what has been said, but enriches it, deepens it, transforms it by adding fresh nuances and bringing in new elements, renders it more concrete and vivid and telling."

/4/ See Wheelwright's term "soft focus," discussed above, p. 11.

/5/ Cf. Martin Buber (quoted by Meir Weiss: 301): "The psalm interprets itself in that it points to what is essential to its understanding through repetitions."

/6/ On threefold repetition in folk narrative see Axel Olrik (132-34). According to Olrik, "Nothing distinguishes the great bulk of folk narrative from modern literature and from reality as much as does the number three" (133).

/7/ Benjamin N. Colby (188) notes that contrast or polarization is a way of concentrating attention on single attribute dimensions.

/8/ Roman Jakobson (368-69) reminds us that the constituents of a poetic sequence, because of the presence of "parallelism" (i.e., repetitive pattern), prompt "one of the two correlative experiences which Hopkins neatly defines as 'comparison for likeness' sake' and 'comparison for unlikeness' sake.' "

/9/   This interpretation is similar to N. K. Gottwald's (cf. 831, 834-35) description of rhythm in Old Testament poetry. He says, "The basic unit of poetic composition is the line, which constitutes normally one half . . . of the parallelism. It expresses a complete thought and has grammatical and syntactic unity." Rhythm arises from this parallelism of lines: "Meter, insofar as it exists in Hebrew poetry, is actually the rhythmical counterpart of parallelism of thought. Rhythm is not due to syllabic quantities but to the less definable instinct of balancing parts whose exact accentual values are not measurable and probably never were. . . . In Hebrew poetry regularity of stress is subordinated to regularity of balanced ideas. Thus the tendency to fill out lines with incomplete parallelisms by means of compensation . . . is due to the desire to oppose word-masses of about the same weight while varying and emphasizing the thought." Gottwald suggests that, in analyzing Hebrew verse, one must take account of "the caesura or stop, both in its sharper form at the end of lines and in its feebler form within lines. The groupings that result from these breaks are essentially thought-units and the word-masses balance, not because of prior metric convictions, but because the poetic thought pulsates in a series of advancing, recapitulating, and contrasting movements. . . . Parallelism of thought, and corresponding word-mass, is the substance and mode of Hebrew poetic expression" (cf. also Buss: 45-46, Kosmala, and Burney: 59-62).

/10/   Although this foot is long, the fact that it is both a grammatical sense unit and corresponds to the participles with pronoun objects which precede it supports this grouping.

/11/   The phrase "of the sky" in Luke 9:58 has a similar function. See below, pp. 161-62. Matt 10:8 also shows how rhythm is maintained in spite of variations and developments in the text. The rhythm of two feet per line encompasses not only the first four commands but also the last two pairs of words, which have a rather different function in the passage.

/12/   Joachim Jeremias (cf. 1971:20-27), following Burney, believes that each of the different rhythms which he detects (two beat, three beat, four beat and kīnā) expresses a different mood. These generalizations are dubious. Only through close examination of the complex unity of form and content in individual passages are we able to move beyond statements about rhythm in general to an understanding of the particular significance of the rhythmic pattern in a particular passage.

/13/   I make no sharp distinction between simile and metaphor, since this distinction is not decisive for the question of tensive quality which we are considering.

/14/   H. R. Jauss (33) makes a similar point when he speaks of the "productive meaning of negative experience." He quotes G. Buck, who asserts that in negative experience "the experiencing consciousness changes. The action of a negative experience is one of becoming conscious of oneself. Whatever one becomes conscious of are the motifs which have been guiding experience and which have remained unquestioned in this guiding function. Negative experience has primarily the character of self-experience, which frees one for a qualitatively new kind of experience."

III. STUDIES OF TEXTS

Each of the texts which we are about to study is formed by the interaction of various factors. The interpreter must respect this interaction by refusing to isolate or overemphasize particular characteristics. Although some of the texts share specific characteristics, it would be misleading to make any single factor an ordering principle for them all. I wish to avoid this in the following studies of texts. To be sure, there is a significant distinction between sayings in brief narrative scenes in which there is sharp interaction between saying and setting and other sayings in which the narrative setting is a minor factor. Many of the latter texts are part of larger groups of sayings in the Gospels. In order to give due consideration to the significance of narrative setting in texts of the former type, we will study four clear examples together (see pp. 152-85 below). Apart from this the order of the following studies is somewhat arbitrary, although there are some significant ties between adjacent texts. Matt 6:25-33 is an appropriate place to begin since it is a good example of the interaction of a number of formal features in a text. Matt 6:1-6, 16-18 follows Matt 5:39b-42 because it provides further examples of the "focal instance" as part of a more elaborate text. Similarly, Mark 10:42-44 follows Mark 7:15, 10:9, 8:35 because it is a more elaborate example of the "antithetical aphorism." In studies 6-13 we will find some features similar to the texts in the earlier studies. However, they are grouped according to content, Luke 6:37-38 and Matt 7:3-5 being joined by the theme of judging our fellow men; Luke 17:26-30, Matt 11:21-24, and Luke 12:54-56 by themes of eschatological warning and judgment; and Matt 19:12, 10:34-36, and Mark 10:29-30 by a concern with the disciple and family life. This grouping is useful because it encourages us to compare the different rhetorical strategies which may be adopted in dealing with similar subject matter. Following these texts we will consider four texts in which the interaction of narrative setting and saying

59

makes a major contribution to the impact of the whole.

1. Matt 6:25-33//Luke 12:22-31. The Birds and the Lilies.

25   Therefore I tell you,
         Do not be anxious about your life, what you shall eat [or what
                 you shall drink,]
             Nor about your body, what you shall put on.
         Is not life more than food,
             And the body more than clothing?
26   Look at the birds of the air:
             They neither sow nor reap nor gather into barns,
             And yet your heavenly Father feeds them.
             Are you not of more value than they?
27   [And which of you by being anxious can add one cubit
                 to his span of life?
28   And why are you anxious about clothing?]
         Consider the lilies of the field, how they grow;
             They neither toil nor spin;
29   Yet I tell you, even Solomon in all his glory
                 was not arrayed like one of these.
30   But if God so clothes the grass of the field,
                 which today is alive and tomorrow is thrown into the oven,
                 will he not much more clothe you, O men of little faith?
31   Therefore do not be anxious, saying,
             'What shall we eat?'
             Or 'What shall we drink?'
             Or 'What shall we wear?'
32   For [the Gentiles seek all these things; and] your
             heavenly Father knows that you need all these things.
33   But seek first his kingdom [and his righteousness,]
             And all these things shall be yours as well.

                                                     Matt 6:25-33

Compared to many sayings in the synoptic Gospels, this text is
rather long and complex. There is some evidence of secondary
expansion. Matt 6:27 (//Luke 12:25-26) clearly interrupts the
natural connection between what precedes and what follows. This
damages the careful form of the rest. Matt 6:28a, which has no
parallel in Luke, was probably constructed by the Evangelist to

smooth the transition after vs. 27. Matt 6:32a//Luke 12:30a may
be secondary, for it brings in à consideration which has no support
in the rest of the composition, and Matt 6:32b does not continue
32a but supports vs. 31. Both Evangelists add material at the end
(Matt 6:34, Luke 12:32), but here they go separate ways,
indicating that these also are secondary additions. We will
consider the passage apart from these additions, which will make
its form stand out more clearly. Whether the remaining material
was always as extensive as now, or whether it represents an
expansion of a shorter kernel of material, is uncertain /1/. In any
case, this remaining material has a careful form which is worthy of
attention .

> Do not be anxious about your life, what you shall eat /2/,
>> nor about your body, what you shall put on.
> Is not life more than food,
>> and the body than clothing?

The first verse of the passage establishes a repetitive pattern. Both
sentences are twofold, referring first to "life" /3/ and eating and
then to the body and clothing. This pattern is basic to what
follows, for Matt 6:26 has to do with food and 28b-30 with
clothing, the two sections being parallel in general structure. Matt
6:31 returns to the prohibition of vs. 25, creating an "envelope"
structure. This is then supported in vs. 32b with the thought of
God's care (taken from vss. 26, 28b-30) and in vs. 33 by a
command antithetical to vs. 31.

   In order to understand the role of this repetitive pattern, we
must see how it interacts with other features of the text to help the
text fulfill its function. We get some insight into that function
when we see that Matt 6:25 attacks squarely the anxiety which
springs from man's insecurity with respect to such basic needs as
food and clothing. This is a very powerful enemy to attack, for our
anxiety is very deep. It suffuses our personal and communal
existence, shaping the life of society and individual. It leads to the
development of elaborate systems of production, and of equally
elaborate systems of protection from those who might take our
products away. Within these structures of care each of us plays out

his life, seeking some measure of economic protection against threats which may at any time turn out to be more powerful than the protection we have devised. In the face of all this, we are hardly able to take seriously the command "Do not be anxious."

Our involvement in these structures of care is too deep to be uprooted by a simple command. Indeed, much of the time we seem to know no other reality, so that a change could only take place if we were to see the world in a fundamentally new way. Can words help us to such insight? They would have to be a special kind of words, for they must penetrate below our present sense of reality, which controls what we do and what we recognize as important. They must show us a reality which we do not now recognize as real. They must show the fundamental importance of something which does not fit our standards of importance but calls them in question.

One way of allowing such a reality to appear within our world is through the use of image or symbol. The image is part of the everyday world, the world which we recognize as real, and yet, as *image*, it is the concentrated representation of something else, something which does not appear except through the image. As image it becomes heavy with significance. We gain a sense of both the breadth and the importance of the meaning there concentrated, and of the fundamental challenge to other perceptions of reality. I would suggest that the birds and flowers of our passage are such images. This may sound strange, for they seem quite innocent and ordinary. We may encounter birds and flowers daily and yet experience no challenge to our sense of reality. How can they function here as images in which some deeper reality appears?

Every image, of course, is selected from our ordinary world. It only becomes an image through its interaction with other words. This means that we must look closely at the linguistic setting of these words in order to discover whether they are able to function as images. Both the section on the birds and that on the lilies are introduced by strong words referring to perception (Matt: ἐμβλέψατε,   καταμάθετε,   RSV: "look," "consider;" Luke:

κατανοήσατε, RSV: "consider") (cf. Rengstorf and Behm). We are not to look casually but observe carefully, so that we will understand the hidden meaning which we ordinarily overlook. This can happen only if the birds and the flowers are removed from the context in which we normally see them. Rather than being incidental features of man's ordinary world, a world which is dominated by structures of care, they must stand out. They must be set over against the ordinary world. They must become foreign, with a meaning of their own which does not fit easily into the structure of human concerns. The speaker helps this to happen through contrasting the birds and the lilies with man's life. The birds "neither sow nor reap nor gather into barns." The lilies "neither toil nor spin." The elaborate structures of care in which we are involved are absent, and yet life goes on. A strange fact when we begin to think about it! This makes the birds and flowers seem strange to us. Or, perhaps, they make *our* world seem strange. When this happens, they are taking on the force of images. They are becoming heavy with meaning, for we see that our sense of reality itself is at stake.

Wishing to argue with the text, we may point out that birds are also concerned with food; indeed, they spend most of their day seeking it. Even so, the contrast remains between man's elaborate structures of care and the comparatively simple, direct supplying of needs in the life of other creatures, and it is on this contrast that the text wishes us to meditate. It is also true that birds do not always get enough to eat, nor do flowers always grow to full beauty. Nevertheless, they do about as well as care-ridden man, and the text assumes that, on the whole, their existence is good, not tragic.

Merely mentioning the difference between man's care and the simple existence of birds and flowers is not likely to have the desired effect. Our ways of seeing and thinking are too deeply ingrained for that. It is necessary to turn up the volume. The text must be forceful. This is a clue to the structure of this passage. It would have been possible to refer only to birds or only to flowers, or to refer to both birds and flowers in one sentence. Instead, the text goes through the pattern twice, for this is more forceful. Twice we are made to consider a fact which contradicts the elaborate structures of care within which we live, twice this is related to God's care, and twice we are left with a question, a question which demands that we respond and recognize this strange world as our world. Furthermore, the repetitive pattern builds to a climax. The part about the birds is comparatively gentle in its language /4/. The part about the lilies is not only longer but more forceful. The latter builds upon the former. The first part suggests something strange, something which does not fit with our view of the world. We carry this over to the second part, which makes it appear even stranger by speaking as forcefully as possible. This is the reason for the more elaborate structure and greater length of the part concerning the lilies. There the language becomes extravagant. The lilies are not merely clothed; they are clothed with a grandeur that not even Solomon could match. This is stressed by the choice of emphatic phrases in Matt 6:29: "I tell you," "not even Solomon," "in all his glory." By this comparison the lilies are removed completely from the realm of the ordinary. They are given a position which sharply contradicts the ordinary estimate of field flowers, and this surplus of significance reflects their function as images. Yet in vs. 30 the glorious lilies are simply used as footing for a giant step beyond. There the insignificance of lilies is emphasized so that God's care for us may be presented with extreme force. The glorious lilies are now called χόρτος ("grass" or "hay"), and their ephemeral life is underscored ("which today is alive and tomorrow is thrown into the oven"), sharply contrasting their state "today" and "tomorrow" /5/. This shows that the text is not based on a romantic or sentimental view of flowers. Nor is the death of flowers viewed as tragic, which would weaken the emphasis on God's care. Grass has the life span appropriate to it. The surprising thing is that even in its short life there are signs of God's care /6/. The reference to the lilies as ephemeral grass is placed right after the conjunction in the Greek clause, which is again a sign of emphasis. At the end of the clause, in the other position of emphasis, stands the word ἀμφιέννυσιν ("clothes"), which recalls the grandeur of the lilies stressed in the preceding verse. Thus the passage emphasizes as strongly as possible the tension between the insignificance of the field flowers and the grandeur of their garb. God's extravagance with respect to the field flowers then becomes the basis for the argument that he is "much more" gracious with men. Here also the text is striving for forcefulness, as we see when we note that, in comparison with Matt 6:26, the word "much" and the mocking direct address "O men of little faith" have been added.

The concern for forcefulness in Matt 6:29-30 is clear. The effect of this is to make the lilies stand out the more strongly in their strangeness, to make them images of God's lavish giving to his world, and to cause them to resonate against the patterns of "little faith" which constrict our lives. The repetitive pattern is significant because it contributes to this forcefulness. Simple repetition would contribute something. Here, however, the pattern is not simply repeated but developed, which greatly increases its effectiveness. The revelatory force of the pattern quickly grows through this repetition with development, for the second instance can begin with what was achieved in the first, and the increased force of the second reacts upon our understanding of the first.

Our text contains features which are similar to poetry, especially its repetitive pattern and use of images. On the other hand, it is highly rhetorical; it is argumentative and demands a response. Our first impression is that the text's argument is rather weak. The conclusion seems to overshoot its basis; there seems to be a lack of proportion between the conclusion and the reasoning. This seeming lack of proportion is a sign that we are dealing with a strange kind of argument. This argument has force only if the birds and flowers become resonant images for a reality which transcends them. Thus the language of the text can attain its rhetorical goal only if it takes on the power of poetry, an indication that we are dealing with the "depth rhetoric" discussed earlier.

Ordinarily remarks about birds and flowers have no power to challenge our basic perception of the world. Birds and flowers are incidental facts within a world dominated by structures of care. It is only the artful form of this text which gives birds and flowers the power to become resonant images in which we find concentrated a reality great enough to challenge the reality by which we ordinarily live. As these simple aspects of everyday life are subjected to the pressure of repetitive pattern, contrast, and emphatic diction, they are stripped of their setting in everyday life, opposed to the reality by which we ordinarily live, and set forth with all the force appropriate to a matter of fundamental importance. Therefore, when we meditate on these carefully formed words, they begin to vibrate with deeper meaning. The imagination casts up corresponding images from forgotten memories: memories of a cardinal singing in a fir tree, of a frozen creek with pockets of air undulating beneath the thin glaze of ice, memories of a world of beauty and goodness which is simply there, flooding and free, prior to all our strivings /7/. We begin to wonder which is the real world, the world of our anxiety, or this other world of which the birds and flowers are images. Thus the text induces a sense of strangeness about our life and a sense of the presence of something more, something deeper, which offers an alternative for action and makes finally unimportant our structures of care. We experience a heightened awareness and the disturbing impingement of another reality. This opens a new possibility for life, a possibility which the text describes as seeking the Kingdom (Matt 6:33). While the direct command to not be anxious at the beginning of the passage is unlikely to be effective, when that command returns in Matt 6:31, there is a greater chance that we may consider this a serious possibility, one founded on a reality deeper than our reality, provided the intervening words have done their work. Of course, we are talking about a highly personal experience, reaching to the depths of personal existence, and whether it will indeed take place depends not only on the text but also on us. However, the form of this passage indicates that it is striving for this goal. This passage shows, then, how rather mild comparisons of man's life to that of birds and flowers may be lifted to resonant images through interaction with elements of forcefulness, including contrast, repetitive pattern, and emphatic diction, and how this resonant language can perform a function which weaker language cannot: It can address the hearer at the level of his personal world, the prerational configuration of meanings and goals out of which he lives, and activate his imagination so that he can begin to see self and world from a new perspective. Thus the text does not simply command but seeks to make possible what it commands.

2. Matt 5:39b-42. Turning the Other Cheek (The "Focal Instance") /8/

39b Whoever strikes you on the right cheek,
       Turn to him the other also;
40   And for him who would sue you and take your tunic,
       Leave for him your cloak as well;
41   And whoever will force you to work for one mile,
       Go with him two miles.
42   To him who asks you, give,
       And him who would borrow from you, do not refuse.

We feel uneasy about interpreting the command to turn the other cheek literally. However, few interpreters attempt to explain *why* this is not literal language. Nor do they give a clear account of the nature and qualities of this language, if it is not literal. The problem with this command is particularly acute in light of the recent self-assertion of minority groups in our country. Is what this command implies always good? Is it good when applied to an oppressed group rather than an individual, or does turning the other cheek in such a situation show lack of concern for the suffering brother? Such reflections often lead to simply ignoring this command. What help is it if it sometimes leads to evil results and if all we can say in its defense is that it is not meant literally? We can escape from this problem only if this command leaves room for the changing complexities of human situations and yet is able to help us in those situations. But are there reasons for believing that this is so?

Certain aspects of the form of these sayings provide clues to the way in which this type of language functions when it is properly understood. Matt 5:39b-42 shows a consciousness of form by the fact that each of the four sayings is approximately the same length (the saying concerning loans in vs. 42 being repeated to give it the required length /9/) and has similar syntactic form. Each begins either with a ὅστις clause or an adjectival participle (the two constructions alternate) and ends with a clause in which an imperative or subjunctive of prohibition is the first element. The feeling for form in the tradition is indicated by the fact that Luke's version of these sayings (Luke 6:29-30), in spite of significant differences in wording and content, varies only slightly from this syntactic form /10/.

The parallel syntax marks Matt 5:39b-42 as a formal unit containing a series of four parallel commands. To go further we must discuss some other formal characteristics which go beyond syntax /11/. Note that each of the commands deals with a specific situation and that each of the commands is extreme. What conclusions can we draw from the fact that we find here specific, extreme commands arranged in a series? Let us begin with the fact that these commands deal with specific situations. A command dealing with slaps on the cheek has a rather limited application literally. It just doesn't happen that often. And the Gospel of Matthew is even more specific, for it speaks only of a slap on the *right* cheek. This involves a surprising narrowing of focus. The commands in vss. 40-41 also refer to quite specific situations. They even indicate the property at stake in the lawsuit and the distance of the forced labor /12/. These commands do not generalize concerning love or non-resistance. They do not attempt to encompass many situations but speak specifically of a particular situation which might arise. In this respect they differ from the general statement concerning non-resistance in vs. 39a. This general statement is a secondary addition to this unit of tradition, as is shown by the following considerations: 1) It is not found in the Lukan parallel. 2) It is formulated in contrast to vs. 38 and is formally parallel to vs. 34a, indicating that it stems from the time of the collection of scattered sayings into the major section of antitheses in Matt 5:21-48. 3) While vs. 39a uses the second person plural pronoun, vss. 39b-42 use the second person singular. 4) Vss. 39b-41 speak of more than non-resistance, as will be shown below. The fact that the commands in these verses remain on a level of specificity which enables the hearer to visualize a concrete situation means that they speak with greater vividness and impact, a fact which is important for the mode of language with which we are dealing.

Although these commands deal with specific situations, we unconsciously assume that they have implications for many other situations as well. We take them as examples which are relevant to many situations which have nothing to do with cheeks and coats and forced service. I think that we are right in doing so, even if we recognize that the general statement in vs. 39a is secondary. This can be justified in the following way: Because the four commands are formally parallel, they constitute a series. The effect of such a series is to establish a pattern which can be extended to other instances. The hearer gets the point, he understands what is being said, when he grasps the pattern and can extend it to new situations, especially the concrete situations in which *he* finds himself. This view is supported by the variations within the early Christian tradition in series of sayings with a common pattern /13/. The fact that there is considerable freedom in wording and detail, and considerable freedom to form new sayings by analogy and delete others, but at the same time a strong tendency to preserve the basic pattern common to the sayings, is a witness to the fact that the early church *understood* this type of language. It is a witness to the fact that the church understood these words as an invitation to extend and adapt this pattern to the situations in which they found themselves. It is a witness to the fact that the church understood such a series to be open-ended. This has important implications. If we are dealing here with a mode of language which is deliberately open-ended, then the hearer must recognize that the meaning of the text cannot be restricted to what it says literally. The text means *more* than it says explicitly, which gives it an indirect and allusive quality.

This observation can be carried further by considering the extremeness of these commands. One of the reasons for the surprising narrowness of focus is the desire to present an extreme instance. Thus the reference to the *right* cheek in Matthew, which is not found in Luke, seems to be due to the fact that such a blow is extremely insulting /14/. Vs. 40 seems to refer to the situation of the very poor, for ordinary garments would figure in a lawsuit only if the man had no other valuable property. Thus the loss of both the tunic and the cloak, the two standard garments, would probably leave the man not only penniless but naked. The fact that the suit involves the undergarment rather than the cloak /15/ reflects the Jewish legal situation. According to Deut 24:13, the cloak of a poor man, given in pledge for a loan, could not be kept overnight, since it served also as a blanket. Thus giving up the cloak means giving up something which could not legally be taken away. Vs. 41 refers to forced labor, probably involving the carrying of some burden /16/, something irksome in itself and especially so if imposed by a foreign invader. Obeying vs. 42 is very likely to leave a man without money to live on. The extremeness of these commands is due in part to the situations chosen, though these might be excelled by a case of bodily injury. It is due even more to the surprising behavior which is commanded in these situations. Not even the command to not resist in vs. 39a catches the extremeness of the commands which follow. Vss. 39b-41 do not merely speak of non-resistance. They do more than insist that one should not resist a slap on the cheek, the taking of one's tunic, or forced labor. In each case an *action* is commanded, and this action is the precise opposite of our natural tendency in the situation. Our tendency when hit is to hit back. The opposite is commanded: we are to let ourselves be hit again. I would suggest that these almost absurd commands were conceived by the simple device of reversing man's natural tendency. Note that no consideration is given to whether this will be helpful to the other person. The commands are not based upon prudential considerations as to what will result in the greatest good for the other. Turning the other cheek is commanded because it is the opposite of what we naturally tend to do in the situation. In this way the command becomes as extreme as can readily be imagined. It stands in deliberate tension with the way in which men normally live and think.

This tension is essential to the way in which this mode of language functions. Whenever the interpreter weakens this tension so as to make these commands practical, he is doing the opposite of what the speaker wishes to do and shows that he has misunderstood the mode of language. The immediate and proper effect of such language on the serious hearer is something like this: His mouth falls open and he exclaims, "We should do even that? Then what about all the rest of my attempts to protect myself against others? What about the argument I just had with so-and-so?" And so forth.

These commands are an attack on our natural tendency to put self-protection first. Because they do not fit together topically but refer to different sorts of situations (a blow, a lawsuit, forced labor), the similarity in meaning for which the similar form sets us seeking is found not at a superficial level of topic but at the deeper level of a surprising rejection of our tendency to put self-protection first. Although these commands refer only to a few specific situations, we experience a general, fundamental attack. This response can be explained in the following way: Because of the tension between the command and normal life, the attention of the hearer does not come to rest in the literal sense of the command. He knows that it is extreme, conflicting not only with particular acts but with the whole pattern of behavior which pervades his life. Because the conflict occurs at this basic level, much more is at stake than behavior in the situation explicitly mentioned. A command which will not fit within the pervading pattern of life calls that pattern into question and indirectly suggests another pattern to replace it. Thus a particular command is able to preside over a whole pattern of life extending far beyond its literal content. This may also be put in another way: Because it is extreme, the command indirectly refers to everything up to and including the literal sense. Thus the limits of the literal sense have been broken down. It is not "just that" which is commanded but "even that." Thus the command acquires a whole field of implications to which no clear limits can be set. The tension which is an essential part of metaphor gives the metaphor its power to point beyond the literal sense of words. In a similar way, the tension which is part of these commands points the hearer beyond the literal sense to the many situations in which he encounters other men. The command becomes the focal point of this field of situations to which it indirectly refers. Therefore I would like to call this mode of language the "focal instance." It is the focus or point of clarity within a larger field of reference of which the instance is a part, a field which appears because of the tension in this extreme instance. The focal instance, then, is characterized by 1) specificness and 2) extremeness. Extremeness means that it stands in deliberate tension with a basic pattern of human behavior /17/. Specificness means that there is a surprising narrowness of focus due to the desire to present an extreme instance. No attempt is made to encompass a major area of human behavior under a general rule or to cover such an area by systematic discussion of the legal and ethical problems of different classes of situations. Thus consideration of an area of behavior seems to be incomplete, and yet the specific instance is indirectly suggestive for many other situations. I would describe Matt 5:39b-42 as an open-ended series of focal instances.

The characteristics of this mode of language will stand out more sharply if contrasted with another mode. Let us briefly consider the saying on divorce in Matt 5:32. Although the syntax of Matt 5:32 is somewhat similar to 5:39b-42 /18/, other formal characteristics show that the mode of language differs significantly, exposing 5:32 to use as a legal rule while 5:39b-42 is protected from such use. In contrast to 5:39b-42, 5:32 has the following characteristics: It is possible (with difficulty) to enforce this implied prohibition as a general rule in its literal meaning, as we see from Christian history. Since this is so, our attention is focused on its limited, literal sense and on the external behavior which conforms to this rule. When so understood, these words do not jolt the imagination or lead us to think beyond the matter explicitly discussed. Furthermore, Matt 5:32 deals with a general area of human behavior and permits clear deduction as to the range of its application, or, when complications arise, it invites clarifying amendments. It makes use of general legal categories: divorce and adultery. What specificness we find is not due to a search for the extreme instance, the least possible example of unfaithfulness between husband and wife. The contrast with Matt 5:28, a focal instance which deals with adultery, makes this clear. What specificness we find is due to casuistry, to the desire to make clear the classes of situations to which the rule applies. This is shown by the variations among the four versions of this rule (Matt 5:32, 19:9, Mark 10:11-12, Luke 16:18). These words mean only what they say explicitly and so must be adjusted explicitly to different legal situations. Exceptions also must be explicitly stated. Here we find a concern for legal clarity. Each version of the rule attempts to make a clear statement of what is forbidden so that there will be a minimum of ambiguity about application to individual cases. Such clarity is only possible through the restriction of language to its literal sense.

The open-ended series of focal instances has none of the characteristics listed above. 1) Matt 5:39b-42 does not provide an enforceable standard of general behavior. While the acts commanded are possible in isolated cases, the pattern of life suggested by the whole series conflicts with basic human concerns, much more basic than a desire for divorce. 2) This text does not deal explicitly with a general area of behavior. 3) It does not permit clear deduction as to the range of its application. In this case it is a mistake to expect legal clarity. Instead, this mode of language has other strengths. Because of the tension within the focal instance and because the series is open-ended, this mode of language refers indirectly to a whole field of situations to which no clear limit can be set. This is the source of the great hermeneutical potential of

such language, its power to speak again and again to new
situations. Furthermore, this mode of language does not raise the
same sort of problem as the legal rule when applied to new
situations. The legal rule, which must state everything explicitly,
can never do justice to the complexities of unique situations. The
focal instance, however, refers to its field of situations only
indirectly. It does not try to spell out explicitly the situations in
which it must apply. Thus the focal instance leaves room for the
uniqueness of complex situations. It does not try to anticipate
each new situation by encompassing it in a general rule. Perhaps
there are exceptions to what the focal instance seems at first to
imply. Perhaps other factors must be taken into account before
one acts. It is not the business of the focal instance to spell out such
exceptions. Because it speaks indirectly, it says neither yes nor no
to them. It is important that a focal instance be concise and
forceful. Therefore simple situations are chosen and no
complicating factors are introduced. However, this does not mean
that focal instances are relevant only to simple situations. Rather,
it means that this mode of language gives the hearer the freedom
of responsible decision in light of the particularities of his
situation.

However, the focal instance does not leave the decision maker
without help. It helps not by deciding for him what he is to do but
by throwing a strong light on his situation from one direction,
forcefully calling to his attention one factor in the situation. The
command does not do the hearer's thinking for him; it starts him
thinking in a definite direction. Its meaning for a particular
situation becomes apparent not through a process of legal
deduction but only through the imaginative shock felt by the
serious hearer, a shock which arouses the moral imagination,
enabling the hearer to see his situation in a new way and to
contemplate new possibilities of action. It is proper to speak here
of the "moral imagination" for at least two reasons: 1) Many of
our decisions are made routinely, and we think of them as already
determined by the situation. However, the focal instance
challenges the "ruts" in which we move and stimulates us to think

of new possibilities, to imagine the creative act which breaks out
of such ruts. 2) The relation between the command and the act is
not one of strict deduction, a direct unfolding of the implications
of a premise. Rather, an element of "insight," of seeing things in a
new way, is involved. A mode of language which is not willing to
remain within the limits of legal clarity but is shaped for the
maximum personal impact on the hearer is best able to awaken
this moral imagination. Thus the focal instance serves as an
illuminator of the hearer's situation. The hearer is invited to lay
the saying alongside his own situation and, through the
imaginative shock produced, to see that situation in a new way. It
is only when this happens that the specific meaning of the
commandment for him can become clear /19/.

Perhaps the following illustration will help to show how Matt
5:39b-42 might serve as an illuminator of the hearer's situation.
Let us imagine that the administrator of a social agency is
informed that one of his most trusted subordinates has been
caught in a serious crime. He reacts with anger. His trust has been
betrayed, and those who oppose what the agency is attempting to
do among the urban poor now have an excuse for cutting back the
agency's funds. In this situation he reads Matt 5:39b-42.
Assuming that he takes what he reads seriously, his reactions
might pass through the following stages: He may see immediately
that these commands are meddling in his business. In terms of vs.
39b, he has been slapped on the cheek. His first reaction to the
command may be a deeper anger. This will be accompanied by the
feeling that the command is impractical. The one who betrayed
him simply cannot be continued in his position and allowed to do
the same thing again. After all, an administrator cannot think of
one man only; he must think of the many people to whom he is
responsible, those above him who dispense funds and the poor
whom he is trying to help. However, these strange commands
cannot be forgotten. They work at the back of his mind, and as
they do, he realizes that at first he had been primarily concerned
with himself. He had been angry at this betrayal of his trust and
this threat to his treasured program. As he recognizes this, he

begins to consider other possible responses: "Even if I do have to suspend him from his position, there are some other things which can be done. Perhaps my testimony at the trial will help him to receive a suspended sentence. If so, I might be able to help him get a job somewhere . . . There is the problem of replacing him, too. Should I look for a safe middle-class fellow or for another 'high risk' type? Maybe it is worth running the risk . . . "

Here we see thought set in motion by these commandments, thought which is not direct deduction from them but which arises through wrestling with a complex situation when that situation is illumined by these forceful words.

Although I have compared the tension in metaphor with the tension in the focal instance, there is a clear distinction between the two. In metaphor the expected word is replaced by a word from a quite different realm of discourse. The tension, and so possibility of new insight, arises through a fusion of these two realms of discourse, normally kept quite distinct. The focal instance is not taken from a different realm of discourse; it is an instance of the field of meaning to which the saying refers. However, it is not just one example among others. It is an extreme instance and therefore is able to call in question our established patterns of thinking and acting. The focal instance may also be compared with hyperbole. Both make use of extreme language in order to increase the impact upon the hearer. However, hyperbole refers to things which are obviously impossible: a log in the eye or a camel passing through the eye of a needle. The focal instance stands at the edge of the possible. One *can* turn the other cheek, though it clashes with deeply-ingrained patterns of behavior.

Brief reference to some other occurrences of the focal instance in the synoptic Gospels will help to show the various ways in which it is used. The focal instance plays an important role in the section of antitheses (Matt 5:21-48) within the Sermon on the Mount. Matt 5:22 is a good example. Note the extreme judgment on seemingly small matters and the quite specific epithets ("*raka*" and "fool") referred to in the second and third sayings of this open-ended series. A focal instance need not be part of a series.

Matt 5:28 is not followed by other sayings of the same pattern (though it is part of the larger formal pattern of antitheses). Matt 5:23-24 is not bound to what precedes or follows it by common syntactical form and is fully able to stand by itself. It has been secondarily joined to the surrounding material to make a longer series of focal instances, consisting of 5:22a-b-c, 23-24, 25-26 /20/. Matt 5:23-24 illustrates the characteristics of the focal instance well. The adverbs "there . . . first . . . then" deliberately exclude the more normal possibilities of taking care of the reconciliation before coming to the temple or waiting until the sacrifice is complete. Instead, the extreme situation is chosen. The use of this saying in Matthew even after the temple had been destroyed, so that a literal application was no longer possible, suggests the early church's awareness that this saying refers indirectly to a wide range of situations. The command to love enemies is probably also to be understood as a focal instance, as is suggested by its placement in the series of extreme and fairly specific sayings in Luke 6:27-28 (cp. Matt 5:44). A good example of a series of focal instances outside the Sermon on the Mount and parallel material is Matt 23:8-10. The texts mentioned above are commands and prohibitions, or indirectly command through proclaiming judgment on a certain type of action. Although this seems to be the most common type, a focal instance need not be a command, as Luke 12: 52-53 (cp. Matt 10:35) shows. Another variation is illustrated by Matt 8:21-22//Luke 9:59-60. Here we have a short dialogue consisting of request and response by Jesus. This is a formal characteristic which deserves investigation for its own sake, but the extremeness of the specific command (Forget your duty to bury your father) means that this pericope shares the characteristics of the focal instance (Luke 9:59-60 is discussed below, pp.162-63).

The list of texts above is not exhaustive but merely illustrates some of the variations in the usage of the focal instance within the synoptic Gospels. Furthermore, much work remains to be done in showing the significance of the conclusions above for the interpretation of particular texts.

3. Matt 6:1-6, 16-18. Righteousness in Secret.

1 Beware of practicing your righteousness before men in order
                to be seen by them; for then you will have no reward
                from your Father who is in heaven.
2 Thus, when you give alms,
        Sound no trumpet before you, as the hypocrites do in the
                synagogues and in the streets,
        That they may be praised by men.
    Truly, I say to you, they have their reward.
3 But when you give alms,
        Do not let your left hand know what your right hand is doing,
4   So that your alms may be in secret;
        And your Father who sees in secret will reward you.
5 And when you pray,
        You must not be like the hypocrites;
                for they love to stand and pray in the synagogues
                and at the corners of the main streets,
        That they may be seen by men.
    Truly, I say to you, they have their reward.
6 But when you pray,
        Go into your storeroom and shut your door
                and pray to your Father
        Who is in secret;
        And your Father who sees in secret will reward you.
16 And when you fast,
        Do not look dismal, like the hypocrites, for they make
                their faces disappear
        That they may appear to men as fasting.
    Truly, I say to you, they have their reward.
17 But when you fast,
        Anoint your head and wash your face,
18   That your fasting may not be apparent to men
                but to your Father who is in secret;
        And your Father who sees in secret will reward you.

In Matt 6:2-6, 16-18 we find commandments concerning three
important aspects of Jewish piety: the giving of alms, prayer, and
fasting. These are presented in three sections which are formally
similar, indicating that they belong together as parts of a repetitive
pattern. Matt 6:1 also binds these three commands together,

announcing the theme which they have in common and so providing a heading for this part of the Sermon on the Mount. To the second command, which deals with prayer, a collection of other material on prayer has been added (vss. 7-15). Here a concern to collect material dealing with the same topic has triumphed over concern with the repetitive pattern. However, when this additional material on prayer is ignored, the repetitive pattern is quite clear.

The pattern common to the three sayings is rather complex and is sufficiently flexible to allow differences in detail appropriate to the different topics of alms, prayer, and fasting. Yet the formal pattern is clearly maintained. This is to a large extent due to the exact repetition of certain elements, which thus constitute a kind of refrain. The elements which vary among the three sections group themselves around these repeated elements in such a way that it is clear that they, too, correspond from section to section. Thus, in spite of all the variations, the following general pattern emerges: "When you . . . (reference to an aspect of Jewish piety), (negative command) . . . as the hypocrites . . . (description of what the "hypocrites" do in extreme language) . . . that they may be seen [or "praised"] by men. Truly, I say to you, they have their reward. But you . . . (reference to the religious practice), (extreme command which contrasts sharply with what the "hypocrites" do) . . . in secret; and your Father who sees in secret will reward you." We are dealing here with repetitive pattern not only in the sense that the total pattern is repeated three times but also in the sense that there is a general parallelism within each instance of the pattern. Each saying is an antithesis, contrasting what the "hypocrites" do and what "you" are to do /21/. Antithesis is often supported by some kind of parallelism, for words must be brought into relation for contrast to be clear. Here each half of the pattern begins with a reference to the religious practice in question, followed by a command. The clause "that they may be seen [or "praised"] by men" corresponds to the phrase which ends with "in secret" in the second half /22/, and then each half ends with a statement about reward.

These texts follow a rather intricate repetitive pattern. What is the significance of this fact? Once again, this shows a concern with forceful language, language which can achieve resonance. The parallelism within each saying is present in order to support a basic antithesis. This antithesis makes the command stand out against its opposite, which adds to its force. Furthermore, the use of repetitive pattern results in a coupling of corresponding elements, both within each section and among the three sections, which gives to the whole a tight unity and results in a complex interplay of meaning (see p. 42 above). Thus words do not simply carry their own meaning as isolated lexical units or as elements of a sentence. They gain in meaning through interplay with other elements of the text. Corresponding words and phrases interpret and reinforce each other. For instance, the full range of meaning in the command "sound no trumpet" in vs. 2 only becomes clear through the contrast with its extreme opposite in vs. 3 and through its relation to other instances of similar behavior in the following commands. Through interaction with these corresponding elements, it becomes clear that it implies much more than its literal meaning. Note that the only two possibilities mentioned in vss. 2-4 are to "sound a trumpet" or to "not let your left hand know what your right hand is doing." This would seem to ignore the wide range of possibilities between these two extremes, such as our casual hints of our own generosity. In fact, however, reference only to these two extremes turns them both into forceful images for a wide range of behavior. Instead of encompassing the many possible ways of giving alms in some explicit formulation, the range of possible behavior is placed either under the sign of "sounding a trumpet" or of "not letting your left hand know what your right hand is doing," so that both expressions refer indirectly to many actions beyond those mentioned explicitly. This is so because of the interplay of meaning which results from the antithetical pattern.

The significance of repetitive pattern can also be seen in the repeated words which constitute the "refrain" within each command: " . . . that they may be seen [or "praised"] by men.

Truly, I say to you, they have their reward. . . . in secret; and your Father who sees in secret will reward you." These elements of refrain which close the two halves of each section not only bind the three sections together by making the repetitive pattern stand out. They also give emphasis through repetition to the thoughts which they contain. This is especially true because the repetitive pattern maintains some subtlety and interest, the refrains mixing with elements which vary, and yet are similar, from section to section. Indeed, there seem to be some deliberate alterations in wording and grammatical form to provide variety within the pattern. Word for word repetition has a dulling effect if it goes to any length. However, when it is broken by variation, the return of the same words hits us strongly. Whatever characteristics the words already have are magnified and their importance is emphasized. In our text this means that the sharp contrast between what is seen by men and what is not seen, between reward from men and God's reward, gains in power, and the decision between them becomes heavy with significance.

Furthermore, the parts which vary among the three sections are also affected by the repetitive pattern. Because they occupy the same place in the pattern, our attention is called to the fact that there is something similar about sounding a trumpet when giving alms, praying on the street corners, and looking dismal when fasting, which suggests a pattern of meaning which may apply elsewhere. Here also, then, we see how repetitive pattern can release words from their literal limits. The return of these similar thoughts also provides emphasis. However, what is emphasized through repetition depends on the nature of the material which is repeated. Repetition can only strengthen characteristics which the language already has. Thus we must look more closely at this language in order to understand what will come to the fore when it is placed in a repetitive pattern.

In vss. 2-4 we see immediately that the commands are formulated in extreme language. The command "sound no trumpet" is either a metaphor (see Grundmann: 193), or, if it does refer to an actual practice /23/, it is one which was probably not a real possibility for a man of ordinary means. This language is chosen because it is striking and extreme. It is the strongest image for advertising one's generosity that could readily be imagined in the first century. These words are not concerned with accurate description, and it would be a mistake to use them as a basis for statements about the actual practices of Jews at that time. The text is deliberately setting up an extreme type, for in such caricature a tendency is revealed most clearly. This view of vs. 2 is supported by the antithetical command in vs. 3, for here also the text goes to the extreme. In this case we have hyperbole, for what is commanded is literally impossible.

The same extremeness can be observed in the second and third sections. Vs. 5 again refers to an extreme type. It was common for Jews to pray in public, including the open streets, at the hours of prayer (cf. Strack-Billerbeck 1:397, 399-400). However, the "hypocrites" of our text "love" to pray in public, including "the corners of the main streets" /24/. The last phrase refers not merely to a public place but to the place of *greatest* visibility. Thus the text refers to an extreme manifestation of the tendency. The command in vs. 6 is even more extreme. The "room" (ταμεῖον) referred to is not an ordinary living or workroom but a storeroom or closet, used as a place to hide. This, together with the closing of the door, makes the precautions against being seen humorously elaborate. The difficulty of following this command in any literal sense is apparent in light of the Jewish custom of fixed times for prayer during the workday /25/. Since one might be far from home at these times, one could pray anywhere, except for places of impurity or in situations which made concentration too difficult (cf. Strack-Billerbeck 1:397, 399-401). The command in vs. 6, however, restricts prayer to the most private place in one's own home, ignoring all the problems which would arise for anyone wishing to follow the Jewish practice of fixed times of prayer during the workday /26/.

There are similar aspects to vss. 16-18. The description in vs. 16 is emphatic because of a play on words involving hyperbole. The verb ἀφανίζουσιν (RSV: "disfigure") is chosen in order to form a play on words with φανῶσιν (RSV: "be seen"). Such a play on words catches the hearer's attention and makes the saying more striking. In this case it also involves hyperbole, for ἀφανίζουσιν really means "render invisible" or "unrecognizable," or even "destroy," "ruin" (cf. Bauer: 124). The sense "render invisible" is supported in this context by the play on words with φανῶσιν. This probably refers to the same thing as looking "dismal," which, in the light of vs. 17, may involve neglect of normal bodily care and cleanliness, but to speak of making one's face disappear is a very strong way to put it. In contrast to this the disciple is commanded to "anoint your head and wash your face." Anointing and washing were associated with normal bodily comfort and even with joy and festivity. Therefore, the self-renunciation signified by fasting could also involve renunciation of anointing and washing. According to the Mishnah, washing and anointing were forbidden during the fast on the Day of Atonement (Yoma 8:1), and during the fast in connection with prayer for rain, washing and anointing were at first allowed, but as the situation became more serious and the fast more strict, they were forbidden (Taanith 1:6). There are a number of uncertainties here: whether these rules go back to the first century A.D., whether the prohibition of washing includes washing the face, and whether the practices of the communal fasts were also followed for the voluntary fasts of the individual. However, we can at least assert that renunciation of anointing and washing, though not always required, was part of the ideal of what would constitute a strict fast. This view of the situation is required by Matt 6:17 itself, for the command has no point unless the opposite was common practice or a commonly accepted ideal. So we must assume that the command stands in sharp contrast to the current understanding of what would constitute a strict fast. Once again the command contains something which is odd or extreme.

One other feature of these commands is worth noting. The second command in each saying, which indicates the right way for the disciple to act, falls into rhythmic or patterned speech. This may be the unconscious by-product of a desire to be forceful, rather than something which was consciously planned.

Nevertheless, the rhythmic repetition of short clauses in a pattern does add to the force of the language. (The following translations attempt to reproduce the pattern of the Greek words by following the Greek word order slavishly. For the meaning consult a standard translation.)

vs. 3: μὴ γνώτω   ἡ ἀριστερά σου

      not let know   the left hand your

      τί ποιεῖ   ἡ δεξιά σου

      what does   the right hand your

vs. 6: εἴσελθε εἰς   τὸ ταμεῖόν σου

      go into   the room your

      καὶ κλείσας   τὴν θύραν σου

      and shutting   the door your

      πρόσευξαι   τῷ πατρί σου

      pray   to the Father your

        τῷ ἐν τῷ κρυπτῷ

      who is in secret

vs. 17: ἄλειψαί   σου τὴν κεφαλὴν

      anoint   your the head

      καὶ τὸ πρόσωπόν σου   νίψαι

      and the face your   wash

In the first two cases the rhythm is established by the use of short clauses of two major words each (a verb form and a noun) with the same word order and end rhyme. In the third instance we have chiastic word order, which probably arises from the desire to put the verbs in the emphatic positions at the beginning and end of the command. That the chiasmus was felt is especially clear from the variation in the placement of the word "your."

From the discussion above it is clear that the three sections follow the same pattern not only with respect to their general structure and use of a common refrain, but also in the mode of language of the parts which vary. The negative images of the first half of each section all show clear tendencies toward the extreme. They are caricatures in which an inclination is magnified so that we see it in its most blatant and ridiculous form. The commands in the second half of each section are equally extreme, for the first (vs. 3) is clearly hyperbole, and the other two refer to behavior which is decidedly odd in the light of current Jewish practices or ideals. The common sense reaction of most men today, and probably also of most men in the first century, is that these commands go too far. It is impossible to keep one's religious life entirely a secret. To be sure, parading one's piety is a bad thing, but one needn't go to such extremes to avoid it, for the problem is not that serious. However, these commands assault our common sense with extreme words. What is the significance of such extreme language?

First, the speaker wants us to see that the danger *is* more serious than we suppose. The language is forceful because our assurance that such hypocrisy is no great problem with us is a major part of the problem. The commands must help us to see a deep and pervasive danger which haunts man's religious life, a danger which we have great trouble in seeing because it springs from one of our deepest needs, the need for "reward," which clearly includes recognition and honor (vs. 2: " . . . that they may be praised by men. . . . They have their reward."). The text realistically reflects the depth of man's need for such reward. Man is insecure, for the validity of his life is open to question. He must be assured that his life is worth while, and he seeks this assurance from others. The resulting search for such approval can dominate the whole of a man's life, even his religious behavior, perhaps *especially* his religious behavior, since religion claims to deal with what has ultimate significance for man. Moreover, just because this reward is so important to us, we are afraid to let it out of our control. Therefore we search for this reward within the sphere of things and men over which we have some power, and religion becomes a tool of manipulation. Against this the text insists that the disciple must dare to live for God's reward alone. However, this seems dangerous, for, as the text says, God is "in secret," and over him we have no control. Looked at in light of the depth of man's need for recognition and honor, we must admit that our religious behavior is riddled with the attempt to win approval from men. By this attempt we make our value and meaning dependent on social approval. We worship a false god, who enslaves us. Furthermore, the assumption that there is an easy alliance between God's approval and man's approval allows religion to turn God into the mythological sanction for the prevailing system of rank and reward /27/. It is only the extremeness of the text which forces us to meditate on the matter at this depth. It is only because the text attaches a weight to this problem which far exceeds the common sense view that we are forced to look until we see something which is so deep and broad that it explains this excessive weight.

Second, the extremeness and specificness of the commands in vss. 3, 6, and 17 call attention to the fact that they belong to the type which I previously called the "focal instance" /28/. Earlier I explained how the focal instance, because it stands in deliberate tension with normal behavior and remains quite specific rather than attempting to generalize, is able to imply more than it says. The imaginative shock produced sets the hearer thinking about many other situations, for he knows that it is not "just that" which is commanded but "even that." Thus the words acquire a larger field of meaning to which no clear limits can be set (cf. pp. 71-76 above). This holds for the commands in vss. 6 and 17 as well. They refer to specific and surprising acts which serve as the focal points of clarity for a larger field of meaning. We know that if we sneak away to the closet or fruit cellar to pray but later brag about our strange behavior, we have not fulfilled the commandment, even though we have not offended against the literal sense of the words. For the command implies more than its literal sense. It stands for

many strange stratagems which we may adopt to keep our practice
of religion from appearing as a claim to honor, stratagems which
only the fully awakened imagination can devise. Similarly, it will
take imaginative thinking to decide what concrete form our
response to vss. 3 and 17 should take.

In the material we have been discussing there is a further
element which adds to what I have said about the focal instance.
In each of the three sections the final command is preceded by a
reference to the behavior which is to be avoided. This is also
extreme and specific, and the two extreme instances within each
saying stand in sharp contrast to each other. This makes the two
instances stand out the more sharply as extremes. It also makes
even clearer the intention to refer indirectly to many possible
situations. The sayings completely ignore the middle range of
behavior. Most of us neither "sound a trumpet" nor keep our "left
hand" from knowing what our "right hand" is doing. However,
this does not mean that the command ignores us and the situations
we face. Rather these two extremes refer indirectly to all possible
situations in which religious practice may appear to lay claim to
human honor. The two extremes are like magnetic poles which
determine the field of force between them. Just because they are
extreme, everything else falls within their field of force. Just
because the ordinary range of behavior is given no explicit
attention, it is interpreted indirectly from the two extremes. In any
situation there may appear a subtle variation of "sounding a
trumpet," but, if we are alert to the danger, we may devise in each
situation the act which corresponds to "not letting your left hand
know what your right hand is doing." The exclusion of middle
ground is not a sign of the irrelevance of this language but of its
power to speak indirectly to many different situations. It is a sign
that the text is turning the clarifying power of the extreme against
the muddiness of ordinary experience, for the extreme can make
us sharply aware of a tendency which likes to conceal itself but
which can be recognized once we have had a clear view of its
undisguised form /29/. Such language cannot be judged by the
literal truth of the words. Attempting to do so turns the text into

nonsense. The text asserts its truth in its power to reveal something about us, opening our eyes to a deep tendency within our lives and awakening our imaginations to devise the new act which can counter this tendency /30/.

This forceful and allusive language is placed within a repetitive pattern, and it is the properties which this language already has which are strengthened through repetition. The forcefulness and imaginative power of these words increase, increasing the chance that we will recognize the danger to which we are normally blind. As the pattern returns a second and third time, it also suggests that the series could easily continue, so that the pattern may have implications beyond the subjects of alms, prayer, and fasting /31/.

4. *Mark 7:15, 10:9, and 8:35. What Goes In and What Comes Out; Joining and Separating; Saving and Losing (The "Antithetical Aphorism").*

In this section we will investigate some short sayings which are neither markedly metaphorical nor focal instances and in which repetitive pattern is incidental to the construction of an antithesis. We will discover from the form of these sayings that they, too, are shaped for maximum personal impact, seeking thereby to change the perspective from which an area of life is viewed.

An aphorism is a short, pithy statement of a principle or precept, often containing something ingenious, striking, or witty. It expresses a truth of broad application and yet it frequently opposes truth as commonly seen. Some examples (Auden and Kronenberger: 5, 26; italics in this source):

> Man is least himself when he talks in his own person.
> Give him a *mask* and he will tell the truth.
>
> > Wilde

> Fanaticism consists in redoubling your effort when you
> have forgotten your aim.
>
> > Santayana

In the Gospels we find a number of antithetical aphorisms. These are brief, pointed sayings which contain a sharp contrast. The saying tends to divide into two halves, with the same key words, in negative and positive form, or with antithetical terms. Thus there are word links between the two halves. As the saying develops, the speaker reverses the terms or ideas in a sort of word-play. We can speak of this as rhetorical wit, as long as we recognize that this playing with words has a serious purpose /32/. These word links unify the saying, emphasizing the interaction between related pairs of words and concentrating the hearer's attention on what is essential (see above, pp. 42, 44). This brings into sharp focus a basic tension within the saying. This concentrated tension is usually reinforced by conciseness, for whatever does not support the tension is omitted. The saying also gains force by its absoluteness. The claim is sweeping; no qualifications are added. Since the saying is general, one might mistake it for abstract, legal language. This would be a mistake because legal language is concerned with clarity of statement and cannot afford to play with words in this way. The absoluteness of the antithetical aphorism is further indication of a concern with forcefulness. It wishes to challenge a basic assumption of the hearer and force him to begin thinking anew. Distracting qualifications provide ways of escaping this challenge, either through arguing over peripheral matters or through reducing these words to a minor addition to what the hearer already knows and does.

We find such an antithetical aphorism in Mark 7:15:
There is nothing outside man going into him which can defile him,
But the things coming out of man are what defile man.

Notice the sharp contrast established through the use of the same terms ("man," "defile") or contrasting terms ("going into," "coming out") to form an antithetical construction. It is clear that the second half of the sentence was formed by twisting the words of the first half and not as an independent thought. Furthermore, no place is given to qualifications. The assertion is absolute and is expressed fairly concisely.

However, Mark 7:15 is not a perfect example of its form. It does show the unity and concentration of the antithetical aphorism, for the second half of the sentence introduces no new major words. But the saying is not as concise as it might be. Not all of the references to "man" and "him" are strictly necessary, and the grammatical construction would be simpler if "defile" were the main verb in each clause. Furthermore, the antithetical meaning is not reinforced by syntactic parallelism, for the two halves of the sentence are constructed rather differently.

The tendency toward a particular form somewhat different than Mark 7:15 appears in the variations in the tradition. In Matt 15:11 the saying is more concise and the antithesis is reinforced by syntactic parallelism. Brevity is achieved without change of meaning, except that Matthew specifies Mark's "into him" by substituting "into the mouth," which leads to the antithetical phrase "out of the mouth" in the second half of the saying. This suggests an unnecessary limitation of Mark's "things coming out of man" to sins of speech, although Matthew may have intended no such limit, for the explanation in 15:18-19 is not restricted to such sins of speech. There are some other indications in the tradition that the form of the saying in Mark was not felt to be fully adequate /33/. Nevertheless, Mark 7:15 exhibits the sharp contrast resulting from antithetical use of a few key words and the absoluteness which are characteristic of the antithetical aphorism.

The use of this form results, first of all, in a certain loss of conceptual clarity. What are "the things coming out of a man"? This could include many kinds of words and action. Rather than being sharp and clearly limited, the phrase is fuzzy and so is open to the many specifications which other experience may suggest. This phrase, which would appear strange in isolation, is dictated by the antithesis basic to the whole saying. This antithesis is more important here than conceptual clarity.

Such fuzziness invites a variety of specifications, depending on the situation of the hearer. We find one attempt at specification in Mark 7:18-23, a passage which commentators have recognized to be a secondary interpretation of vs. 15 (cf., e.g., Lohmeyer, 1959:142; Taylor: 344-47; Klostermann, 1936: 67, 70-71). This passage also shows how the mode of language can shift in spite of continuity of content. In vss. 18-23 each half of the saying in vs. 15 is considered separately, which dissolves the tension in the original saying. Vs. 19 attempts to explain and argue, doing so in a rather pedantic way. This attempt at argument, which is valid only if one admits the presupposition that what does not enter the heart does not defile, involves a different mode of language and calls forth a different kind of response. It invites a rational evaluation of the argument, followed by intellectual assent or dissent. No argument is found in vs. 15, nor does the form of the saying allow it. Vss. 21-23 offer further argument and specify the meaning of "what comes out of man" by attaching a list of vices. Vs. 15 allows specification. However, its potential of meaning stretches far beyond the list in vss. 21-22, and this list, since it is composed of general and widely recognized vices, has none of the sharpness of vs. 15. The interpreter may need to be *more* specific in applying vs. 15 to his situation.

The tension in this saying no doubt reflects the situation of tension to which it was originally addressed. Even without the context in Mark, the choice of the term "defile" and the reference to what is "going into" man suggest that this situation involved a conflict over cultic food laws. However, the interpreter does not do justice to the saying if he sees it as only an indication of how radical Jesus was or as only permission to ignore the Jewish food laws. Going only so far provides no understanding of the antithetical aphorism as a mode of language. The formal characteristics of this saying indicate a desire for maximum personal impact. Its absoluteness, leaving the assertion as strong as possible, its play with words, setting them in striking combinations, its concentration on a few major words, making their differences stand out in tensive contrast, all contribute to the saying's impact. The characteristics of this text also indicate an intention to force the hearer to decide. Just as psychological tension may lead to a decision, so the formal tension of this saying can bring about a decision. It seeks to do so without introducing new arguments or evidence. This does not mean that argument and evidence are irrelevant to decisions, even decisions about cultic impurity. However, listing all of the arguments and evidence is not the same as making a decision, which involves the personal will. Especially in decisions regarding the deeply personal and religious, the marshaling of arguments and evidence seldom leads directly to decision. In these cases much depends on the perspective from which the evidence is viewed. Decision on such matters means that a new concern becomes dominant; one begins to see the matter from a new perspective. It is the function of this antithetical aphorism to awaken a new dominant concern. After all the arguments and evidence are in, the decision as to what is important in man's life before God still has to be made. The saying must force that decision by speaking directly to the personal will. It must point forcefully to a new perspective, shocking us into seeing the matter in a new way, so that the lines of evidence become part of a new *Gestalt*. Everything depends on the saying's force. That is why this saying must be shaped so that, ignoring all the advantages of clarity and argument, it can achieve the greatest personal impact.

In this saying the cultic food laws are understood to be the point for such a decision. To modern Christians no decision seems necessary at this point, but within the context of first century Judaism this was not so. Moreover, the saying is not simply a declaration of freedom from cultic food laws. The concern for defilement is neither ridiculed nor denied but is radically refocused. Observance of the food laws is rejected so that it may be replaced with a new concern, a concern so pressing that there is no room for it and observance of the food laws. The defilement which is caused by the words and acts which arise within us and relate us to the external world, *that* must be the overriding concern. The saying is less a declaration of freedom than a radically different vision of the meaning of defilement. The new vision of defilement changes the understanding of what separates man from God, for that is what defilement is all about. It is in order to induce this new vision of defilement that this saying assumes the form which will give it maximum force.

The antithetical aphorism gains much of its force through sharp attack on a prevailing perspective. The saying is arresting because it resonates against a customary viewpoint in which the hearer has invested himself, and so the hearer feels it as a challenge to *him*. This makes it very difficult for most modern men to feel the force of this saying. The prevailing perspective has completely changed. The view of cultic defilement which the saying attacks, thereby gaining its force, is now regarded by the majority as obvious foolishness. The forcefulness of such language is essential to its function, but a shift in the prevailing perspective has robbed the saying of its force. In this situation, what can the modern interpreter do? He must find an area of modern life which represents a comparable prevailing perspective and allow the saying to resonate against it. Perhaps one of the simplest ways of doing this, because it involves the smallest shift in subject matter, is to recognize the modern *rejection* of cultic defilement as such a prevailing perspective. Then the saying regains some of its original force if we simply give the first half a concessive sense in line with modern views: "To be sure, there is nothing outside of man going into him which can defile him, *but* the things coming out of man, *these do* defile man." This changes the way in which the saying gains its force, but it does honor the saying's concern for forceful language and stays close to the subject matter. The alternative is to apply the saying to something quite different than cultic defilement. This can also be justified, provided the new application is chosen with sensitivity both to the meaning of an area of life for modern man and the meaning of the saying in its original setting.

In Mark this antithetical aphorism is placed in a setting which emphasizes both its importance and the difficulty men have in understanding it. It is introduced in 7:14 by a call for all to hear and understand /34/. In vs. 17 it is designated a *parabolê*, a term which is used in the New Testament in the broad sense of the Hebrew *mashal*, including not only parables but proverbs, riddles, and other kinds of figurative or obscure speech (on the meanings of this term see Jeremias, 1963:20). Mark seems to understand a *parabolê* to be inherently difficult to understand or accept (cf. 4:10-13). In 7:17-18 the disciples must ask further concerning the *parabolê*, and their lack of understanding is emphasized. Why should the Evangelist /35/ understand the saying in 7:15 to be difficult to understand or accept? It is neither a parable, nor a strange figure of speech, nor a riddle. Nevertheless, the Evangelist is correct that the saying presents a problem to understanding. The understanding which it requires is not a matter of adding new facts or ideas to a proven stock but of radically shifting one's perspective, so that a major area of life looks quite different. The problem is not in understanding the concepts in the saying but in seeing life in this new way, through the eyes of the aphorism. For the antithetical aphorism wishes to change us and our world, as is made clear by its sharply antithetical form and its forcefulness.

Much of what has been said about Mark 7:15 applies also to the antithetical aphorism in Mark 2:27: "The sabbath was made for man, not man for the sabbath." The antithesis, the playing with words, the absoluteness are all clear. In some respects this is an even better example of the form for it is extremely concise, and the antithesis is reinforced by syntactic parallelism. The lack of concern with qualifications and with the practical problem of establishing rules of behavior is quite apparent as soon as one considers the implications of such a saying within the context of Jewish piety. The saying does not spell out a rule which will directly solve questions of how to behave on the sabbath. Starting from this aphorism, various practical conclusions could be reached, from an almost total disregard of the sabbath law because of human need to observance of the sabbath law except in unusual cases, since the sabbath is good for man. The aphorism does not predetermine the conclusion but requires the hearer to think about these things in a radical way. It is the aphorism's rejection of a common assumption and announcement of a new priority which sets thought moving in a new direction. However, here as in Mark 7:15 a shift in our assumptions has robbed the saying of much of the force necessary to its original purpose.

In Mark 10:9 we find another antithetical aphorism: "What God has joined, let not man separate." The structure is somewhat different than the preceding examples, for it does not consist of denial and affirmation of two opposite possibilities but of a prohibition and the relative clause which is its object. However, the relative clause ("what God has joined") is emphasized by being placed first. This, together with the fact that the two clauses contain antithetical terms consisting of subject and verb in the same order, gives the relative clause sufficient weight to balance the main clause, and we feel a sharp antithesis in spite of the fact that the two clauses are not syntactically equivalent. The antithesis results primarily from the two contrasting verbs "join" and "separate." However, the verbs also suggest a possible conflict between their subjects, and so "God" and "man" become contrasting terms also. It would have been quite possible to prohibit divorce without this antithetical playing with words, but the use of an antithetical aphorism has its own purpose, which a legal rule cannot fulfill. This saying also illustrates well the conciseness and absoluteness of the antithetical aphorism.

In discussing Mark 7:15 I indicated that the antithetical aphorism by its forcefulness intends to jolt the hearer into a new perspective on an area of life. It does this by sharply challenging his old perspective. This is true of Mark 10:9 also. The old perspective is indirectly expressed by what is prohibited. The dissolution of marriage was an option open to the marriage partner (or, at least, to the husband), and, although the necessary grounds might be understood more strictly or more loosely, the use of such an option was no offense to God, provided certain regulations of the law were followed. Within the legal limitations, divorce was a man's private business. The antithesis within Mark 10:9 brings to sharp expression the challenge to this perspective. The possibility of separation is brought up against God's act of joining man and woman. There is no longer an option which man may exercise without offense to God. The whole marriage relation is understood in light of the active presence of God realizing his will in the union of man and woman. There is no possibility of the destruction of this relation with impunity. Thus the saying resonates against the old perspective, and the resulting tension is reflected in the antithetical form of the saying. This gives to the saying sufficient force to set forth God's acts of joining as the root from which new thought about man's tendencies to separate may grow.

This does not mean that the saying proposes a stricter legal rule to replace the legal rules which were in effect. The use of an antithetical aphorism indicates a purpose different than setting forth a legal rule. It indicates that the force of the words is more important than stating clear standards of behavior for the different situations which people face. This is apparent from the fact that the saying, in its forceful absoluteness, seems bent on encompassing all possible situations related to marriage, thus obscuring differences which are very important. The saying retains its full force and appropriateness not only in situations where a man or wife /36/ may contemplate divorce from the marriage partner but also in cases where a third party may interfere with a marriage (e.g., philanderers, mothers-in-law) /37/. It is fully relevant to situations in which divorce is not even contemplated but in which there is damage to the unity of man and wife which might lead to a decisive break in their relation. And it continues to be relevant even after divorce has occurred, when it brings sharply to mind the need for a new start in the face of a serious failure. The difference from a legal rule is clear when we compare Mark 10:9 with a command such as "Don't get divorced," which, if we were to ignore the significance of form, might appear to be an adequate translation of it. This command could function as a legal rule, but it would apply to only a part of the situations encompassed by the antithetical aphorism. Even in the case of situations addressed by both, the legal rule functions in quite a different way. The legal rule is content to regulate behavior; the antithetical aphorism does not immediately decide questions of behavior, which may involve complex considerations, but helps the hearer to see the situation in a new way. Thus, like the focal instance, the antithetical aphorism can act as "illuminator" of many different situations but makes no attempt to decide which is the lesser of two evils, as must often be done in practical decisions /38/. To draw the conclusion that, if this command is taken seriously, there must be no such thing as divorce is to understand it as a legal rule. The effect of the command is, rather, to bring sharply into focus the conflict between the many ways in which the marriage relation may be damaged and God's will that husband and wife be joined as one. This may require us to recognize that there are situations in which we can only admit that we are sinful men.

Just as with 7:15, this antithetical aphorism is followed by material related in theme but different in mode of language, for vss. 11-12 are much closer to being a legal rule (see pp. 72-73).

Mark 10:9 is the climactic statement in a longer discussion of divorce which begins at 10:2. Whether 10:9 was always a part of this setting or not, the setting supports it, first by allowing the alternate perspective to be expressed so that it may be attacked (vs. 4) and then by amplifying in advance the reference in 10:9 to God as the one who joins husband and wife. In vss. 6-8, with the help of the Old Testament, God's joining of husband and wife is rooted in God's decision to create man and woman, who, drawn to each other, unite as "one flesh." I would suggest that we experience the reality of this "one flesh" when we share through marriage in a community of life with a sexual basis. This reality shows itself not only in the happy home but also in the suffering which results from a home falling apart. In the suffering perhaps more than in the happiness a man and a woman may discover how deeply involved they are. They may discover that they are no longer simply individuals, for in the poisoning of their marriage a part of them is dying. This unity of "one flesh" in marriage, here rooted in God's purpose since creation, may be understood as a major manifestation of God's larger purpose of uniting men in love. Therefore my attitudes and actions within this special community of life not only concern me and another person but also concern my relation to the God who wills that men be joined in love.

Although this aphorism neither solves our legal problems nor makes our practical decisions for us, it can perform the function for which it is fitted by its form. It can do this simply and directly, in much the same way as in the first century, for most modern men share the view of marriage which is here attacked. Marriage is essentially a private affair. Society is only secondarily involved, and God hardly at all. When the saying challenges such a view, it is challenging us. This challenge should set us thinking, perhaps along these lines: God's purpose of uniting persons in love finds special expression in the intimate relation of marriage. The greatness and the failures of the particular marriage in which I share appear with new clarity when judged in light of this purpose. The saying wants us to recognize how much is at stake in marriage and to consider how our experience in marriage relates to the purpose of the God who takes pleasure in uniting man and woman.

A further example of the antithetical aphorism is found in Mark 8:35, which reads in the RSV translation:

> For whoever would save his life will lose it;
> And whoever loses his life for my sake and the gospel's will save it.

This saying occurs in five other places in the Gospels. Matt 16:25 and Luke 9:24 are close parallels to Mark 8:35. Matt 10:39, Luke 17:33, and John 12:25 show more extensive differences from Mark 8:35 in wording, but in all six versions the saying consists of two clauses and makes strong use of antithesis. We will focus on Mark 8:35, which represents the form of the antithetical aphorism well, although the presence of the phrase "and the gospel's," found only in Mark, somewhat distends the second clause.

In this saying the antithesis is more elaborate than in previous examples. Not only are the two clauses antithetical, but there is antithesis within each clause, for the two verbs "save" and "lose" are opposites. The verb $\dot{a}\pi\acute{o}\lambda\lambda\upsilon\mu\iota$, which could be translated here as "destroy" or "kill" as well as "lose" /39/, stands in sharp contrast to the possibility of saving one's life, and this contrast is strongly emphasized by its repetition in reverse order in the second half and by the word order of the first half, which, in

Greek, brings the two verbs into immediate conjunction. This strange combination of opposites, with reversal of the two terms in the second clause, illustrates the striking use of words typical of the antithetical aphorism. The saying also exhibits the conciseness and absoluteness typical of such sayings. As in the previous examples we have studied, all of this contributes to forcefulness.

There is a tendency among interpreters to explain the saying by distinguishing between two senses of ψυχή ("life"). Thus Vincent Taylor (382) says, "In the saying ψυχή. . . is used in a double sense, first of a man's ordinary human life and then of his true self or personality." This explains how one can both lose his life and save it. I doubt that this helps us to hear this saying in the way in which it wants to be heard. It is noteworthy that the saying uses the same word as object of the verbs throughout (ψυχή or its pronoun), thus obscuring the point which interpreters wish to clarify. This is not merely the result of carelessness, for in this way the paradoxical tension of the saying is strengthened. The saying *intends* to be a paradox. The significance of this fact begins to appear when we note the result of removing the paradox. When the paradox is ignored, it is possible to fit this saying into a religious system of thought which appears reasonable, at least to its adherents. Then the saying is reduced to a religious commonplace: self-sacrifice (or the martyr's death) on earth will bring happiness in heaven.

However, the saying dares to be unreasonable and gains power because of this. The paradoxical form of this saying allows it to take the opposing perspective seriously, for this other perspective is heard within the saying itself. We are reminded of our deep concern to preserve our lives and of the fear which any threat to our lives causes. Furthermore, we have firm convictions as to what it means to "save" and to "lose" one's life, and these convictions are reflected in the way in which these verbs are used in the first part of each clause. However, within the saying, this vision of our situation is crossed by another, and the paradox is the formal reflection of the conflict between these two visions. In the sharp antithesis, in which saving becomes losing and losing saving, we feel the grating vibration of two visions of life rubbing against each other. No effort is made to persuade us to accept the new perspective by reason or common sense. The speaker risks everything on the forcefulness of the words. Evidently argument from what is reasonable would not be adequate. What is reasonable is reasonable within a particular horizon of meaning, and within the established horizon this saying does not fit. It must seek to break open the old horizon and challenge its logic. It must shake our deep assurance that we know what saving life and losing life mean. It attempts this by taking the meaning of our words away from us, turning them inside out, forcing us to face the possibility that we should fear what we have always wanted and should do what we have always feared. Such a shaking, if it begins in us, attacks our fear and concern themselves. Only this shaking of our deep, largely unconscious convictions can do this. On the other hand, if the saying fit within our lives as something reasonable, the possibility of bringing about significant change would be lost. The saying would only be an additional item within the established vision of life, not a new beginning point. This the saying wishes to prevent, as its sharply paradoxical form makes clear /40/.

Thus the form of the saying makes it more difficult to accept but also more significant. We hear the new demand as a radical challenge to the rules by which our lives are governed and so can recognize how radical the response to this challenge must be. When the modern interpreter allows the paradox of the saying to dissolve in his interpretation, the saying becomes a prop for an established religious world view rather than a challenge to the vision of life which dominates us even when we espouse that world view. Our conscious world views seldom reach to the springs of life. This saying wishes to penetrate that far. The new vision of life which it carries is not a new world view which we may adopt if it is intellectually convincing. It is a challenge to the concern for our own lives which lies much deeper than our world views. And this new vision of life preserves its strangeness, its mystery. What we see is seen indirectly, through the surd introduced into the logic by which we live. Because of the paradox, the promised saving of life appears not as a natural consequence of our action but as a *wonder*, and so long as we feel the paradox it remains a wonder. This wonder is the sign of a reality which does not explicitly appear within the saying and which is, perhaps, most adequately expressed in this indirect way. For neither God nor heaven appear here as fixed entities of a religious world view /41/. Rather we see the shadow of a reality which makes itself known in its challenge to our existence. All of this is possible only because of the paradoxical form of this antithetical aphorism.

The phrase "for my sake," which Mark 8:35 shares with the parallel sayings in Matt 16:25, 10:39, Luke 9:24, ties this paradoxical possibility of saving one's life through losing it to the experience of following Jesus as a disciple. This linkage is reinforced by the setting of these words in Mark, for they are spoken by the Christ who has chosen the way of suffering and who is calling his disciples to follow him in that way. Thus the saying indirectly catches up the Gospel story of suffering, self-giving, and resurrection, pointing up *its* paradox and sharing in the richness of this larger event. The addition of "and the gospel's" to "for my sake" in Mark 8:35 suggests that this experience of discipleship continues to shape the life of the church in its mission after the death and resurrection of Jesus.

With appropriate adaptation, much of what has been said about Mark 8:35 can also be applied to such sayings as Matt 23:12// and Mark 10:31//, which are similar in form. There are a number of other aphorisms with contrasting elements, e.g., Matt 10:26-27//, 12:30//, 22:14, Mark 4:25//, 9:35b//, 9:40//, Luke 9:48c, 16:15b, 18:27. These vary somewhat in form, and each would have to be studied in light of the way in which form and content interact to produce a significant utterance. However, what has already been said may be sufficient to suggest how this might be done. Mark 7:15, 2:27, and 10:9, which are found in expanded controversy settings, should be compared to Mark 2:17, 3:4, and 12:17, other sayings with contrasting elements found in controversy dialogues /42/.

5. Mark 10:42-44. Being Great as Servant.

42b   You know that those who are supposed to rule over the Gentiles
         lord it over them,
       And their great men exercise authority over them.
43   But it is not so among you;
       But whoever would become great among you shall be your servant,
44   And whoever would be first among you shall be slave of all.

The sayings about being great and being first are antithetical aphorisms. In other passages we find a similar aphorism without the additional material in Mark 10:42-43a and without the doubling of the aphorism in 43b-44 (cf. Matt 23:11, Mark 9:35 [partial doubling], Luke 9:48c) /43/. Since the material in Mark 10:42-44 could also circulate as a single aphorism, we must inquire into the reasons why a speaker or writer might choose to use this longer version. As we look at the passage more carefully, we will see that it is a rather successful attempt to strengthen the powers already present in the antithetical aphorism.

The parallel sentences in vss. 43b-44 show the characteristics which we have found to be typical of the antithetical aphorism: conciseness, absoluteness, sharp antithesis. The aphorism in Mark 8:35, which we have already studied, was also a double saying, but there the two sentences were antithetical. Here they are synonymous, and so the amount of information added by doubling the saying is small. However, we have noted previously that repetitive pattern can increase the forcefulness of words, especially when the second instance of the pattern is stronger than the first. Such is the case here. "First" in vs. 44 is a stronger form of "great" in vs. 43, for it refers to the ultimate in greatness. The importance of this word is emphasized by placing it last in the Greek clause in vs. 44 /44/. Similarly, "slave of all" in vs. 44 is stronger than "your servant" in vs. 43. Both of these phrases are emphasized by placing the crucial noun last in the clause. Thus vs. 44 says the same thing as vs. 43b but says it more powerfully. It is able to build upon the first instance of the pattern and increase its forcefulness.

However, the pattern of this passage is more extensive. The

double antithetical aphorism is balanced by a double statement
about the rulers of the nations in vs. 42. In vs. 42 also the similarity
of meaning between the two halves of the saying is supported by a
formal similarity (οἱ ...κατακυριεύουσιν αὐτῶν ; οἱ ... κατεξουσιάζουσιν
αὐτῶν), so that a pattern begins to be established. Over against this
budding pattern, vs. 43a is a sharp interruption. The negation
which it expresses is underlined through breaking the pattern with
a sentence of quite different form. However, the sense of pattern is
regained when the double statement of vs. 42 is balanced by the
double aphorism in vss. 43b-44. This formal balance enforces the
thought, for the two double sentences stand in antithetical
relation. The pattern helps us to compare them and so underlines
the contrast. Moreover, this develops the contrast which is
already present within the double antithetical aphorism. There we
find reference to becoming "great" and being "first," though these
are paradoxically linked to being a slave. The paradox is even
stronger because vs. 42 first presents greatness as crass power and
position /45/. Here we are reminded of what greatness means in
human society. Over against this the striking strangeness of
identifying greatness with the servant stands out with increased
force. Thus this passage shows considerable sensitivity to the
powers of the antithetical aphorism. The expansion does not add
foreign elements, thereby weakening the antithetical aphorism,
but strengthens the characteristics which are proper to it.

The narrative context adds an additional aspect to the contrast
in these verses. Before we come to vss. 43-44, we are not only
reminded of the oppressive power of the world's rulers but are also
presented with the disciples' jealous rivalry for position (cf. 10:35-
41). The struggle for dominance appears not only in the Gentile
world but also among Jesus' followers, with whom most readers
of Mark would identify. The writer's skill leads us to bring these
ideas of greatness with us as we approach vss. 43-44, where they
are confronted with a strikingly different view. The shock of this
confrontation gives vss. 43-44 the power to challenge man's strong
desire for dominance, for the contrast in our text seeks to assure

that these words can only be affirmed after a great negation.

Vs. 45 is also intended to support vss. 43-44, as the conjunction "for" shows. The concern of scholars with the question of the historical origin of this interpretation of Jesus' death has tended to tear the verse loose from what precedes it and turn it into an independent, doctrinal statement. Perhaps this has been encouraged by the fact that formally it is not well integrated into the passage. The thought of what precedes is carried on by the phrase "not to be served but to serve," but vs. 45 is a new type of sentence which does not fit the pattern of the preceding passage. It is more complex, makes no attempt at parallelism, and introduces an important new thought. Therefore it tends to stand out for its own sake and, perhaps, to compete with what preceded it. However, the interpreter should honor the Evangelist's intention that it support, not detract from, vss. 43-44. This it can do because it also speaks very forcefully, although in a different way from the antithetical aphorism. It gains its power by calling to mind Jesus' death for others, a powerful image which already carries depth of meaning for readers of the Gospel. This powerful image underscores the challenge of vss. 43-44 by calling the reader to follow in the way of the Son of Man /46/.

If the modern reader is to encounter the full force of this passage, he must be careful not to give to the concepts of "servant" and "slave" connotations of religious dignity. In the Biblical world being an important slave of a great lord might be a position of honor, but being "slave of all" was not. Slavery was a familiar social institution, and the original hearers of these words were not likely to have romantic ideas about it. It was a position of degradation, not of honor and power. Similarly, we weaken the proper force of the passage when we understand being "great" and "first" as referring to some sort of religious or "spiritual" greatness which we may add to our other types of greatness or which, at least, provides a clear alternative to other forms of greatness, thus establishing firm ground for our strivings. When we are less religious and more honest, we know what being "great" means: it means power and position. This is what vs. 42 points to, thereby helping us to be honest. Thus vss. 43b-44 are full of paradoxical tension, for greatness and being a slave do not go together. To be sure, something happens to the ideas of being "great" and "first" when they enter into this paradox. What happens is not that we are given a new goal for which to strive, a clear and reasonable ideal of greatness, but that greatness is taken out of our hands, for it is promised to the one who has decided in his life to make no claims to greatness. For such a one greatness can only come as a strange and wonderful gift and be based on something quite different from his achievements for himself in the world.

Under the pressure of this tensive language the concepts of "servant" and "slave" are stretched beyond their normal, literal meanings, without leaving them completely behind. The range of meaning of these words is determined less by normal usage than by the contrast with the greatness for which we strive. The connotations of dishonor and subordination remain, but being "slave of all" indirectly suggests many different acts in many different situations which may or may not involve literal slavery.

There is no attempt to spell out these acts concretely nor to decide whether there are situations when self-assertion may still be necessary, perhaps to protect the possibility of service. It is not the purpose of this passage to give general rules for the solution of practical problems, though it will indirectly affect practical decisions if it is able to awaken in the hearer a new vision of life.

We encounter situations as opportunities or threats to our values, and these values reflect the basic perspectives from which we see our world. One of the most pervasive and powerful ways in which we see the world and structure it as value is in terms of our own power and prestige. It is this basic perspective which our passage attacks. Here we see the significance of the forceful antithesis which shapes this passage. The prevailing perspective is allowed expression in order that a radical reversal may take place. Our desire for greatness is paradoxically tied to the opposite of greatness, the role of slave, and the force of this thought is increased by the additional elements of repetition and antithesis which we have noted. Such drastic measures with language are necessary in order to attack at the root the rule by which we live. The words must be forceful to strike so deep.

The world to which these words point remains strange to us. There is no direct, logical connection that we can see between being a slave and greatness. Indeed, we know that servants are usually walked on by all around them. If we are slaves to others, who will care for our dignity? Is there a reality from which we may live with meaning and dignity while being slaves of all? The saying points to a paradoxical possibility which has no basis within our ordinary, closed world.

I have pointed out how the antithetical aphorism has been strengthened in this passage by repetition and by contrast with vs. 42 and the narrative setting. However, our armor is thick. Are the words strong enough to pierce? Evidently the Evangelist was not sure, for he has gone even further in his effort to give the words power. In doing so, he again uses the devices of antithesis and repetition. Within the Gospel of Mark Jesus' three announcements of his coming death (8:31, 9:31, 10:33-34) are the basis for a repetitive pattern of major scope. Each announcement is accompanied by indications that the disciples do not understand, are afraid, or reject what Jesus says. This reaction is not only expressed in the narrator's descriptive comments but is also graphically portrayed in a scene following each announcement. Peter rebukes Jesus, the disciples discuss who is the greatest, James and John want the positions of honor at Jesus' right and left hand. Each of these scenes is followed by strong teaching on discipleship in which it is made clear that the disciples must follow Jesus in suffering and selfless service. Two passages which we have examined (8:35, 10:42-44) are part of this teaching, and 10:42-45 is its climax. When the reader comes to 10:42-45, therefore, he is coming to the climax of a threefold pattern. He has already encountered similar antithetical aphorisms at 8:35 and 9:35, as well as related forceful teaching. Furthermore, the impact of this teaching has been increased by the contrast with the disciples, who represent the prevailing perspective under attack. In 10:42-45, therefore, the Evangelist not only gives force to his

words by the repetition and antithesis which we find there but also
builds upon a repetitive and antithetical pattern of much broader
scope. He has taken great care to give his words the greatest force
which his tools permit. This is necessary because, as the
Evangelist's portrait of the disciples makes clear, it is not easy to
hear words which challenge our fundamental view of life and wish
to replace it with another.

6. Luke 6:37-38. Judge not.

37 Judge not, and you will not be judged;
       Condemn not, and you will not be condemned;
       Forgive, and you will be forgiven;
38 Give, and it will be given to you;
          A measure good,
                pressed down,
                      shaken together,
                            running over,
                                  will be put into your lap.
       For by the measure with which you measure
          it will be measured back to you.

In the antithetical aphorism we encountered a serious sort of
playing with words. One term called up its opposite, both
vocabulary and sentence structure being determined by a pressure
toward sharp antithesis. This conflict of words was the formal
reflection of a conflict between the prevailing perspective and the
new vision which the saying wished to awaken. Such meaningful
playing with words is not limited to sayings which contain a
contrast. There are other sayings in the synoptic Gospels which
allow a word to appear in one form and then use it in another
form, tying parts of the saying together by word links. The word
play does not establish a contrast but, through a double use of one
or more words, suggests a similarity between two different
situations. Thus the pattern brings together situations which we
may normally keep apart. This type of formulation is found in
Luke 6:37-38.

In vss. 37-38a we find a series of four short sayings with the
same form. Each exhibits the conciseness and lack of qualification

characteristic of the aphorisms which we previously examined. In fact, these sayings are very short, consisting almost entirely of two different forms of the same verb. The word play consists in this shift in the form of the verb, especially the shift from active to passive voice /47/. The series consists of two negative versions of the saying balanced by two in the positive. The formal consistency encourages the hearer to understand them as a group and to allow one saying to interpret the other. Thus the parallel to "condemn" and the contrast with "forgive" makes clear that the word "judge" in the first saying refers to an unfavorable judgment, as it does fairly frequently in the New Testament /48/.

The careful form of these sentences is again the result of a concern for forceful language which can address a deep-seated problem. Simple instruction is not enough to combat our tendency to ferret out the faults of others and expose them to our condemning gaze. We have much at stake in this process, for our own egos gain by comparing ourselves with our inferiors. Our sense of right and wrong supports our efforts, for we can often show that our neighbor has broken the law of man or of God. Therefore our text does not merely instruct; it attacks with full force. We encounter not a single saying but a fourfold repetitive pattern. Little new information is added by this repetition, but the text does gain in energy and passion. The rhythmical repetition is a sign of the importance of these words, which cannot be allowed to die without achieving their goal. Even more significant is the way in which the double use of a single verb in each of the four sayings enforces the command. Behind the passive forms of these verbs stands God as the implied actor /49/. Thus the sayings link man's condemnation or forgiveness to God's condemnation or forgiveness. It is this link which is the primary source of the forcefulness of these sayings, for by this means the hearer is caught in his own need. These words neatly turn our concern for ourselves against us. The same self-concern which leads us to condemn others forces us to recognize that such behavior will no longer do. Our harsh attitude toward others now carries with it a threat to ourselves; the judgment we practice drags our own judgment after it. It is more comfortable to live in two worlds at the same time, the world of forgiveness and the world of strict judgment. Then we can ask for mercy for ourselves but demand full payment from others. The command forces us to choose between these worlds. In doing so the text attacks at the very spot where we thought our position was strongest. It speaks to the sense of justice which we invoke in condemning others. The text proclaims that we will receive exactly what we give, judgment for judgment, forgiveness for forgiveness. What could be more just than that? But this justice leaves no room for our demand of justice from our neighbor. This justice won't allow us to judge strictly but requires us to forgive, since we ourselves do not dare face God's strict judgment. Forgiveness is our only chance; therefore we must forgive.

These commands wish to reorder radically the way in which we understand our relations to others. This web of relations, which we order according to rights and debts, must now be seen in terms of God's demand for forgiveness. The text hopes to achieve this by a simple device: playing with a word, turning the active verb into the passive. This device, simple as it is, is no mere decoration. It is the hinge pin which links our relation with God to our relation with our neighbors. What we tend to separate must be held together. This simple device accomplishes this. We may intellectually affirm that our relation with God is linked to our relation with man but deny this in action, for our actual behavior responds to a vision of life deeper than our intellectual convictions. Though bare of all arguments, the text, with its little linguistic surprise, catches our attention and takes root in our memory, carrying with it a vision of life which challenges the one by which we live. For the threat of God's judgment and the offer of God's forgiveness are brought forcefully to bear upon our attitudes toward others through this simple device of playing with a word.

Luke 6:37-38, like some other synoptic commands, combines a radical demand with a sharp awareness of the depth of evil in man's life. The demand is radical not because man is inherently good and so can achieve great things but because man is radically dependent on God's forgiveness and so must learn to live in the order established by that forgiveness. The demand is extreme but not idealistic, for it arises not from an optimistic view of man but from a sharp awareness of the depth of man's need for forgiveness. We are dealing with an ethic which knows the profundity and pervasiveness of human self-centeredness but which dares to do battle with this enemy because it believes in another reality which has come to lay claim to the heart of man.

Vs. 38 contains additional material which introduces the metaphor of a "measure." The final sentence of the verse (RSV: "For the measure you give will be the measure you get back.") is found also in the other synoptic Gospels, in Matt 7:2 in connection with the command to not judge, in Mark 4:24 in quite a different setting. The Markan setting may suggest that the saying circulated separately from the saying about judging. Its syntactic form does not match Luke 6:37-38a exactly. However, this saying also links God's judgment to man's action in relation to others by playing with a word. Thus there is a certain appropriateness to its location in Luke /50/.

Nevertheless, we must ask whether this saying contributes to the force of what precedes it. When the form and force of words are important, rather than only the information which they supply, additions can undermine the force of a passage by breaking the form, qualifying the thought, or introducing extraneous considerations. One can say less by saying too much. The problem here, however, is not that the form of the passage is damaged but that there are some dangers in the concept of measure. The sayings in vss. 37-38a link God's judgment to man's judgment of his fellows. However, one might come to understand this link as a calculable relation whereby God's judgment may be manipulated. Introducing the idea of measure would seem to strengthen this possibility, for it leads the hearer to think of a manageable quantity which may be exactly calculated.

Another problem may arise in connection with vss. 37-38a. These sayings speak most forcefully when we are sharply aware of our own need for God's forgiveness and of God's willingness to respond to our need. A lively sense of this need and this hope makes both the commands and the promises of these sayings speak vividly. If this is a radical ethic, it is nevertheless an ethic for sinners. This means, however, that a limited awareness of our need and of God's grace will also limit the impact of these commands.

The problems raised in the last two paragraphs can help us to understand the significance of the sentence concerning "good measure," found only in Luke's version of this passage. This sentence serves as a bridge to the final sentence of the verse by introducing the concept of "measure." It also breaks with the rather rigid form of the preceding commands. However, we find here another variety of carefully formed and forceful speech, which gives this sentence power to contribute to the total impact of the passage rather than detracting from it. It contributes by placing vividly before our imaginations the nature of God's giving /51/, thus attacking the second problem discussed above. Here the giving which is promised in response to our giving shows itself as true gift, for it overflows the expected measure. This also combats the tendency to interpret the preceding commands in terms of calculable quantities with definite limits which make these commands manageable within the prevailing patterns of our lives. The dangerous concept of measure is not avoided but adopted and stretched out of shape. This measure is used in a surprising way, which increases the impact of the metaphor. It is a measure not used to measure, that is, not used to limit what is given. However, we see this clearly only when we consider the form of the words, for, once again, the intention of the text is reflected in its form and is only fully effected through this form. The impact of the sentence rests upon the careful climactic pattern constructed with the adjective and adjectival participles which modify the noun "measure." We find five words in a row with the same ending, which underscores the repetitive emphasis in the heaping up of the adjectival modifiers. The four adjectival elements are arranged so as to begin with the shortest and mildest and end with the longest and strongest /52/. Thus the pattern of the words and the meaning reinforce one another and the whole phrase builds up to a strong climax:

μέτρον	καλὸν	πεπιεσμένον	σεσαλευμένον	ὑπερεκχυννόμενον
measure	good	pressed down	shaken together	running over

In this way we are not merely told that God's gift is gracious. We gain a sense of how wonderful it is as these words pile up, one upon the other, each one carrying us farther from the normal practice of measuring and the limitation which it implies. We are not merely told that God's gift is overwhelming. We feel it overwhelm us in the words. This vivid metaphor for God's giving and forgiving fills the whole passage with power and reacts upon our understanding of what it must mean for us to give. The final sentence of vs. 38, which in itself might suggest an element of calculation, now serves instead to apply this vivid picture of an overflowing, unmeasured measure to our actions also, suggesting that we must give in this way, since this is how God desires to give. Thus the passage attacks strongly our vision of life as a network of rights and debts which must be upheld by condemning the wrongdoing of others and substitutes a vision of an order imposed by God's forgiveness. And the vivid picture of God's uncalculated giving shows how far we must go in our forgiveness.

As with other commandments which we have discussed, no attempt is made to deal with the complications which arise when we seek to relate such teaching to practical decisions. We are not told directly and simply what we are to do with a man who has become a danger to society. This mode of language does not address us on that level but speaks to our basic vision of the world of human relations. Nevertheless, such teaching can make a difference in our practical decisions, for our vision of life expresses itself again and again in our decisions, even when we are not aware of it.

We discussed above the use of two forms of a single verb in the sayings in vss. 37-38a. We find a similar use of one word to refer to both the action of man and to God's response in the "sentences of holy law" discussed by Ernst Käsemann. Examples of this form within the synoptic tradition are Mark 8:38//, Matt 10:32f.//,

5:19, and 6:14f. Käsemann also includes Mark 4:24f., a parallel to the last sentence of the passage we have been discussing. He wishes to distinguish between these pronouncements of "holy law" and material which is merely "parenetic warning or prophetic threat" (67). He admits that there is similar material which is clearly parenetic, but insists that these pronouncements use legal form and reflect a situation of eschatological immediacy in which God himself is establishing his right in the world. This interesting thesis has recently been challenged by Klaus Berger (1970-71), who argues that Käsemann's "sentences of holy law" have the same form as the exhortations of wisdom teachers and so are neither law nor necessarily connected with a situation of eschatological expectation. He also questions the connection which Käsemann sees between these texts and the *jus talionis* /53/. Berger's arguments, though questionable in some respects, do raise serious doubts that the form of these sentences is distinctly legal. Furthermore, our study of Luke 6:37-38 suggests that the double use of a word in these sentences serves a function which might best be characterized as "parenetic warning or prophetic threat." This double use of a single word serves to reveal forcefully to the hearer the dangerous situation which he faces. It expresses the threatening conflict between God and man and the appropriateness of God's punishment, an appropriateness which makes it inescapable. For the guilty hearer must recognize that the punishment *fits*, that it is properly *his*. This is forced on the hearer's attention by the repeated use of the same word, for in its second occurrence the word fits. In this way the saying can shed new light on certain situations, forcing men to see them in a new way, and attacking the common tendency to regard them as not very serious. This feature of the language suggests, then, that these sentences are concerned with personal impact and resulting insight, and so have much in common with parenetic warning and prophetic threat.

There are, of course, other sayings which strive for forceful speech through using a single word, or words from a single root, in two different connections. Matt 5:7, 26:52b, and Luke 12:48b are examples.

7. *Matt 7:3-5 // Luke 6:41-42. The Log in the Eye.*

3   Why do you see the speck that is in your brother's eye,
      But the log in your eye you do not notice?
4   Or how can you say to your brother, "Let me take
          the speck out of your eye,"
      And look! the log in your own eye?
5   Hypocrite!
      First take from your eye the log,
         And then you will see clearly to take the speck
          out of the eye of your brother.

                                                          Matt 7:3-5

These verses directly follow Matthew's version of the passage we have just examined. In Luke they are separated from the passage on judging by two short verses. The two passages are related in subject matter, which makes their placement together understandable. However, they are different in form, for, although both speak forcefully, they gain their force in quite different ways. Here we see how a similar goal may be gained by different strategies.

The whole passage is dominated by a single metaphor, that of having something in the eye. The metaphor gains in power through being developed in a hyperbolic antithesis. The idea of a log in the eye is, of course, hyperbole; it is beyond the limits of the literal. This hyperbole indicates a desire to make the contrast extreme. What is in the eye of "your brother" is very small; what is in "your eye" is as large, or larger, than can be imagined /54/. Evidently the extreme tension resulting from this grotesque contrast is important if the saying is to have its proper effect. While literal credibility is of no importance here, metaphoric shock is. The striving for impact through extreme language is so obvious that we cannot avoid asking what the speaker could accomplish in this way /55/.

These words are a sharp attack upon a particular stance of man toward his fellow man. The charge of a log in the eye already constitutes such an attack, and the force of this attack is increased by other features of these verses. The attack is more forceful because it is made in a highly personal way. The hearer is directly addressed in the second person singular. The first two sentences are questions. Questions, whether rhetorical, used to seek information, or to give indirect commands, demand a response. The hearer is personally confronted and an answer is demanded, although the questions in this text are so tendentious that no answer is possible except the acceptance or repudiation of the charge. The question is emphasized by repetition. Matt 7:4 adds no new information and would not be missed if omitted from the passage /56/. However, it adds to the force of the words by repetition with a subtle change. Vs. 4 pictures a concrete situation face to face with the "brother" in which the hearer is exposed to social embarrassment. The hearer's fear of being shamed, of being publicly exposed, is here used as an additional way of strengthening the personal attack in these words. This is somewhat sharper in Matthew than in Luke, for Matthew's phrase "Look! The log in your eye!" (obscured in RSV) presents the moment of the hearer's embarrassing discovery of what everyone can see but him. Furthermore, the very ridiculousness of the picture of a log in the eye enforces the hearer's fear of being ridiculed. Finally, the passage ends with a direct command accompanied by the epithet "hypocrite," and the contrast between speck and log is repeated for a third time /57/. We see, then, that the hearer is not allowed to lose sight of this extreme contrast for a moment, and that its force is increased by repetition and by the highly personal way in which the attack is made.

Why should anyone address us in this way rather than in polite and reasonable language? Because the starting point for reasonable discussion is not present. It is not a question of discussing what all reasonable men see but of uncovering what we do not see because we are blind. Of course, we are willing to admit that we have faults, but this admission does not undermine our basic confidence in our own judgment. However, the passage wishes to expose a deep tendency which warps our judgment even when we admit that we have faults. This requires language of imaginative power, language strong enough to change the images by which we understand ourselves and others, becoming a new set of glasses through which self and world appear different. This language is concerned with nothing less than how we as selves are constituted. The self it addresses is no *tabula rasa* but is already deeply structured. Therefore, a new structure can arise only by attacking the old. Furthermore, the extremeness of the attack makes clear that the problem is deep and pervasive, not a problem which can be overcome through a few adjustments in behavior but one which affects our very selves and which can be overcome only when a new image of the self takes root in the imagination. That is why forceful language is so important.

In this passage the hyperbolic contrast reverses the tendency which it attacks. Our tendency to see our own faults as small and those of others as large is called in question because we are required to apply the same kind of vision in reverse, as if we turned a telescope end for end. Now our faults appear huge and those of others very small. Is this perspective truer than the one which it seeks to replace? This is not a question which can be answered by weighing the quantity and quality of our faults compared to those of others. To argue in this way is to miss the point. A log in the eye corresponds to no measurable quantity; indeed, this image is a deliberate caricature. The truth of these words is affirmed not through a process of weighing quantities of fault but much more immediately. The feeling inside of being wounded is already an affirmation of their truth. The words have struck home; they have had their effect; they have shown us something about ourselves. These words can have their effect even without our recognizing a specific, major fault in ourselves. It is enough that our self-assurance has been undermined so that we can no longer be certain that our awareness of others' faults does not conceal a blindness to our own. The fact that, through these words, we can *imagine* the situation to which they point, that we can *imagine* such blindness and the shameful exposure which must follow, means that the essential work of these words has already been done.

The tendency being attacked is presented here in extreme form, in caricature, and we have come to see that such extreme language has its own important purposes. It contributes to the force necessary to attack at the required depth, at the level of pre-rational vision of self and world, and to replace the old with a new imagination. Thus it speaks to a deep level of the self, rather than to particular acts and decisions. However, it is also relevant to these particular acts and decisions. One's vision affects one's acts. These extreme words may lead us to act differently by making us sharply aware of a tendency which appears in subtler forms in the situations which we face.

Approaching such a passage with a model of language oriented primarily toward conveying information, making assertions, and supporting these with arguments not only robs it of its power but also makes its truth very doubtful. This approach would seek to distill a clear statement from the passage in defiance of the passage's own mode of speaking. The resulting understanding of this text would be something like this: The text asserts that our own fault is much worse than our brother's and that we must correct our fault before correcting that of our brother. This "truth" extracted from the passage is actually something quite different than our text, for something different happens between text and reader in the two instances. This interpretation eliminates the imaginative force of the original and so does not provoke the reader to see himself in a new way. Instead it invites the reader to judge the statement according to the usual canons of logic and evidence, which makes everything doubtful, for it is not at all obvious to us that we are so much worse than others. Thus the original text has been lost because its form, and the particular intention embodied in that form, has been ignored.

In the New Testament we seldom find the complex development of a metaphor or interplay of several metaphors which is characteristic of much poetry. However, in this passage we do find effective use of the metaphor of having something in the eye. The metaphor becomes powerfully expressive not through a complex development of its compacted meaning but through hyperbolic contrast combined with the repetition and personal force discussed above. There is nothing obscure about the central thrust of this metaphor, but neither is it vapid, which is largely due to the forcefulness of the language in which it is developed. Through this metaphor these verses are able to present a concrete, arresting picture, one which sticks in the imagination and is able to indirectly illumine a whole range of situations. It has the importance of a general assertion, for the meaning of metaphor is not limited to a word's literal sense. At the same time, it has the force of a specific, striking picture. In contrast, the words in Luke 6:37-38a, though related in subject matter, could only achieve general significance by moving away from the concrete image. However, they had their own way of achieving imaginative force.

8. Luke 17:26-30. The Days of Noah and of Lot.

26 As it was in the days of Noah,
   So will it be in the days of the Son of Man.
27   They were eating,
      They were drinking,
         They were marrying,
            They were being given in marriage,
      Until the day when Noah entered the ark,
         and the flood came and destroyed them all.
28 Likewise as it was in the days of Lot —
      They were eating,
         They were drinking,
            They were buying,
               They were selling,
                  They were planting,
                     They were building,
29   But on the day when Lot went out from Sodom fire and brimstone
         rained from heaven and destroyed them all.
30   — So will it be on the day when the Son of Man is revealed.

The common tendency to summarize New Testament texts in terms of the "ideas" which they convey would lead us to say that this text teaches the idea that the end of the world, expected in apocalyptic thought, will be sudden and surprising. This tendency arises from the unexamined assumption that the text wishes to convey clear ideas, just as academic language does, and that the task of the interpreter is to put the message of the text into clear statements and relate them to their historical setting. As a result we reduce the text to concepts which we may hold at a distance and examine. If we look closely at the form of this text, however, we will see that the idea above is not an adequate translation, for the text is striving for something more than the teaching of such an idea.

The text is based upon two similes, which are expressed quite simply in vss. 26, 28a, and 30: the "days of the Son of Man" will be like the days of Noah and Lot /58/. In these verses the similes are presented without particular force and so are only mildly poetic at best. However, they provide the basis for the intervening material, which does strive for imaginative force. The effect of this intervening material depends greatly on the way in which verbs are used. In vs. 27 we find first a series of four verbs in the imperfect tense, all referring to customary events of ordinary life. No other words are attached to them, not even conjunctions /59/, resulting in a strong pattern of rhythmic repetition of similar words. This rhythm is cut off by the phrase "until the day," which leads into three short clauses, in each of which the verb is placed in the first optional position, a position of emphasis /60/. This emphasizes the dramatic action in these clauses. It also emphasizes the difference between the first series of verbs, in the imperfect, and these verbs, which are in the aorist tense, a difference which signifies the interruption of the continuing rhythm of everyday life by a particular, decisive event /61/. Thus there is a tension within the verse which is expressed not only on the conceptual level but also by the form of the text. The text invites the hearer to feel the familiar, comfortable rhythm of life and recognize his involvement in it. To make this possible, the text not only refers to common activities but also uses the imperfect tense of a rhythmic series of verbs without adjuncts. Feeling the rhythm of ordinary life, we feel more sharply the interruption of this rhythm and its replacement by a series of verbs and their adjuncts which stand opposed to the first series both in meaning and tense. The latter series comes to a climax in the strong threat "and destroyed them all." The shortness of the last two clauses in vs. 27 emphasizes the quickness of the surprising change.

The characteristics of the text which we have already discovered are strengthened by repetition of the overall pattern in vss. 28-30. The comparison with the days of Lot parallels the comparison with the days of Noah rather than adding something new. Therefore we cannot explain vss. 28-30 from a desire to convey further ideas. As we have noted before, however, repetition is important when language must be forceful in order to achieve its purpose or when the words bear more than ordinary weight. Even greater force can be achieved if repetition is combined with the heightening of certain features. This is the case with the saying concerning the days of Lot. In vs. 28 we again have a series of imperfect verbs in asyndeton referring to activities of ordinary life. However, we now have a series of six, instead of four, and only the first two are the same as vs. 27. This change is not required by the situation, for either series of verbs could be applied to the contemporaries of both Noah and Lot. The change is made in order to develop the rhythm first encountered in vs. 27. The first pair of verbs is the same as in vs. 27, which quickly establishes the relation between the two sections and enables the second to build on the first, picking up and developing its power. Once this is established, the series can be expanded. This is done in two ways: First, other aspects of ordinary life are chosen. We find reference to commerce and productive work rather than to marriage. Thus our vision of the fabric of our ordinary world is broadened. Second, there is a lengthening of the rhythmic pattern from four to six. This makes the rhythmic repetition of verbs more emphatic and increases the tension. A rhythm, once established, encourages us to expect its continuance, and there is no reason why the series of verb pairs could not be extended. At the same time, however, we anticipate that the rhythm will be broken off, as in vs. 27, and this causes suspense. We anticipate the end but we don't know when it will come, and we are made to wait slightly longer than in vs. 27, which gives more time for the tension to develop. Then, once again, the rhythm of ordinary life is interrupted by a decisive, destructive event. So vss. 28-30 not only repeat but intensify vss. 26-27. This shows that the repetitive pattern is being used to help this text achieve resonance (on the meaning of resonance see p. 45 above).

The text reaches its goal only when the hearer begins to experience the rhythms of ordinary life in a new way. For most of us most of the time ordinary life is a closed world. We do not see beyond it. Its rhythms give structure to our lives and, therefore, a kind of security. Our text makes us more sharply aware of these rhythms than we usually are, but, at the same time, changes their meaning. The rhythms of ordinary life become like the ticking of an alarm clock — we anticipate the alarm. The text makes the ordinary world stand out by emphasis and places it over against something else. But this means that it is no longer ordinary. Instead of being the reality which we can take for granted, it has become contingent. Our awareness of the rhythms of life now carries with it an awareness of their limits. The text's careful form serves to lead us to this awareness. This form would not be necessary if the text merely wished to convey information about how the world will end.

Note that nothing definite is said about the kind of destruction which might come. This remains hidden behind the similes. Thus the indirectness of its language gives the text some freedom from the apocalyptic conceptions which were associated with it in early Christianity.

The artfulness of Luke's text will stand out more clearly if we compare it with Matthew's version. Matt 24:37-39 not only lacks any parallel to the saying about Lot, and so lacks Luke's repetitive pattern, but is also less forceful in other ways. In contrast to the short clauses with strong and prominent verbs in Luke, Matthew uses a complex sentence in 24:38-39. In this sentence the verbs denoting strong action are subordinated to weaker verbs, and the contrast between the rhythm of ordinary life and the decisive event which ends it becomes a minor part of a sentence which basically asserts a comparison. The insertion of the words "they did not know until" contributes to this. These words reflect a secondary use of the material by the Evangelist, for they support the statement in 24:36 that no one knows the time, a statement which circulated independently of the saying about Noah, as the parallel in Mark 13:32 shows. Thus the Evangelist understands the saying about Noah to support the assertion that men do not know the time of the end, a point which requires no special forcefulness in language. However, Matthew's version resembles Luke's sufficiently to indicate that its original intention was the same as Luke's text. This suggests that Luke's version represents a sensitive development of the original intention of the text, even if we cannot be sure that the doubling of the saying by referring to Lot and other details in Luke were an original part of the tradition /62/.

9. *Matt 11:21-24//Luke 10:13-15. "Woe to You, Chorazin!"*

21   Woe to you, Chorazin!
     Woe to you, Bethsaida!
          For if in Tyre and Sidon had been done the mighty works
               done in you,
               Long ago in sack cloth and ashes
                    they would have repented.
22   But I tell you,
               For Tyre and Sidon it shall be more tolerable on the day
                    of judgment than for you.
23   And you, Capernaum, will you be exalted to heaven?
     You shall go down to Hades.
          For if in Sodom had been done the mighty works done in you,
               It would have remained until this day.
24   But I tell you that
               For the land of Sodom it shall be more tolerable
                    on the day of judgment than for you.

                                             Matt 11:21-24

This passage announces the judgment which awaits three towns of Galilee because of their failure to repent at the mighty works of

Jesus. The form of these words shows that they are intended to do more than convey information about the future.. Judged by the criterion of efficiency in supplying information, there are strange aspects to our text. Reference to the three cities of Old Testament fame is really irrelevant, since it is the fate of the Galilean towns which is the subject of the announcement. Furthermore, to make assertions about what the cities of Tyre, Sidon, and Sodom *would* have done is odd, for, as a matter of fact, they did not repent and, in the case of Sodom, there is no longer even a possibility of repentance. The large amount of repetition in Matthew's text makes no sense from this viewpoint, and a number of details of the text look like an odd sort of posturing that adds nothing to the informational value of the words. However, as soon as we recognize that these words seek imaginative force, the formal features of the text fall into a meaningful pattern.

There seems to be a common body of "facts" perceived both from the perspective of the text and from the perspective which it attacks. That Jesus performed "mighty works" in Chorazin, Bethsaida, and Capernaum is taken as a basis for argument rather than a point to be argued. But these "facts" are seen from different perspectives; they are integrated into different personal worlds. These events may have been perceived by the residents of these Galilean towns as a minor disturbance to the routine of life, as a dangerous temptation to stray from the true faith, or as a sign that God had especially honored these towns. However, the people evidently did not see them as revealing their own godlessness and pointing to judgment, for the speaker is attempting to awaken such perception by challenging the self-assurance of the hearers. To do this the form of the text must give its vision of the situation sufficient force to be seen for what it is, a vision which cannot be integrated into the old perceptions of a personal world because it radically attacks them.

Perhaps there is still a possibility that the hearer will repent and escape the judgment. This is not indicated by any ideas expressed in the text, for it speaks of the future only in terms of judgment. However, the hope that is not expressed directly is expressed

indirectly through the mode of language used, for the text is
formed for warning and not merely for prediction. Whether or not
the speaker was conscious of his hope for repentance, the form of
his words shows a concern that these towns understand their
situation, that their blindness be overcome, that there be a change
of mind, something which is most likely to take place through
language with imaginative force.

The text as given by Matthew and Luke is very similar in
wording and word order. The most important differences are the
settings in which these words are placed and the fact that Luke's
text ends with the words "You shall go down to Hades," while
Matthew continues with two more sentences. It is possible that the
original text ended where Luke does and that the extra sentences
in Matthew, which closely parallel material in the first half of the
text, were added by the Evangelist because of a desire for
parallelism. However, other observations point to the possibility
that Luke has shortened the text. Another saying concerning a
judgment less tolerable than Sodom's circulated in the early
tradition. It is now found in Matt 10:15 and Luke 10:12. The
connection with the passage we are studying is so close that they
must go back to a common root. However, the saying in Matt
10:15 and Luke 10:12 shows several significant differences which
indicate a different use of the material: it is not addressed to
specific cities of Galilee but to the disciples and concerns any city
which may reject the missionaries who come to it. In Matthew this
mission saying and the woes to the towns of Galilee are separate.
Luke, however, noting the similarity between them, places the
woes after the mission saying. This means that the judgment less
tolerable than Sodom's is already mentioned at the beginning of
the passage. To speak of it again in connection with Capernaum
would be repetitious, which provides ample reason for the
removal of the last two sentences of the original text. To this can
be added another consideration. In the rest of the New Testament,
it is Sodom, not Tyre and Sidon, which serves as the type of the
sinful city which God destroys /63/. To compare a city with
Sodom is, therefore, stronger than comparison with Tyre and

Sidon (noted by Grundmann: 314). In a passage concerned with force, it is natural to refer to Sodom in the second, climactic half of a two part saying, as in Matt 11:21-24, or to refer to Sodom and Gomorrah instead of Tyre and Sidon, as in Matt 10:15. Instead, Luke 10:13-15 refers only to Tyre and Sidon, although the preceding mission saying, which previously circulated separately, refers to Sodom. This is explained if the Evangelist omitted a second reference to Sodom when he joined the woes to the mission saying.

There is no reason to refer to any of these cities, Tyre, Sidon, or Sodom, except as a way of increasing the impact of these woes. In the Old Testament the corruption and rebellious pride of these cities calls forth God's judgment /64/. The evil of these cities and the fate which follows it, obvious to the Jew on the basis of the Old Testament, become the point of leverage for addressing the towns of Galilee. Moreover, the speaker does not merely assert that the Galilean towns are like these infamous cities; he refers to the cities only to move beyond them by asserting that they would have repented at such mighty works and that the judgment will be easier on them. The cities which all judged to be evil are made to look good by comparison. The towns of Galilee could hardly be put in a worse light /65/.

This is supported by other features of the text. The word order is used to emphasize the basic contrast between the evil cities and the Galilean towns by placing references to them in the positions of emphasis at the beginning and end of clauses.

If *in Tyre and Sidon* had been done the mighty works done *in you*,
    Long ago in sack cloth and ashes they would have repented.
But I tell you,
    For Tyre and Sidon it shall be more tolerable on the day
        of judgment than *for you*.

. . . . .

If *in Sodom* had been done the mighty works done *in you*,
    It would have remained until this day.
But I tell you that
    For the land of Sodom it shall be more tolerable on the day
        of judgment than *for you*.

Additional force is achieved by direct address in the second person with each town addressed separately: "Woe to you, Chorazin! woe to you, Bethsaida! ... And you, Capernaum! ... " /66/ Furthermore, in Matthew we find a repetitive pattern with elements of climax. What is said of Chorazin and Bethsaida is also said of Capernaum, the first two being compared with two cities and the last with one /67/. It would have been possible to treat all three towns as a group and avoid such repetition. However, emphasis through repetition helps the words to gain the power they need. Repetition also enables the words to Capernaum to bring the previous words to a strong climax. The climactic force of Matt 11:23-24 is indicated by a number of features of these verses. While two Galilean towns are grouped in vss. 21-22, Capernaum stands alone in vss. 23-24. It is compared to Sodom, a more forceful type of the corrupt city upon which God's judgment falls (cf. above, pp. 124-25). Furthermore, an addition is made at the beginning of the words to Capernaum. These added words reflect the taunts which Old Testament prophets addressed to cities and rulers, though they are not an exact quotation. Isa 14:13-15 seems to be the closest parallel (cf. also Ezek 26:20). If this is the source of these words, however, the source text has been handled freely in order to make it sufficiently compact not to disturb the basic pattern of the New Testament text. This also makes the antithesis in the source stand out all the more sharply. This antithesis is neatly enforced by rhyme, for the similarity in sound between the two verbs in end position invites us to compare them, thus emphasizing the contrast in meaning.

μὴ ἕως οὐρανοῦ	ὑψωθήσῃ;
To heaven	will you be exalted?
ἕως ᾅδου	καταβήσῃ[68]
To Hades	you will go down.

These words refer very concisely to two extreme positions. The first, exaltation to heaven, might possibly reflect historical knowledge of Capernaum's unusual pride in being the center of Jesus' ministry (cf. Grundmann: 314). This is doubtful, however, for the antithesis is sufficiently explained by the Old Testament source and the desire for rhetorical force. Capernaum's exaltation to heaven is mentioned only in a question expecting a negative answer /69/. However, the mere mention of the possibility serves as a foil for what follows, accenting the descent so that it is felt as a sharp plunge. And this plunge will carry them all the way to Hades, the underworld, the realm of the dead.

The forcefulness of these words should now be clear. Not only are the towns of Galilee said to be less open to repentance and subject to a harsher judgment than the cities condemned in the Old Testament, but this extreme comparison is accentuated by the word order and repetitive pattern, and is brought to a climax with the words to Capernaum, where we find, in addition, a sharp antithesis. And all of this is presented in forceful direct address. This concern for force reflects the fact that these words must fight against another perspective, a perspective which seems invulnerable because it is generally assumed but which becomes doubtful as soon as a conflicting possibility catches the imagination. Past assumptions lose their obviousness when a different possibility takes root in the imagination and begins to grow. Thus a key factor in the fight is the ability of words to awaken the imagination to envision a possibility contrary to the general assumption, a possibility, moreover, which men do not want to envision, because it challenges the security which the prevailing perspective provides. The "mighty works" of Jesus, which have been a source of interest and, perhaps, pride, must now be seen as signs of condemnation by the people of these towns. The lack of response, which previously seemed unimportant or excusable, must now be seen as the fatal factor determining the present situation.

These words are addressed specifically to three towns in a very small area of first century Palestine. This specificity adds to the force of these words in their original historical situation. Does it prevent them from speaking to us in our quite different situation?

On the contrary, particular historical (or legendary) events can be illuminating for later times. The story of Sodom did not cease to be important in the Biblical tradition even though that city belonged to the distant past. Similarly, these words to Chorazin, Bethsaida, and Capernaum did not lose their importance when they became part of writings used in churches far from these towns. Indeed, the mission saying in Matt 10:15 and Luke 10:12 is specific evidence that the early church applied these words to other towns as well. It is especially the force of these words which makes them capable of such an afterlife. If these words merely conveyed information about three ancient towns, they would be of little interest to us. Since they dig deeper, however, seeking to awaken a new vision of the hearer's situation, and since they preserve the power to do this in their form, they can speak again to particular situations in which there is similar insensitivity to God's call in recent events. Through these words we may discover that we share the guilt of those who have shrugged their shoulders at the mighty works in their midst.

The discussion above may be suggestive for understanding Matt 12:41-42//Luke 11:31-32, for there are similarities in form and content. There also the text seeks to awaken men to the seriousness of their situation by a forceful comparison with well known Old Testament figures and makes use of a repetitive pattern.

10. Luke 12:54-56. Interpreting this Time.

54b   When you see a cloud rising in the west,
        You say at once, "A storm is coming";
        And so it happens.
55   And when you see the south wind blowing,
        You say, "There will be scorching heat";
        And it happens.
56   Hypocrites!
        The appearance of earth and sky you know how to interpret;
        But how is it that you do not interpret this time?

The text divides easily into three parts. Vss. 54-55 present two specific instances of accurate prediction of the weather. Vs. 56 first makes a general statement about the ability displayed in the preceding verses, and then sharply contrasts this with a failure to act in a similar way in a third situation.

Günter Klein has argued that in an earlier stage of the tradition vs. 56 circulated separately and that vss. 54-55 are a later expansion of the thought of vs. 56a (cf. 373-90, especially 388-90). Among other evidence, he points to the relation between this passage in Luke and Matt 16:2-3, which, according to Klein, is an independent tradition of the same saying, whether it belongs to the original Gospel of Matthew or not /70/. Luke 12:56 is fairly close to the parallel text, while the preceding words are quite different. This can be explained on the supposition that vs. 56 and its parallel are the root of the tradition and that in the course of time two independent expansions of the tradition took place. The truth or falsity of Klein's arguments do not essentially affect our project, which concerns the present form of Luke 12:54-56. However, these arguments do show the danger of making historical critical judgments without adequate appreciation of the literary function of parts of the text. In the background of Klein's position is his view that vss. 54-55 detract from, rather than contribute to, the original purpose of vs. 56. In what follows I will show that these verses have an important function in the text and support vs. 56 in a significant way.

Although vss. 54-55 are more specific than vs. 56, the basic idea of these verses is present in summary form in vs. 56a. Thus they contribute nothing essential in the way of information or ideas. However, if the text as a whole is not primarily concerned with conveying information or ideas, these verses may still have an important function. The antithetical form of vs. 56 is a clue to the function which they serve. The hearer's ability to interpret the appearance of earth and sky is contrasted with his failure to interpret "this time." The contrast calls this failure sharply to the hearer's attention, for it stands out against the contrasting background. This is the sole function of vs. 56a, for the text is certainly not concerned with predicting the weather for its own sake. The hearer's ability is emphasized in order that the contrasting failure may stand out with greater clarity. The stronger the contrast, the greater the impact of the final reproachful question. A strong contrast requires the foil to be strong. We must receive a vivid impression of man's ability to interpret the signs of nature. Vs. 56a is sharply antithetical, but it does not present us with pictures which enter the imagination and stick there, becoming the irritant around which the imagination can form its pearl. Vss. 54-55, however, present us with two concrete situations, adding vividness to the text. We are not merely told of man's ability in general terms, but pictures are suggested which invite the imagination to inhabit them. In this way we receive a stronger impression of our ability to read the signs of nature and the contrasting failure also stands out more strongly.

The two similar sentences in vss. 54-55 present us with two concrete instances of man's ability to predict the weather. It is clear that the point lies not in the differing detail but in the larger meaning which both instances share. Thus vss. 54-55 imply a wide-ranging and important human power, as vs. 56a indicates, without departing from vivid concreteness. Furthermore, two similar instances presented in similar form are sufficient to establish a pattern, which may then be used to measure what follows. Vss. 54-55 point to man's competence in reading the signs of his world. What follows conflicts with this pattern, for it involves a failure to see what is there to be seen. Within the context of this patterned speech it becomes a strange reality, one which doesn't fit and causes tension, even though outside this context the hearer may be quite comfortable with it. Thus it is clear that vss. 54-55 do not involve a turning away from the concern of vs. 56 to secondary matters but are present to heighten the contrast in vs. 56 and increase its impact.

Just as in texts studied previously, details of the text can be shown to support the interpretation of the text's basic structure given above. In vss. 54-55 certain words appear which are not essential to the thought but which help these verses to perform their function and so indirectly reflect what that function is. Why are the words "at once," "and so it happens," "and it happens" included? There is nothing comparable in Matt 16:2-3 /71/, and they would not be missed if they were omitted. Furthermore, weather predictions are not always easy and successful! These details, however, are meaningful when we recognize that vss. 54-55 have the function discussed above. Any thought of hesitation or inaccuracy in man's ability to read the signs of his world will decrease the contrast in vs. 56. Therefore, it is excluded. Man's ability to understand the significance of what he sees is set forth as strongly as possible so that the failure to understand "this time" will appear all the stranger /72/.

Certain other features of the text also contribute to its force. The entire text addresses the hearers directly, using the second person. The sense of personal confrontation is heightened by the fact that the passage ends with a question. A question, even a rhetorical one, demands a response. The hearer must agree to the judgment of himself implied in the words or else repudiate these words and their speaker. The antithesis in vs. 56 is supported by the word order, for the key repeated verb and the changing object are placed in positions of emphasis at the beginning and end of clauses.

τὸ πρόσωπον τῆς γῆς καὶ τοῦ οὐρανοῦ οἴδατε δοκιμάζειν,

The appearance of earth and sky you know (how) *to interpret*;

τὸν καιρὸν δὲ τοῦτον πῶς οὐ δοκιμάζετε;[73]

but *this time*   how (is it that)   *you do not interpret*?

The strong epithet "hypocrites" is kept in reserve until it can be used to strengthen the accusation which these words imply, while vss. 54-55 are kept free of anything which implies a limit on man's accomplishments.

Within the individual's personal world, events are signs which must be interpreted by fitting them into a pattern of significance. Events which do not fit in some way into the established patterns of significance can have no importance in this personal world and they are scarcely noticed. We become aware of such realities only when the structures of our personal world, our ways of seeing and interpreting, are stretched through being used in strange ways and placed in tension. Then we may become aware of significant reality which does not fit easily into familiar categories. Our text seeks to bring about such stretching. The weather is part of man's familiar world and has unquestioned significance for him /74/. But here our interest in the weather and ability to interpret its signs are used against us. They are placed in sharp contrast to a failure of insight in another area, and the whole text is shaped to make this contrast forceful. Outside of the text we may be quite confident of our insight into "this time" or confident that there is nothing special there to know, but within the text we are not allowed such confidence. The text insists that there is a significant mystery which we have not comprehended. It makes us aware of this mystery by making our behavior appear strange. Our very confidence in our ability to interpret our world is used to make this failure a glaring exception. Thereby something important is gained. What was a matter of no importance or a matter of settled significance becomes the center of active, imaginative thought. It has been presented to us with challenging force and, almost in spite of ourselves, we begin to turn over in our minds the meaning of "this time."

The phrase "this time" is vague /75/. The text wishes to awaken imaginative thought, but it does not tell us what to think. If the text were to spell out in conceptual form what the meaning of this time is, it would defeat its own purpose. It would no longer incite to thought. The subject of thought must be presented as something which eludes us and yet is significant. It must be presented as a beckoning mystery. It is doubtless true that within the historical context in which these words arose they were related to an eschatological interpretation of Jewish history, within which Jesus' ministry had a special role. Much depends, however, on whether this historical observation is used to tie New Testament texts to a hardened system of thought from the past or whether eschatology is understood to be more than such a system and dependent upon the imaginative language which we find in texts like Luke 12: 54-56. To understand this text as simply the vehicle for an eschatological ideology makes that ideology, and its steno-language, primary and leads us to deny any basic significance to the text's imaginative form. This robs the text of its special function, for the text is not formed to convey an ideology but to challenge our hardened perceptions of our world and awaken new thought. This it can continue to do as long as we do not escape from thought by turning these words into ciphers for an ideology.

A text with a basically similar structure, and yet some interesting differences, is Matt 7:9-11//Luke 11:11-13. Here also two concrete situations are pictured, and then the significance of these instances is summarized and compared with a third situation. Here also the pattern is used to give force to the words. Thus some of what was said above will also apply to this passage. However, the first two verses are in question form and picture situations which are decidedly odd: a father giving his son a stone when asked for bread or a snake when asked for fish /76/. The text counts on the fact that the hearers will scarcely be able to imagine themselves doing such a thing. The first two instances establish the pattern in light of which the third instance is to be judged. The vivid oddness of considering whether we fathers might respond to the needs of our children in a harmful or capricious way makes distrust of the heavenly Father appear unnatural, and this is enforced by introducing a note of contrast into the final verse with the phrases "you who are evil" and "how much more." While Luke 12:54-56 introduces natural situations in the first two verses and then summarizes these and makes a third situation look odd by contrast, this passage refers to unnatural situations in the first two verses, suggesting how unlikely they are, and, in the final verse, draws a positive connection between the improbability of our behaving this way and the way God will act, strengthening this by asserting that this is "much more" true of God. While the former passage produces tension by introducing an instance which conflicts with the preceding pattern, the latter produces a sense of relief by the righting of a pattern which was vivid but strange. This way of speaking has force because the oddness of the first two situations carries over to our judgment of our relation to God. The fact that we do hesitate to trust God, thereby attributing to him the strange behavior depicted in the first two verses, now appears odd. Here our own awareness of the necessity of trust within the family and confidence that we are worthy of trust is used against our failure to trust in God.

The structural pattern which we noted in Luke 12:54-56// and Matt 7:9-11// is also found elsewhere. A structure in which two instances of the same pattern are followed by a contrasting instance is found in the parables of the Talents (Matt 25:14-30//) and the Good Samaritan (Luke 10:29-37), as well as in a number of short sayings, for instance, Matt 8:20// (cf. below, pp. 161-62), 10:5-6, 24:26-27, Luke 17:20-21. The structure is basically antithetical, but the contrast is strengthened by allowing a clear pattern to develop through two similar instances before introducing the third, contrasting instance. Of course, more than two instances may be used to establish the pattern. In the parable of the Sower (Mark 4:3-8//) three cases of failure are followed by a fourth of success, and in Peter's confession (Mark 8:27-29//) Peter's answer is made to stand out through contrast with three answers which "men" give.

11. Matt 19:12. Eunuchs for the Kingdom.

There are eunuchs who were born thus from the mother's womb,
And there are eunuchs who have been made eunuchs by men,
And there are eunuchs who have made themselves eunuchs
    for the sake of the kingdom of heaven.

After the teaching on marriage and divorce in Matt 19:3-9 the possibility of living apart from a wife is discussed.Other passages in the synoptic Gospels suggest that vss. 10-12 reflect an important issue in the life of the early church. The early church was sharply aware of the possible conflict between family life and the demands of discipleship /77/. The statement of the disciples in vs. 10 probably reflects awareness of this conflict rather than desire to escape the demands of marriage for selfish reasons, and Jesus'

reply is also best understood in light of this problem /78/. Vs. 11
indicates an exception to Jesus' teaching in vss. 4-9 for some
followers of Jesus /79/. "This word" (RSV: "this precept") refers
to Jesus' teaching on marriage and divorce, not to the disciples'
statement in vs. 10 /80/. It has the same reference as "thus" (RSV:
"such") in vs. 10. This provides a clear train of thought in these
verses, for Jesus' reply in vs. 11 takes up the problem posed by vs.
10, that of the conflict between the demands of marriage and
Christian discipleship, and vs. 12 supports vs. 11 in a clear and
relevant way, pointing to an exception to the previous teaching on
marriage and divorce. If "this word" in vs. 11 referred to the
disciples' statement in vs. 10, Jesus would be seeking to limit the
disciples' assertion that it is not expedient to marry, and we would
expect vs. 12 to support this by pointing to some for whom it *is*
expedient to marry. The reference to eunuchs is singularly
inappropriate for this purpose. The exception indicated by vs. 11
may refer to vs. 5, understood not merely as permission but as
command to marry, thus indicating Jesus' agreement in some
cases with the statement in vs. 10. However, it is not vs. 5 but the
prohibition of divorce which is the new and striking element in the
previous teaching. It would hardly be possible to speak so vaguely
and generally of "this word" if one intended to omit this
prohibition from consideration. It is likely, then, that the
exceptions mentioned in vs. 11 include some married men, who
are released from the commands in vss. 6b and 9 /81/. Although
one could both obey the demands of discipleship and preserve a
semblance of obedience to the teaching in vs. 9 so long as one did
not remarry, the command in vs. 6b is more sweeping.
Furthermore, the tension between the reality of some marriages
and the vision of man and wife as "one flesh" in vss. 5-6 would be
all too apparent, especially since the joining of man and wife
referred to there seems to be quite concrete and sexual rather than
indicating some legal bond which continues when man and wife
have separated /82/. This might well lead to the recognition that
the demands of discipleship require exceptions to this teaching on
marriage and divorce. At the same time, the radicalness of the

language which follows in vs. 12 prevents this from being an invitation to laxness.

Whether vss. 11-12 are meant to apply only to the unmarried or, as I believe, also to married men who are forced to leave their wives for the sake of the Gospel, it is clear that they point to an extreme possibility which is quite different than the normal situation of marriage discussed prior to this. This possibility is not only recognized but, as the form of vs. 12 shows, presented as a forceful challenge. We must now examine vs. 12 to see how this is done.

The bulk of vs. 12 consists of three similar sentences, each approximately the same length and each beginning in the same way: "There are eunuchs who . . . (εἰσὶν εὐνοῦχοι οἵτινες . . .)." The formal similarity between the three sentences invites the hearer to compare them. It suggests that all three belong to the same class, that the speaker is enumerating subdivisions within a larger whole. This view is reinforced by the fact that the first two sentences refer to recognized classes, for the same division appears in rabbinic discussion of the eunuch /83/. Thus there is nothing surprising in these first two sentences. The hearer understands them in the customary, literal way, and they have no unusual force. This pair of sentences creates a presumption that, if the series continues, there will be other classes of the same type, and this expectation is reinforced when the third sentence begins in the same way. It is only the final prepositional phrase which thwarts this expectation. Apart from the phrase "for the sake of the kingdom of heaven," the third sentence would simply indicate one more class of eunuchs in the literal sense. However, this phrase turns the third class of eunuchs into a powerful metaphor, for the sentence contains a combination of ideas which is simply not bearable in its literal sense. This is true not only for modern men but probably for most of the ancient world /84/ and certainly for ancient Jews who obeyed the Jewish law /85/. Castrates were widely despised and in Judaism castration was prohibited. Deliberate self-castration would be a horrible offense against God's law. And yet vs. 12 requires us to evaluate this act positively, for it speaks of a self-castration "for the sake of the kingdom of heaven." The extreme tension produced by this unexpected combination shifts the language from the literal to the metaphoric mode /86/. Since the hearer can no longer understand the word "eunuchs" in the literal sense of the first two clauses, he must seek a new reference for this word. Other situations in which a man is unable to join with a wife as "one flesh" and beget children come into view. These situations are seen in a new way, through the glass of the term "eunuchs" with its strong connotations, which confronts the imagination with a possibility at the extreme edge of human life, a possibility which is now presented with such force that it cannot be ignored.

In studying previous sayings we have noted various methods by which they achieve imaginative force. The force of this saying depends entirely on a metaphor. This metaphor is so striking and extreme that almost by itself it is able to force us to consider an extraordinary possibility. It is especially the specificity of the image, its strong negative connotations, and the surprise of its use in this context which gives the phrase "made themselves eunuchs" its metaphoric power. Since the force of the saying depends on this metaphor, the rest of the saying is shaped to contribute to its power. The first two sentences require the hearer to think of eunuchs literally, and the similarity among the three sentences creates a presumption that the third sentence will also refer to eunuchs in the literal sense. The surprise is reserved until the very end of the third sentence, which suddenly forces us to think of this class of eunuchs differently. The literal use of eunuchs in the first two sentences strengthens the metaphor of the third sentence. It assures that the strong negative connotations of the literal sense will be present in the hearer's mind, thus leading to a shocking surprise when the hearer discovers the same words used positively. The result is a saying filled with extreme tension, a saying which we can neither assimilate nor forget /87/.

Josef Blinzler (268-70) suggests that vs. 12 was originally spoken by Jesus in reply to his opponents' criticism that he and, perhaps, some of his followers remained unmarried and so were not fulfilling God's command to beget children. In contempt the word "eunuch" had been used by the opponents and then was used by Jesus in his reply. The saying would make good sense in such a situation, and we can point to Mark 3:22-26 as an analogous appropriation of the opponents' accusation in order to make a forceful reply. This saying, then, would demonstrate Jesus' willingness to even submit to slander in order that his reply might provoke his opponents to new thought. The reply would catch the opponents by surprise. They would be forced to imagine a possibility for which their assumptions left no room, and the resulting crack in those assumptions would make possible a new understanding of Jesus and his work. The extremeness of the language would make it unforgettable, thus blocking all attempts to ignore Jesus' claim that his behavior is "for the sake of the kingdom." The reply would contribute no new facts or arguments about Jesus, but it would challenge the fixed pattern of meaning into which previously known facts had been arranged, setting free imaginative thought so that a new pattern might emerge.

We do not know whether the saying in vs. 12 was actually used in this way or not. If it was, Jesus' opponents were not the only ones struck by this metaphor. In Matthew the saying is not directed to opponents but to the disciples. In this situation also the force of the metaphor is important. It is able to awaken the disciple to an extreme possibility and force him to decide whether it must be realized in his life. The exact requirements for being a eunuch for the sake of the kingdom are not spelled out but remain hidden behind the metaphor. They may vary from case to case. The striking metaphor does not mark out a single path which all must follow but sets the imagination going, helping the hearer to view his own particular situation in the light of a new possibility. This possibility is deliberately extreme. It is not meant to be inviting. The shame of being a eunuch, indeed, the horror of self-castration, are forced upon the mind. There is no suggestion that this is the easy way out or that those who escape from family life are better off. No one would do such a thing — except for the sake of the kingdom. The overpowering, total demand of the kingdom comes to expression in the extremeness of the metaphor. This extremeness also forces the hearer to a radical decision; no one who understands these words can say yes to them and still hold something back. The metaphor is offensive and yet has such force that it is able to "infect" the imagination, setting it tossing and turning on its feverish bed as it struggles with this foreign body within, making a boy imagine what no "normal boy" would do, making a man imagine what no "respectable husband" would do, the deliberate abandoning of the joys and duties of family life for the sake of the kingdom. By placing the situation of the disciple without family under this repulsive image, the saying gives the joys and duties of family life their full due. By nevertheless affirming the possibility of abandoning these joys and duties, it makes clear that the kingdom's claim is total.

All of this is true so long as we feel the sharpness of the metaphor within its supporting setting in vs. 12. However, when the saying is understood to commend a recognized institution of celibacy, the original force of the saying is endangered. Then we seem to be faced with a choice between two different institutions, the family and the priesthood, both of which are reasonable and proper, and choosing the priesthood loses the repulsiveness of making oneself a eunuch. If the choice is reduced to a choice between institutions, it can be made without any challenge to our fundamental values and without recognizing the total claim of the kingdom. The saying did not originally support an institution but pointed through its metaphor to a possibility which conflicted sharply with the ordinary patterns of life. This tension continues to be essential to the intended function of these words

Gerd Theissen has recently argued that the radical commands in the Gospels would not have been passed on very long if they had not been practiced. He believes that the tradition of Jesus' words was preserved by a group of wandering charismatics and reflects the manner of life of these men who cut their ties with home, family, and possessions. It is possible that this clarifies the setting in the life of the early church of some, though not all, of the texts studied in this book. However, some of these texts remain an extreme challenge even for such men. Furthermore, the practical application of these texts is not as limited as Theissen suggests. These texts are relevant to the lives of Christians who are not homeless wanderers, for, as I have pointed out, their significance is not limited to their literal or most obvious sense (see especially pp. 73-76 above). The choice between family and the kingdom may appear in decisions about the family budget as well as in the decision to leave home. To be sure, within the conflicting claims of daily life the absoluteness of the kingdom's claim tends to be obscured. Both the radicalism of the text and the radical manner of life of some disciples may help to make that claim clear again.

12. *Matt 10:34-36//Luke 12:49-53. Not Peace but a Sword.*

Matthew and Luke present two quite different versions of this saying. Each is forceful in its own way.

34   Do not think that I have come to bring peace on earth;
     I have not come to bring peace, but a sword.
35   For I have come to split
     a man against his father,
       and a daughter against her mother,
         and a daughter-in-law against her mother-in-law;
36   And a man's foes will be the people of his own household.

Matt 10:34-36

The essential thought of Matt 10:34 could have been expressed much more briefly if the speaker had simply announced, "I have come to bring a sword." This, however, would remove the antithesis in this verse, which contributes to the power of these words. The announcement stands out against its opposite, the peace for which men long and which they hope Jesus will bring. This is surely a legitimate hope; indeed, "peace" is one way of expressing the eschatological salvation which God will give at the chosen time through his Christ /88/. Here this hope is brushed aside, and our attention is directed instead to that which replaces our hope, the "sword." In contrast to peace, we naturally think of the "sword" as a symbol of war, and that is indeed part of its meaning here (cf. Bauer: 497). So something important is gained by this use of antithesis. The word "sword" is more forceful because of contrast with its opposite, part of its meaning is clarified by this antithetical setting, and the reader is immediately involved in what is being said because of the sharp rejection of his hopes for peace.

The use of "sword" for "war" is metonymy, the substitution of one word for another to which it is closely related. As is frequently the case, this involves the replacement of something general and ordinary by something specific and vivid. "Sword" also has a metaphorical sense here, for our text is not referring to war in the literal sense but speaks of family disputes as war. A good figure of speech, one which is concrete, vivid, and sufficiently surprising to provoke new insight, is always forceful. This figure is concrete and vivid, but, in itself, not especially bold, for it is used elsewhere in the Biblical tradition /89/. However, it is helped by its setting. The contrast between "peace" and "sword" not only helps us to understand the latter but also contains a minor surprise. The two words do not stand on the same level. The latter immediately calls up a concrete image of a perceptible object; the former does not. We might anticipate the contrast "peace" and "war;" instead we are presented with the contrast "peace" and "sword." Furthermore, the figure is not allowed to die after its first appearance. Vs. 35 explains and supports vs. 34 (cf. "for"), especially the climactic word "sword." It does so by repeating the words "I have come" and substituting the infinitive διχάσαι for "to bring . . . a sword." This infinitive means "to divide in two" or "to separate." Since it explains and develops the reference to a sword, it here refers to the cutting function of that sword, and we could also translate "to split," "to cleave," "to sever" /90/. Then vs. 35a can be translated, "For I have come to split a man against his father." The connection between this infinitive and the noun "sword" contributes to the force of both. It suggests, on the one hand, that the separating is a violent act. On the other hand, it awakens further connotations of "sword." This "sword" not only suggests war in contrast to peace but is also an instrument which

violently severs what naturally belongs together, hacking to pieces
the living organism of the family.

The resulting division is expressed in a series of three phrases
formed in exactly the same way:

> A man against his father
> And a daughter against her mother
> And a daughter-in-law against her mother-in-law.

The reference to these particular members of the family is based
upon Mic 7:6, as is made especially clear by the identical order and
the completion of the verse from Micah in Matt 10:36. This
reference to Scripture may call to mind a broader prophetic-
apocalyptic motif of the breaking of family relationships in the
final tribulation (for supporting references see Siegfried Schulz:
260, n. 578), stirring the fears and hopes associated with this motif.
The three phrases refer to specific relationships within the family.
These are close relationships, especially within the ancient Jewish
family. However, they are not the only relationships which could
be mentioned. For instance, there is no reference to father and
daughter, mother and son, brother and brother, etc. These are
unnecessary, if the mode of language is properly understood, for
we have here a series of focal instances. As we saw above (cf. pp.
68-72), the focal instance consists of a specific and extreme case
which implies more than what is said explicitly. The choice of an
extreme instance gives it a broad range of implication, suggesting
that what holds true even here may be true of other situations as
well. As frequently, the focal instances are arranged in a series, an
open-ended series, for the list could easily be continued by
mention of other relationships. Indeed, the rhythmic effect of the
threefold repetition of the same pattern invites additions, for a
rhythm, once established, suggests its own continuance. However,
three instances are enough. In this passage the series is followed by
a more general statement which makes clear that the same division
may apply to other relationships within the household (vs. 36).
This is expressed very succinctly, so that nothing interferes with
the tension of being both foes and family /91/. Thus the text loses

nothing in suggestive range by speaking so specifically in vs. 35, and it gains in force. We are compelled to think of the closest, most personal relationships and to imagine their severance. The text does not speak in abstractions but presents persons to our imagination, two by two, so that we begin to sense the personal pain in such cleavage.

One further feature of the text contributes greatly to its force. All that we have discussed above is presented not as an unfortunate side effect of Jesus' ministry but as the very purpose of his coming /92/. Obviously this is not a general summary of Jesus' mission; it is not meant to be. But the choice of this manner of speech is significant. The text contradicts our desire to think of such family divisions as temporary and accidental, as problems which can be overcome with time or better counseling techniques. It claims that such divisions are inherent in Jesus' mission and therefore a fate which we cannot avoid if we follow him. It speaks not of temporary personal problems but of the dark will of God, of a cup which we wish would pass from us but which we must drink.

The forceful language which we have noted is directed not toward making discipleship more appealing but toward making it more difficult. Our hopes for peace are brushed aside and replaced with the fearsome image of the sword. Concrete personal relationships within the family are deliberately raised to consciousness, reminding us of the emotional ties by which we are bound, but only in order to proclaim their destruction. The tension which this produces would be better avoided if simple acceptance were the goal. It would be much easier to accept a Jesus who conforms with our desires and supports our family ties. Furthermore, it is doubtful that Jesus *always* breaks up families. Why emphasize the negative side so strongly? The text is not a factual statement of what always happens. It wants us to imaginatively contemplate a possibility and to recognize fully the conflict between this possibility and our hopes and emotional ties. Therefore it makes the tension between them as forceful as possible. Such tension is useful because the goal of these words is not acceptance but change, not agreement that Jesus fits with our established values but a basic reordering of those values. The tension in the text awakens an internal tension which points to a necessary decision. Apart from this tension the decision is avoided or is made only with the lips. Furthermore, the decision cannot be real if it ignores the emotions which accompany family ties. If it does, it will fall apart as soon as our emotional ties make themselves felt. The decision will only be a real reordering of values if we are intensely aware of our desires and emotions and still decide that something else must come first. Once again we see that the forceful form of these words is important in helping them to achieve a significant goal.

49 Fire have I come to cast upon the earth;
       And would that it were already kindled!
50 A baptism have I to be baptised with,
       And how I am constrained until it is accomplished!
51 Do you think that I have come to give peace on earth?
       No, I tell you, but instead division.
52   For from now on there will be five in one house divided
               three against two
               and two against three;
53   They will be divided
               father against son
               and son against father,
                 mother against daughter
                 and daughter against her mother,
                   mother-in-law against
                     her daughter-in-law
                   and daughter-in-law against
                     her mother-in-law.

                                        Luke 12:49-53

In Luke 12:49-53 a saying similar to Matthew's is combined with sayings about fire and baptism. While the absence of these sayings from Matthew suggests that the combination is a secondary development, the ties between vss. 49-50 and 51-53 are sufficiently strong that we must regard vss. 49-53 as a textual unit. This changes the structure of the text. The reference to peace is now preceded by two parallel sentences, each containing a strong image (vs. 49: "fire"; vs. 50: "baptism"). The word order of the sentences emphasizes these images by placing them first ("Fire have I come to cast . . . A baptism have I to be baptized with.") and placing a corresponding verb in final position ("kindled"; "accomplished" /93/). Vs. 51a, in spite of the use of a question introduced by "Do you think that . . .", conforms exactly to the word order of vs. 49a ("Fire have I come to cast on the earth." "Peace have I come to give on the earth?"). By extending the pattern of vss. 49-50 into vs. 51, the shaper of these words is inviting us to interpret these verses together. So the possibility of peace to which our attention is called in vs. 51 is not only contrasted with "division" but also with the stronger images of "fire" and "baptism." This pattern also strengthens the sense of dark necessity in Matthew's text, for the fire and baptism as well as the division are presented as essential aspects of the mission for which Jesus has come. These features heighten the tension between the normal human desire for peace and these words and compensate somewhat for Luke's use of the rather pale word "division" instead of Matthew's "sword."

The similarities which invite us to read vss. 49, 50, and 51 together also suggest how we should interpret "fire" and "baptism" in this passage. While the text shows no concern to attach precise and limited meanings to these images, the contrast with peace requires us to think of their threatening and painful connotations. The baptism evidently refers to suffering or death, as in Mark 10:38-39, perhaps also recalling the threatening waters of which the psalmists spoke (cf. Ps 69:1-2). This baptism applies to Jesus himself, thus reminding us of his share in the tribulation of which the whole text speaks. Fire is frequently associated with judgment in the Bible but may suggest, especially in parallel with the purifying bath (baptism), the possibility that the fire of judgment may purify and refine. The division in families to which vss. 51-53 refer is evidently a third aspect of the suffering and judgment of which the preceding verses speak, which lightly suggests that the division reflects the division of eschatological judgment.

Luke 12:51, like Matt 10:34, contains a strong antithesis. Indeed, it is emphasized. The word "peace" is first in its clause in the Greek text and so in a position of emphasis. It is part of a question, which even though rhetorical, confronts the hearer personally and suggests the need for a response. The answer is strongly worded (οὐχί, λέγω ὑμῖν "No, I tell you") and is elliptical, thus tying the answer closely to the preceding question and emphasizing the contrast between "peace" and "division." In vss. 52-53 the reference to "division" is unfolded in a series of clauses. Verb forms of the noun "division" are used twice, and this threefold repetition of the same root adds emphasis. The reference to five in the family is probably derived from the list of individuals in vs. 53 /94/. Even though this may be the primary reason for the choice of this number, the resulting asymmetrical division of three and two is effective, for it suggests imbalance, instability, tension, in contrast to the balance and restfulness of symmetry. In this way Luke refers to division within the total family group as well as division between individuals in the family.

Luke's text comes to a powerful climax through effective use of short clauses in strong and rapid rhythm. In Matt 10:35 we found three phrases with the same pattern. The effect of repeating short units of the same pattern is rhythmic. This rhythm is much more strongly developed in Luke than in Matthew. The number of units of the pattern is greatly increased, for each of the relationships mentioned in Matthew is also presented in reverse form, and the phrase "three against two and two against three" is added at the beginning of the pattern. The rhythm moves rapidly, for the units of the pattern are short /95/, and so return quickly. The slight pause caused by the word διαμερισθήσονται ("They will be divided") does not interfere with this movement, for we feel the rhythm all the more strongly when the rhythmic phrases return. The rhythm enforces the meaning of the words. When the rhythm is felt, it carries its unwanted meaning with it. The words rush upon us, pile on top of one another, to suggest a general collapse of family relations. Furthermore, each rhythmic unit is paired with another in which the terms are reversed. Little information is added by this procedure, for a mutual tension between the two individuals is probably implied even in Matthew. However, in Luke there is an antithesis in the very pattern of the words. We are not only told of family tension through the meaning which the words convey; we feel it in the pattern of the sounds as the terms are presented and then reversed. Luke's text lacks Matthew's figure of speech, but it gains imaginative force through the images in vss. 49-50, the sharp antithesis in vs. 51, and the rhythmic pattern in vss. 52-53. This imaginative force involves us in a decision concerning basic values, as it compels us to face the conflict between the one who brings division and our desire for peace and a happy home.

13. Mark 10:29-30. Hundredfold Reward.

29 Truly, I say to you,
    There is no one who has left
        house or brothers or sisters or mother or father
        or children or lands,
            for my sake and for the gospel,
30 Who will not receive
    a hundredfold now in this time,
        houses and brothers and sisters and mothers
        and children and lands,
            with persecutions,
    and in the age to come eternal life.

In vs. 30 the reward promised to the disciples who abandon property and family for the sake of Jesus and the gospel is related to two distinct temporal periods. The disciples are told what they may expect to receive "now in this time" and what they will receive "in the age to come." Greater attention is given to the reward which the disciple will receive now. This reward is indicated by a list of six items including both property and family. Since it is said explicitly that the disciple will receive these "now in this time" and "with persecutions," this list must refer to what the disciple will receive within the fellowship of the present church. A reference to material prosperity and a happy family life in a future, less troubled period which would still be part of "this time" in the eschatological sense is excluded by the reference to persecution. Thus the saying suggests that the church is now the disciple's family and that the sharing of goods within the church means that the houses and fields of others are his. Mark 3:31-35 shows that the contrast between the natural family and the family of the church is a theme familiar to the Evangelist, and other passages in the New Testament apply terms of family relationship to relations within the church /96/.

Some scholars have suggested that the original saying ended with "a hundredfold" and that what follows is a later addition, perhaps by the Evangelist (cf. Klostermann, 1926: 118 and Bultmann: 110). This is possible, though not certain. If such a pre-Markan text existed, it would function in quite a different way from Mark's text, for it would be a rather simple and straightforward promise of reward, presumably in the age to come. It would lack precisely the elements in Mark 10:30 which make the saying striking. That there is something odd in what follows "a hundredfold" in Mark is shown by the fact that both Matthew and Luke, though dependent on Mark, as is shown by both location and wording of their versions /97/, drastically simplify this part of the Markan text. Both remove the enumeration of "houses and brothers and sisters," etc., and the reference to persecution in Mark 10:30. Matthew also removes the distinction between "this time" and "the age to come," thus making it possible to understand the reward as entirely a matter of the future age. Both Matthew and Luke reject Mark's insistence that the reward consists precisely in "houses and brothers and sisters," etc., for their references to the reward as "manifold" or "hundredfold" simply indicate the surpassing value of the reward rather than its precise nature. The surprising twist found in Mark is acceptable to neither Matthew nor Luke. This could reflect knowledge of a pre-Markan form of the saying in which this surprising twist is lacking. More likely, the versions of Matthew and Luke reflect what the hearer expects here: a straightforward promise with no surprises, a promise of something which is obviously glorious. This difference between Mark, on the one hand, and Matthew and Luke, on the other, entails a basic difference in the function of the texts. The effect of Matthew and Luke's text on the disciple conscious of his own sacrifices is to comfort and encourage him; the effect of Mark's text is to produce a surprised laugh or an embarrassed smile.

What happens to a reader through a text may depend on the expectations which he brings to it. In order to be effective a text may seek to control the way in which the reader approaches it by encouraging certain expectations. This the Evangelist does by the way in which he attaches the saying to preceding material. The saying is preceded in vs. 28 by Peter's statement, "Lo, *we* have left everything and followed you." The Greek pronoun ἡμεῖς ("we") is used only for emphasis. Here the emphasis is caused by contrast with the rich man of vss. 17-22. What the disciples have done, according to Peter's claim, corresponds to Jesus' command to the rich man in vs. 21, which this man was unwilling to fulfill. The conversation with the rich man is introduced with the question, "What should I do to inherit eternal life?" (vs. 17) The outcome of the encounter implies that the rich man fails to gain his goal because he rejects Jesus' command. The themes of vss. 17-22 are developed further in vss. 23-27 by discussion of the relation of riches to the eschatological reward of "entering the kingdom of God" or being "saved." When Peter in vs. 28 claims that the disciples have fulfilled Jesus' command to the rich man, the reader is prepared to hear Jesus promise that they will receive the reward which the rich man sought /98/. The reader of Mark comes to vss. 29-30 with a particular expectation which has been aroused by the text. This the text could easily do because this expectation of eternal life as a reward for sacrifice was already a part of the beliefs of the Gospel's original readers. Through Peter the text gives this view of life a spokesman, thereby making it available for reflection. In the text Jesus responds to this expectation, for he does speak of reward, and vs. 30 ends by referring to the "eternal life" previously mentioned in vs. 17. But before the end of vs. 30 something happens which is *not* expected.

The two verbs "left" and "receive" form a contrasting pair, which is emphasized by the fact that they are used with the same series of objects: "house or brothers or sisters," etc /99/. The pairing of these verbs leads one to expect that "left" and "receive" stand on the same level of meaning, that the receiving will simply reverse the previous loss, except that the reward will be a hundredfold. This would be a materialist's bonanza as well as a population explosion within the family /100/. The extravagance of such an idea is already an indication that something strange is happening. The shift from the expected meaning is made fully clear by the "frame" placed around the enumeration in vs. 30. Before the series the phrase "now in this time" is placed and after the series we find "with persecutions." These phrases are essential, for they are the clues to the twist in meaning which is taking place. The phrase "with persecutions" is especially jarring. It is reserved until the end of the clause. The reader may get this far with his expectation of a simple and glorious reward, but he can go no farther. Without this frame the reader could only think of having houses, brothers, etc., in the same sense in which he had them before. However, the frame makes this view impossible. The reward cannot belong to some materialistic heaven nor to some miraculous period of peace and prosperity on earth. It belongs to the Christian's life now in the midst of persecution. The meaning which seemed to be implied has proved impossible. The reader's expectation has been frustrated and he must grope for a new meaning. The perceptive reader will soon see that the Evangelist is talking about what the disciple shares within the fellowship of the church. However, this perception does not remove the tension from this saying. This new view of the Christian's reward remains odd.

We see signs of this oddness in the text's stretching of the word "receive," which now refers not to a simple reversal of the disciple's loss but to receiving property and family in quite a different way from before. More important, the reader has an investment in the expectation which the text first aroused and then twisted. The expectation was encouraged by the text, but it was his own. It was familiar and probably reflected his own beliefs and desires. The surprising twist effected by vs. 30 means that there is a sharp incongruity between this expectation and the text's promise, an incongruity which can lead to laughter. This effect is accentuated by the emphatic, even grandiose, style of the first part of the saying. The introduction with "Truly, I say to you," the emphatic "no one," the solemn sevenfold enumeration "house or brothers or sisters or mother or father or children or fields," the extreme "hundredfold," lead one to expect that something grand will follow. Then the text refers to what seems ordinary and probably insufficient. It may be true that there is fellowship in the church which is something like a family. It may be true that members of the church occasionally share food and shelter. But is this the great reward promised to the disciple who has "left everything and followed" Jesus? This reward is not simple, pure, and glorious, as the text itself reminds us by the phrase "with persecutions." The tension between the reader's expectations and the surprising words of the text persists, for the text is suggesting an understanding of the reader's situation and reward which conflicts with his own.

To this is added, "And in the age to come eternal life." Here, at last, the reader's hope is affirmed. This is not simply a concession by the speaker or writer, for the reference to persecution shows that he is aware of the fragility of the church's situation and the inadequacy of the church's life as a final answer to man's quest for life. However, this addition does not destroy the force of what precedes it. It is short, contains no surprise, and so carries no special force. It allows the words which precede to remain in the center of attention.

There is an incongruity between the reward which the reader expects and the reward which he is actually promised "in this time." The context and beginning of the saying lead us to expect one thing; the climax in vs. 30 promises something different. The text suggests that "left" and "receive" are on the same level of meaning, but we discover that the word "receive" has been twisted or stretched. The first part of the saying suggests that the "hundredfold" reward will be something grand; then we discover that it is speaking of the ordinary life of the church in which the disciple already shares and that we are being promised a reward "with persecutions." Such incongruity is humorous. The reader's surprised laugh or smile shows that he has understood the text. The text has played a joke on us, but it is a joke with a serious purpose. When we laugh, we see ourselves differently, for we are laughing at ourselves, our grandiose expectations, our eagerness for a glorious reward, our blindness to the present. The text debunks our martyr complex, our certainty that "we have left everything" and so some great reward is due us, for it insists that what we have already received far exceeds what we have left. The text debunks our eagerness for the final reward freed from the relativities of history and suggests that we do not recognize a hundredfold reward when we already have it. The text challenges our blindness to the deep meaning of the fellowship which we already enjoy, a blindness partly caused by our concern for our own future reward. As is true with jokes in general, this illuminating laugh is based upon careful literary form. We laugh and see ourselves differently only because the text has been shaped to surprise us with a sharp incongruity.

EXCURSUS:
THE CONTRIBUTION OF NARRATIVE SETTING
TO THE IMAGINATIVE FORCE OF SYNOPTIC SAYINGS

We have noted in connection with several texts above that the narrative setting contributes in a significant way to the force of the saying (see pp. 103-04, 149). Many other synoptic sayings are part of brief stories which report conversations between Jesus and another person. In these stories, which Rudolf Bultmann (11ff.) called "apophthegms," the saying of Jesus forms the climax, but it is reported as Jesus' response to a question or challenge on a particular occasion. There are similarities between the sayings in these stories and the sayings which we have already studied. Therefore we are not moving into entirely new territory. However, the interplay between Jesus' words and their setting is particularly

sharp in some of these stories, and setting as well as saying appear
to be carefully formed to increase imaginative force. We must now
give some attention to the contributions of dialogue and narrative
to the imaginative force of sayings in preparation for examining
some of these little stories.

A first indication of significant form is the fact that these stories
are stylized. Their brevity, concentration, and pointedness
contrast with the complex muddiness of much of our experience.
While actual conversations usually go on at some length with
inconclusive results, many of these stories contain only a single
exchange and end with a striking word of Jesus. In real life we
would expect the critic or questioner to reply, if only to defend
himself or ask for clarification. Historical curiosity would suggest
that the story should also include some indication of the
impression which Jesus' saying made on the questioner. However,
this is often omitted, for verisimilitude and the satisfaction of
historical curiosity are less important than the force of Jesus'
words, resulting from their climactic position, and the reader's
own response, invited by leaving the response open in the story.
The stylization of these stories also appears in the fact that, while
issues are often complex and are sometimes raised in groups, there
is little room for such complexity in these stories, which must
maintain a basic simplicity and brevity so that nothing will detract
from the sharply pointed saying. The story is there for the sake of
the saying, and in most cases we are told nothing except what
contributes to the force of the saying. Modern men, who are
psychologically curious, may especially feel the lack of
portraiture. We learn next to nothing about the individual traits
of those who encounter Jesus. We are tempted to fill this gap with
our own fantasy. However, if this has no basis in the text's own
"lineaments of provocation," it is simply fantasy and not the
legitimate activity of the imagination.

This does not mean that these stories lack dramatic impact.
However, the impact comes not through convincing portrayal of
character but through the tension which is expressed in the
structure of the story itself. In these stories there is interaction

between Jesus' word and the word (or, occasionally, the act or attitude) of another. This commonly causes Jesus' word to stand out through contrast. We feel it resonate against the assumptions of Jesus' conversation partner, assumptions which the reader may share to some extent. As I indicated in an earlier discussion of tensive language (see pp. 53-56), this constrast prevents the easy assimilation of Jesus' words to the questioner's perspective and gives them the power to challenge that perspective at a deep level. We find in these stories, then, another variety of tensive language, one in which the tension assumes narrative form, with two speaking and acting persons as the poles.

Every story capable of holding our interest contains tension, and a major element of tension usually determines the structure of the story. V. Propp, whose analysis of Russian fairy stories has been a major stimulus to the study of narrative structure, discussed these stories in terms of "functions" and "moves." A "move" is a series of plot elements ("functions") which arises from an act of villainy or a lack and which comes to an appropriate resolution through the overcoming of the villainy or lack (59, 92). Between the initiating problem and its resolution there stretches an arc of tension which holds the series of acts together as a meaningful unity, for other events are meaningful in that they help or hinder the resolution. In other types of stories also it is important to note the arcs of tension which determine the plot and give events their meaning. It is not always easy to do this, for there may be more than one type of tension in a story, and events relevant to the resolution of each may interweave (cf. Propp: 92-94). This is true even of some of the brief stories in the synoptic Gospels.

A remarkable feature of some synoptic stories is that there is no real resolution. When the story concerns someone who seeks to follow Jesus, we expect to hear whether he is successful in doing so or not. However, in Luke 9:57-62 each encounter ends with Jesus' words, and we do not learn what happens to the would-be disciples. Furthermore, Jesus' words in this text do not resolve tension but increase it. Here the story remains the servant of the imaginative power of the saying, rather than coming to its own resolution. The story remains open-ended, which invites the reader to make his own response. These encounters begin as stories of men undertaking a quest, but the minor tension involved in their quests is overpowered by the tension in Jesus' words, which reaches beyond the context of the story to the reader.

The further kind of tension made possible by narrative, the tension of plot, is frequently developed as a tension between the actors in the plot, i.e., between Jesus and his conversation partner. This happens not only when the conversation partner is a hostile Pharisee but also when he is a disciple or would-be disciple. This gives a dramatic quality to these little dialogues. Amos Wilder, noting that the Bible does not contain any technically dramatic genres, nevertheless maintains that "the category of the dramatic" is appropriate for discussing dialogue in the New Testament, for "a play of any consequence rests usually upon a momentous transaction or encounter of some kind. In this sense many aspects of the style and discourse of the New Testament are dramatic" (51). He notes in particular the "radical personal challenge and encounter" found in the early anecdotes about Jesus (53) and detects an affinity between this dialogue form and the nature of the Christian message: "The personal dramatic character of the Gospel itself necessarily involves confrontation, not instruction in the ordinary sense but the living encounter of heart and heart, voice and voice, and . . . this has inevitably registered itself in the ongoing story of the Christ and in the style of the New Testament. . . . The early speech-forms made much of the dialogue involving Christ, because each follower thus found himself not only within the reach of the sound of Jesus' voice but in fateful give and take with him" (54).

As Wilder indicates, the fateful give and take involves the hearer or reader of the story and not just the actors in the story. However, there is a significant difference between the words of Jesus which are part of these little stories and some of the sayings previously examined, which were part of a large block of teaching. In the latter case the narrative setting was vague and distant, which encouraged the reader to understand himself as the "you" being addressed by Jesus. When the narrative setting is prominent, the reader is reminded that this is a story about another time and place /101/. The fact that the reader is not addressed directly can increase rather than decrease the text's power. The dramatic scene invites us to step outside our ordinary lives and imaginatively experience personal involvement in another situation. It tempts us to loosen our hold on our personal worlds in order to participate in an experience which is not our own by playing a role vicariously. Since we are not addressed directly and so not directly threatened, we may be willing to risk this imaginative involvement. However, the imagination is the unguarded door through which our sense of reality may be attacked.

When Jesus' conversation partner is an honest inquirer or a disciple identification with him is often easy. When the conversation is with an opponent of Jesus, the Christian reader will assume that he should stand with Jesus and defend him. However, he may discover that Jesus does not defend himself in the expected way, creating difficulties for the defender as well as the opponent. The dynamics of this process of identification are sometimes subtle, involving special features of a particular text and the individual characteristics of the reader. The story does not necessarily assume a single point of identification in the story. By speaking to the reader indirectly, it allows him to choose his way of identification, thereby revealing or determining his inner being.

Sometimes the climactic saying of the story is couched in general terms; sometimes it is directly related to the particular situation of the inquirer. In the latter case as well as the former Jesus' words may have significance beyond the time and place of the story, for this depends less on the generality of the saying than on its imaginative force, its power to stir the imagination of the reader. Jesus' reply to the man who wished to go and bury his father may be full of unsettling significance for Christians who have never had to face that particular problem (see Luke 9:59-60, discussed pp. 162-63 below). This imaginative force results not

only from the characteristics of Jesus' words but also from the
additional contributions of the narrative setting discussed above.
Close examination of four texts will illustrate how these factors
operate in particular cases.

14. *Luke 9:57-62. Following Jesus.*

57 And as they were going along the road, a man said to him,
"I will follow you wherever you go." 58 And Jesus said to him,

"Foxes	have	holes,
And birds	of the sky	nests;
But the Son	of Man	has
Nowhere	to lay	his head."

59 To another he said, "Follow me." But he said, "Let me first
go and bury my father." 60 But he said to him, "Leave the dead to
bury their own dead; but as for you, go and proclaim the kingdom of
God."

61 Another said, "I will follow you, Lord; but let me first say
good-bye to those at my home." 62 Jesus said to him, "No one who
puts his hand to the plow and looks back is fit for the kingdom of God."

In these verses we find three very brief scenes in which Jesus
responds to three men who plan to follow him. Each of the scenes
is dominated by a saying of Jesus. Indeed, it is clear that the scene
is depicted in order to provide an appropriate setting for Jesus'
word. Here we can study the narrative setting in its simplest form
and ask about its function in relation to Jesus' word.

The three sayings of Jesus in these scenes differ in form. If they
were transmitted apart from their settings, there would be no
formal connection between them. In spite of this, they constitute a
series that has its own unity. The unity arises from the fact that all
three scenes concern following Jesus and all three are very brief
narratives of conversations, consisting basically of a statement or
request and Jesus' reply. This thematic and formal similarity
encourages the reader to view these scenes together, seeing them
as parts of a series /102/.

Noting what is omitted will help us to see the distinctive style of
these narratives. This is not the mode of narration which every

storyteller automatically adopts. It would be used only by a storyteller who is sharply focused on his goal, a goal which demands strict concentration on a single concern. The reader's curiosity is given no satisfaction. The men remain anonymous. They are supplied with no personal characteristics. There is no attempt to lead up to the encounter by supplying relevant background, nor is the narrator concerned with colorful details. We are not even told how the men responded to Jesus' words, which means that the narrative tension is unresolved, since we do not learn whether these would-be followers of Jesus pass these tests of their intention or not. An ordinary dialogue would not stop where these do. The man would object, seek clarification, or defend himself, and then Jesus would reply again. But there is nothing of that here. The extreme brevity of these stories is not accidental, nor is it simply the result of ignorance, for it is easy enough to make up plausible details. It is the result of a desire to concentrate all attention on Jesus' powerful word.

In all three scenes the climactic word of Jesus is shaped to be forceful. In all three scenes the interaction between the request and Jesus' word contributes to this force. These scenes may be compared in structure to some jokes, although they are not funny. Jokes are commonly based on an incongruity of perspectives, which can be achieved in dialogue form through a straight line and a punch line. The joke would not be funny if it consisted only of the punch line. The ordinary perspective must be presented first so that the incongruity will be sharply felt when this perspective is twisted in the punch line. Hence a "straight man" is useful, one who presents the expected view which serves as the foil for the joke. The three scenes in Luke 9:57-62 do not contain the kind of witty interplay that results in humor. Only the surprising reference to the dead burying the dead in vs. 60 approaches wit, and even that is more biting than humorous. Nevertheless, there is an interplay between request and reply in each of the three scenes which is important for their purpose. In each of these scenes the would-be disciple proposes a course of action and in each case Jesus' reply challenges that proposal. These proposals seem either

laudable (vs. 57) or, at least, reasonable. Vss. 59-62 refer to the
kind of adjustments between discipleship and other demands
which all Christians do, in fact, make, and , in the case of vss. 59-
60, the conflict of Jesus' reply with the expectations of his
contemporaries is very sharp indeed. Thus the would-be disciple
presents the expected and accepted view, and so has a role
something like a "straight man." The result is not humor but a
sense of the extremeness of the challenging word which follows.
The hearer encounters Jesus' word *over against* the laudable or
sensible intentions of men. The text makes agreeing with Jesus
difficult by placing his words in contrast with the sensible point of
view, a point of view which, by and large, we also share. It is
deliberately trying to make things hard for us in order to block the
natural tendency to simply add discipleship to the configuration
of duties and values by which we live. Discipleship is not merely
another commitment which we may add to the long list of our
commitments but is *the* commitment, demanding a reordering of
our lives from the bottom up. We are forced to recognize this
because of the conflict of perspectives within these little dialogues.
Just as the joke requires both straight line and punch line to make
people laugh, these little scenes require both the expected and the
extreme to make people see.

In this text tension is embodied in dramatic scenes. The tension
is between two persons in a situation which we are allowed to
witness. As I indicated earlier (see pp. 155-56), the fact that the
reader is not addressed directly can invite his imaginative
involvement and increase the power of the text. However, these
little stories are not far removed from direct address to the reader.
Although they tell of another time and place, Jesus' challenging
words are dominant, his challenge strikes the reader as well as the
inquirer in each story, and, as indicated in the preceding
paragraph, the inquirer represents the reader's normal point of
view. Furthermore, the would-be disciple remains largely a blank
into which the reader may insert himself. He is anonymous and
without distinctive characteristics, thereby permitting the reader
to identify with him easily. The personal characteristics can be

supplied by each reader, and the final response of the would-be disciple, omitted in the story, is supplied by each reader's reaction to Jesus' challenge.

The requests of the would-be disciples are also significant in that they help clarify the issues to which Jesus' words are addressed. Lack of such clarity may or may not detract from the force of a saying. For instance, the saying in vs. 62 would retain its force apart from vs. 61. The metaphor of "looking back" would have no clear application but still could be powerfully suggestive of many situations. Indeed, there may be a danger that vs. 61 will unduly limit the significance of vs. 62. On the other hand, vs. 60 would clearly lose force apart from the request in vs. 59, for it would be rather puzzling and would lose the sharpness which results from denying this particular request. While it may be important for the text to provide some understanding of the issue to which a saying is addressed, this need in itself does not account for the dramatic scene with dialogue. It would be possible to provide sufficient understanding without picturing such a scene. For instance, the saying in vs. 60 could have been introduced in some such way as this: "Concerning family funerals Jesus said, 'Leave the dead to bury their own dead . . .'" The saying would be just as clear, but there would be significant loss in the values of the setting discussed above. Jesus' words would seem more like general instruction and less like personal challenge.

Now we must look at the text in greater detail. In vss. 59 and 61 the willingness of the man to follow Jesus is qualified by a request. However, this is not the case in vs. 57. There the statement is entirely affirmative, and the addition of "wherever you go" suggests eagerness. There is nothing to indicate that the man is insincere, yet his statement is not praised nor is it unequivocally accepted. Instead, Jesus' answer forces the eager disciple to stop and think. More may be demanded than he is prepared to give. Eagerness is no more a virtue than hesitation; what is required is personal commitment made with full understanding. Such a commitment can take place only if the disciple is brought face to face with the realities which may prove to be obstacles. This may require more than mentioning this negative reality; it may be necessary to bring it to his attention forcefully so that he must come to terms with it. The careful form of these verses serves this end.

Not only does the contrasting tone of the man's statement and Jesus' reply sharpen the impact of the latter, but Jesus' reply itself has an antithetical structure. The saying is threefold, and the third instance contrasts with the preceding two. We have discussed previously how such a pattern awakens the feeling that further instances should conform to the first two, so that a contrasting third instance is set off strongly (cf. pp. 43-44, 130-31, 136-37). It stands out as odd in light of the preceding pattern. The foxes and birds are mentioned here only in order to establish this pattern. The reference to animals and birds is effective, for, when the contrast is introduced, it suggests that *even* animals and birds have what Jesus /103/ does not have. The antithetical pattern is also reinforced by rhythm. This rhythm is partly a by-product of the parallelism on which the antithesis in the saying is built. But it also reinforces this parallelism, and so the antithesis, for we not only note the similarity of the meanings but also feel the similarity in the rhythmic pattern.

αἱ ἀλώπεκες	φωλεοὺς	ἔχουσιν
Foxes	holes	have
καὶ τὰ πετεινὰ	τοῦ οὐρανοῦ	κατασκηνώσεις
and birds	of the sky	lodgings
ὁ δὲ υἱὸς	τοῦ ἀνθρώπου	οὐκ ἔχει
but the Son	of Man	has not
ποῦ	τὴν κεφαλὴν	κλίνῃ
where	the head	he may lay /104/

Although the rhythm is engendered by the parallelism of the first three lines, we are dealing here with rhythm and not just parallelism, as is shown by line four, which follows the same rhythmic pattern though it is not parallel in thought, and by line two, where the words "of the sky" are superfluous in meaning but rhythmically useful. Note that the verbs always occur at the end of a line, helping to mark off the lines as major rhythmic units. This placing also points up the contrast between the verbs "have" and "has not" /105/. All of the features of the text which we have discussed contribute toward making the situation of the Son of Man stand out vividly. The would-be disciple is not merely told that Jesus is a homeless wanderer and that anyone who follows him must share this existence. He is told this in a way that will have impact. The form of these words makes sure that this reality will not be passed over but will be seriously confronted by the eager disciple.

Jesus' reply in vs. 60 is neither antithetical in structure nor rhythmic. Here the tension which arises from the conflict of Jesus' command with the current understanding of a son's duty to his father is quite enough. The man in vs. 59 is requesting time to fulfill a duty of great importance in Jewish society /106/. We must assume that there is good reason for the man to go home, i.e., that the father has either died or is on the point of death, for the text gives us no basis for thinking otherwise. Jesus does not reply by saying that the man is overly cautious and there will still be time later on. Instead, he rejects the duty itself. Such a statement would stand out no matter the form in which it was made. Its force lies in its extremeness, its contradiction of such an important aspect of family and religious piety. However, this force is enhanced by two additional features: 1) The tension of Jesus' words is dramatically developed in a scene of personal confrontation between Jesus and another. 2) Jesus' reply contains a play on words. That the dead should bury the dead may appear at first as a paradox. Then the hearer perceives that the first reference to "the dead" cannot mean the physically dead, since they are still capable of burying others, but must refer to those who reject or make no response to Jesus' message /107/. Thus we have a pun, one which is biting rather than humorous. A pun has its own "logic," with which it knocks

everyday logic into a cocked hat. There is a witty appropriateness
to the dead burying the dead. The common name suggests that the
two groups belong together, that this combination is fitting or
"logical." This odd "logic" attacks the stable structures of the
everyday world, in which it is the son who must bury the dead
father. Obviously this pun will not stand up as an argument, for it
is clear that something strange has happened to the word "dead."
An argument is not attempted. It is sufficient for this odd "logic"
to catch the hearer's attention and provoke a different view of the
situation, for in this way the inevitability of the ordinary view is
called in question. The new perspective remains odd, but the
evident seriousness of the speaker sets us seeking its cause. The
text points indirectly to something which tips the ordinary world
askew, something which the end of vs. 60 calls "the kingdom of
God." Through this forceful pun the hearer may begin to
understand the kingdom's meaning, a type of understanding
which entails a dramatic shift in perspective, an insight, something
more likely to happen through such provocative words than
through arguments.

We have already seen how extreme Jesus' reply is. The problem
discussed in vss. 59-60 is also remarkably specific. It is doubtful
that funerals were a major problem for discipleship either within
the ministry of Jesus or the life of the early church. Yet these verses
speak only of a man who wants to bury his father. As with the
"focal instances" previously discussed, this situation is chosen not
because it is a common problem but because it is an extreme
instance /108/. One can hardly think of a better excuse for
postponing the demands of discipleship, but even this excuse is
rejected. The words have implications far beyond the specific
situation to which they refer. They show the kind of demand that
Jesus makes and so indirectly illumine many other situations in
which duties and desires may conflict with the demands of
discipleship.

The Matthean version of the text we are studying (Matt 8:19-
22) consists only of the two scenes already discussed, but in Luke

we find a third. Once again the brief scene consists of a request and
reply, but this time Jesus' reply centers in a metaphor. The general
bearing of the metaphor seems clear enough: No one who puts his
hand to the plow and looks back can be a good plowman, for
plowing requires steady attention to where the plow is going. The
good sense of this is obvious in the situation of plowing. However,
since this is used as a metaphor, the mind must make a leap. The
structure of the metaphorical situation is being imposed on other
situations where it is not at all obvious that it applies. Following
Jesus is not the same as plowing, but the unexpected conjunction
of these two activities in the metaphor can awaken a new view of
certain situations which the disciple faces. The metaphor acts as a
filter through which the situation is seen. Each such filter causes
certain features of the situation to recede and others to stand out
prominently, thereby changing the meaning of the whole.
Through the filter of everyday expectations, saying good-bye to
one's family is simply the right thing to do. Through the filter of
this metaphor, it is looking back while plowing. The odd reference
to plowing brings with it an odd view of the situation to which it is
applied, and the metaphor is sufficiently striking to catch the
attention of the hearer and force him to glimpse his situation in
this new way /109/.

"Looking back" could refer to many possible situations in
which previous attachments assert themselves in the life of the
disciple. To think only of saying farewell unnecessarily limits the
illuminating power of the metaphor. And yet Jesus' saying is
related to this particular situation by vs. 61. This has some
advantages and need not limit the significance of Jesus' saying. Vs.
61 ties Jesus' words to a specific issue and helps to bring out their
extremeness. Thus vs. 61 turns vss. 61-62 into a focal encounter.
As we have seen, the implications of a focal encounter are not
restricted to the problem explicitly mentioned, for an extreme
reply to a specific request is able to indirectly suggest a similar
demand in many other situations.

At the beginning of our consideration of this text, we noted
that, although the three sayings of Jesus in vss. 58, 60, and 62 are

different in form, the three dramatic dialogues of which they are a part constitute a formal series. Each speaks of discipleship in a brief scene consisting of request and challenging reply, and this similarity is reinforced by word links among the requests /110/. Therefore the members of the series reinforce one another and suggest that many other situations may require similar decisions, for the series could easily be continued. However, the formal series still permits variation. Not only do the sayings of Jesus vary in form, but vss. 57-58, in which there is no request for a temporary excuse, speak to a somewhat different type of situation than the scenes which follow.

The interplay between request and reply, and the forceful way in which Jesus' words are formulated, make us sharply aware of the tension between the customary and reasonable, on the one hand, and what Jesus demands, on the other. We might be willing to accept the idea that the demands of the kingdom are total as a general statement, but these little stories allow us no refuge in general statements. They force us to recognize what this total demand means and how this conflicts with our desires. These stories do not present us with clear rules on how we are to behave when called to a funeral or on other occasions. They simply suggest possibilities to the reader. However, these possibilities are presented with such imaginative force that, once we allow them room to work in the imagination, we cannot ignore them. They set us thinking about the place of Jesus' call within our competing commitments and about the decisions which this call may require us to make.

15. Mark 3:31-35. Jesus' Family.

31 And his mother and his brothers came; and standing outside they sent to him and called him. 32 And a crowd was sitting about him; and they said to him, "Look, your mother and your brothers outside are asking for you." 33 And he replied, "Who are my mother and my brothers?" 34 And looking around on those who sat about him, he said, "Look! My mother and my brothers! 35 Whoever does the will of God, he is my brother, and sister, and mother."

This text is one of the few places in the Gospels which appear to supply information about Jesus' relation to his own family. This is a fascinating historical topic. If we knew more about it, we would doubtless know more about Jesus. However, any discussion of this text which is content to seek historical information about the relation of Jesus to his family cannot be said to be an *interpretation* of the text, for the interest of the text itself lies elsewhere (on the distinction between interpreting a text and using it as a source of information, see above, pp. 6-7). There is no indication of the attitude of Jesus' mother and brothers toward him in Mark 3:31-35 itself. That must be gathered from 3:21. The references to a crowd and to someone coming to "seize" Jesus in 3:20-21 are puzzling because they seem to lead nowhere. What immediately follows refers neither to a crowd nor an attempted seizure. These verses are less puzzling if we understand them to refer forward to vss. 31-35, for there we find reference both to a crowd and to Jesus' family coming to him. Thus the phrase οἱ παρ' αὐτοῦ ("those from him") in 3:21 probably refers to Jesus' family rather than "his friends" (RSV) as those coming to seize him /111/. However, the opposition of Jesus' family is merely presupposed, not emphasized, in 3:31-35. Furthermore, the story ends without telling us whether his mother and brothers got to see Jesus or not, and if so, what the outcome of the encounter was. This surprising lack of interest in important events is the result of concentration upon another interest, which completely dominates the text and determines its form. Jesus' mother and brothers appear in the story because they are useful for a larger purpose. Since the scene comes to a climax with the words of Jesus in vss. 34-35, it is in connection with these verses that this purpose must be sought.

The phrase "mother and brothers" occurs no less than five times in this short scene /112/. This is because the scene hinges on two contrasting uses of this phrase. We might say that the text is a play on words embodied in a dramatic scene. Two contrasting senses of "mother and brothers" rub against each other. We encounter the second, more surprising meaning in vss. 34-35 only after the

common meaning in vss. 31-32. Therefore we feel Jesus'
announcement in vss. 34-35 to be a departure from, and in conflict
with, normal family ties. The antithetical use of a single phrase
enables "mother and brothers" to become resonant metaphors.
Jesus' climactic pronouncement in vss. 34-35 is not only more
forceful because it is made while his own mother and brothers wait
outside, but also this setting reminds us of the full meaning of
"mother and brothers," including the strong emotional
connotations which arise through the daily experience of family
life. The metaphor is kept in contact with its non-metaphorical
root, from which it must draw its power. The New Testament
shows that it became common to address fellow Christians as
"brothers." Repeated use of such a metaphor turns it into a
commonplace. "Brother" simply means "fellow Christian" and no
more. However, this scene is able to awaken the metaphorical
power of such a term. The two meanings of "mother and brothers"
directly confront one another, helping us to sense all that is
involved in these terms. When the second, metaphorical meaning
replaces the first meaning in the text, it also absorbs its power.
While the metaphorical sense easily becomes the weaker of the
two, referring to a relationship less important and less deeply felt,
the structure of this text makes it the stronger of the two, strong
enough to replace the other, strong enough to absorb the rich
meaning found in the close ties of the family and go beyond.

The contrast basic to this scene is dramatically presented; it is
embodied in a vivid scene in which there is tension between
persons and suspense, and the reader is able to imaginatively
experience what it means to be involved in such a situation. This
dramatic element is carried much further than in the very brief
scenes in Luke 9:57-62. There the drama consisted almost entirely
of the words of the two characters in each short scene. Here we
find not only speeches but action, for narration of acts in a
particular setting plays a significant role. However, such
narration is strictly limited to what will contribute to the force of
Jesus' words, which depends primarily upon the contrast between
the two meanings of "mother and brothers." These two meanings

are dramatically represented by persons in the narrative, and the difference between them is accented by spatial separation. This arrangement of the scene expresses the relation of the two parties to Jesus: on the one hand, there are those "outside;" on the other, there are "those sitting about him." This arrangement is the spatial symbol of the relation which Jesus announces in vs. 34 /113/. Most of the description in the text establishes or reflects this division of the scene into outside and inside (cf. vss. 31-32, 34a).

Jesus' response in vs. 33 is surprising in its context. He asks as a question what all others assume to be obvious. Thus the obvious becomes questionable, meanings are loosed from their fixed moorings and begin to float about. Dramatic suspense is also introduced. Jesus' intention is in doubt, and the reader must wait briefly to discover it. This is supported by the fact that the answer does not follow immediately in vs. 34 but is preceded by a bit of description which retards the forward movement of the story and heightens the suspense. Because of its placement at this moment of suspenseful pause, Jesus' act of "looking around on those who sat about him" becomes highly dramatic /114/. The dramatic rightness of the text is clear when we consider the loss of suspense, and therefore of impact, which would result from placing the answer first in vs. 34, followed by the description, and the loss which does occur in Luke 8:21, where both Jesus' question and the suspenseful pause are eliminated. Jesus' announcement in vs. 34 is striking because it conflicts with the expected meaning of "mother and brothers," especially since that expectation has been aroused by the presence of Jesus' family outside. But vss. 33-34a add significantly to this by first questioning the obvious and introducing a suspenseful pause.

Because the reference of the words is made clear by the scene, Jesus' announcement in vs. 34 can be very terse: "Look! My mother and my brothers!" It is possible that these words mimic the message in vs. 32, which also begins, "Look, your mother and your brothers . . . ," the similarity in form accenting the shift in meaning /115/. In vs. 35 Jesus' words move beyond the concrete scene in which he speaks, as is clear from the phrase "whoever

does the will of God." The addition of "sister" to "brother" and
"mother" also shows an effort to broaden the scope of application.
Since vs. 34 points emphatically to a particular group, it was
important to indicate explicitly that this does not imply a
limitation which excludes later Christians. The form of the text as
a whole makes clear that it is not just concerned with reporting
past events concerning other people but wishes to make an impact
on the reader. Vs. 35 contributes to this by suggesting the way in
which the reader may be included in the story /116/. Details of vs.
35 help to give it sufficient force to prevent the scene from sagging
at the end. The unnecessary οὖτος (here a strong "he") is used for
emphasis, the term "mother" is placed at the end because this
relation is the most striking, and "brother," "sister," and "mother"
are connected by "and" rather than "or" because any sense of
limitation here might also limit the force of the words.

The tension in this story is most appropriate if it reflects a
tension in the situation to which it speaks. Then the tension in the
story awakes awareness of the tensive situation, and awareness of
the situation heightens the impact of the story. This story could
hardly be told in the early church without reminding Christians of
the frequent conflict between family ties and discipleship. The
decision which Jesus here makes against his natural family and for
the fellowship of disciples is one which many of his followers had
to make, as is clearly indicated by such sayings as Matt 10:34-37//
and Mark 10:28-30//. The latter passage is especially important,
for there we find applied to the life of the disciples the same motif
of replacement of the natural family by the family of the church
(on this passage see above, pp. 147-52). So Jesus is not alone in the
decision which he makes, and the necessity of that decision
explains why our text ends with an indirect challenge to do the will
of God. Faced with this decision between the natural family and
the fellowship of disciples, the contrasting use of "mother and
brothers" is bitingly relevant, for it brings to expression the
tension which the first readers faced /117/.

However, the story is not simply a call to sacrifice. Those who
follow Jesus in his decision not only lose a family but gain one, for

the story comes to its climax with the announcement of a new family which has Jesus at its center. The story is both a challenge to decision and an offer of a new relationship. In both ways it wishes to preach, that is, to call forth faith and obedience.

We feel the force of Jesus' announcement "Look! My mother and my brothers!" because these words are first applied to Jesus' natural family and then used in a contrasting way, the whole story being carefully formed to heighten this contrast. Such force is necessary because the story points to a decision involving a major reordering of values. If the decision simply involved adding one further association to the web of associations in which we live, such antithetical force would be inappropriate. Since the goal of the story is to bring about and sustain such a reordering of values in the personal world of the reader, we only begin to understand the story when we feel its bite, when we become aware of the possibility of such a reordering in our own lives. There are situations today in which conflict between family ties and doing the will of God is quite possible. The situation of young men who conscientiously opposed participation in the Viet Nam war is a recent example. We may also think of situations in which a father's decision to do the will of God would result in financial and psychological damage to his family.

Since the text speaks indirectly and relies upon its imaginative force to create its application in the life of the reader, rather than attempting to spell out that application explicitly, the extent of that application is indefinite. The fact that Jesus' father is not mentioned does not lessen the relevance of the text to conflicts with fathers. Nor does the fact that other social ties are not mentioned necessarily exclude them from the circle of the text's relevance. To be sure, we must use the concrete situation in the text as our clue and attempt to follow out *its* "lineaments of provocation," stopping before we rob the text of its force through proposing applications which have lost contact with this concrete situation. In my opinion we do not overstep the bounds of a proper caution when we note that the immediate family is the closest and most powerful strand of a whole web of social relations, any part of which may hold us back from doing the will of God. Thus this story of a conflict between Jesus and his family, through its imaginative force and suggestive indirectness, may legitimately set us thinking of a large field of relationships including not only our families but our clubs, churches, and socio-economic classes.

16. Mark 12:13-17. Caesar and God.

13 And they sent to him some of the Pharisees and some of the Herodians, to entrap him in his talk. 14 And they came and said to him, "Teacher, we know that you are true, and give special consideration to no man; for you do not regard the position of men, but truly teach the way of God. Is it lawful to pay the census tax to Caesar, or not? 15 Should we pay, or should we not?" But knowing their hypocrisy, he said to them, "Why put me to the test? Bring me a denarius that I may see it." 16 And they brought one. And he said to them, "Whose image and inscription is this?" They said to him, "Caesar's." 17 Jesus said to them,
"Give to Caesar what is Caesar's
And to God what is God's."
And they were amazed at him.

Even though this controversy dialogue is longer and more complex than most, the final command of Jesus in vs. 17 retains its primacy within the whole. Everything prior to that serves to heighten interest in how the story will come out and to focus the reader's attention on the final, climactic utterance. All that is strictly necessary to the story is the initial question concerning the tax, Jesus' counterquestion concerning the coin and the opponents' reply, and Jesus' final command /118/. However, the additional elements remain subordinate to the final command, supporting it rather than competing with it. This is an indication of careful composition.

Vss. 13-15a emphasize the evil designs of Jesus' opponents and the danger which lies hidden in their question. The question does not refer to taxes in general but to the tax assessed on the basis of the Roman census of people and property, a tax especially hated by Jewish nationalists. The institution of this tax for the first time in Judea was a direct cause of the resistance movement led by

Judas of Galilee (cf. Martin Hengel, 1961:132ff.). It would appear, then, that a positive answer to the question would cause Jesus to lose favor with the many who sympathized with the resistance movement and that a negative answer would be a dangerous attack upon Roman authority. The elaborate compliment in vs. 14, placed in a frame (vss. 13, 15) which makes its falseness very clear, heightens the sense of threat. Jesus is faced not with open opposition but with deceitful trickery. The false compliment stands in sharp contrast with the reality of the situation, and this contrast is heightened by stylistic means. While the discourse in the rest of the story is very terse, vs. 14 is verbose and repetitive. Rather than deepening the thought, the repetition, especially in contrast with the terse discourse which follows, makes the compliment sound overdone and therefore hollow /119/, bordering, perhaps, on sarcasm. Yet for the followers of Jesus these statements are true. Their truth, however, simply increases the tension for the reader. Can Jesus "teach in truth the way of God" and still escape the trap of his enemies?

In vs. 14, where the questioners appear to be in command, the pace of the story is slow. In vss. 15-17 Jesus takes command of the situation, and this is marked by a sharp change in pace. These verses contain a rapid series of exchanges in which no word is wasted. Rather than forcing Jesus to respond to their question, the opponents are now forced to respond to Jesus, first to his command to bring the coin, then to his question about it. They must participate in answering their own question, which makes the answer less easy to escape. The reason for Jesus' request for the coin is not immediately apparent. This puzzle increases interest in the story, for the reader will want to discover how the coin can lead to the desired answer /120/. Jesus' question about the coin in vs. 16 continues the suspense. Nor is it ended by the opponents' reply, for this only states what is obvious, so that the reader is still wondering what is the point of it all. Thus all of the discourse in this little story points forward to Jesus' final response in vs. 17. The quick exchanges between Jesus and his opponents have the interest both of a verbal fencing match and, through the use of the coin, of a dramatic demonstration /121/. The reader can scarcely avoid being interested in the outcome.

Jesus' reply is couched in general terms, referring in sentences of the same construction to "the things of Caesar" and "the things of God." If we assume that this is meant to be a general rule of behavior, a clear and practical guide to action, a division of life into two realms suggests itself. So long as Jesus' words refer to realms which are distinct and identifiable, they can serve as such a rule of behavior. When we isolate vs. 17 from its setting, it is fairly easy to identify "the things of Caesar" with aspects of our familiar world. Generalizing, this becomes the sphere of politics and government, and, having handed this over to Caesar, "the things of God" must then be limited to private religion and personal morality. The chief fallacy here is the initial assumption that Jesus' words are meant to be a clear and practical guide to action. This assumption ignores important features of our text.

The previous discussion of the antithetical aphorism (see pp. 88-101) suggests that Jesus' reply may have a different function. Like an antithetical aphorism, Jesus' reply is a short, pointed saying consisting of two halves. The halves are linked with each other, for each speaks of the same relationship and expresses this in the same syntactic structure, the only important change being the insertion of the word "God" for "Caesar" in the second half. The omission of the verb in the second half also ties it closely to what precedes. So the two halves of the saying are bound into a tight unity in which the parts interact with one another. Our attention is directed to the two proper nouns which occur within the same pattern, and we are forced to think about their relation. Like most antithetical aphorisms, Jesus' reply is very concise. It is general, indeed, absolute, showing no concern for complications and qualifications. At the same time it lacks the clarity characteristic of a good rule of behavior (How much belongs to Caesar? What are the "things of God"?). The chief difference between an antithetical aphorism and Mark 12:17 is that the former is built upon an unambiguous contrast, while the relation between the claims of Caesar and the claims of God remains ambiguous. This concise, absolute, but nebulous command can refer to situations in which the claims of Caesar are legitimate and do not infringe on the claims of God, but it can also apply to situations in which Caesar claims more than his right, in which case the command places a limit on those claims in the name of God, and "the things of Caesar" means "only those things which Caesar may legitimately claim." Thus we may call Jesus' reply in vs. 17 an aphorism, but not an antithetical aphorism.

Nevertheless, the similarity to the antithetical aphorism provides a clue to the function for which Jesus' reply is fitted by its form. Like the antithetical aphorism, Jesus' reply does not directly solve the problems which may arise in the sphere of life under discussion. The only specific thing which it authorizes (due to the setting rather than to vs. 17 itself) is the payment of the Roman tax being discussed. This does not provide a simple answer to any of our questions, even that of paying taxes. (Think, for instance, of taxes to support an unjust war, which raise a different set of ethical issues than the Roman tax.) Rather than providing specific guidance for behavior, the aphorism is shaped to speak to a prior level of our being. The pattern of the words forces us to meditate on the dangerous and difficult relationship between Caesar and God. By placing these two proper nouns in concise, parallel constructions, the saying prevents us from thinking of either separately. We cannot settle questions of political life without considering the claims of God nor seek to live a religious life oblivious to the problems of society. These words should awaken concerned awareness of the (possibly conflicting) claims of Caesar and God. This awareness is the beginning of obedience.

So much can be said by considering the aphoristic form of vs. 17. However, this aphorism is found in a carefully constructed setting, and consideration of its setting shows that more is happening than is apparent from the aphorism itself. While the form of the isolated aphorism suggests that Jesus is speaking of similar, even equal, claims, the controversy dialogue as a whole makes clear that the emphasis falls on the second half of the aphorism and that the speaker wishes to shift concern away from the question of Caesar's tax to the question of the claims of God as they impinge on problems of the state. This emphasis may be contrary to the concern generated by the political situation /122/. The loyal Jew would scarcely have disputed that one should render the things of God to God, while Caesar's tax was a disputed matter /123/. This would seem to make the first half of Jesus' reply the more interesting part. However, vs. 17 by its form holds the claims of Caesar and the claims of God *together*. The possibility of this combination was disputed by some Jews, while there were doubtless others who were quite content to satisfy the claims of Caesar without worrying about God. Thus the emphasis on the second half of Jesus' reply, by which this disputed combination is established, may be appropriate in the Palestinian situation.

In any case, there are a number of features of our text which show that that is where the emphasis properly falls /124/. We have already seen how the entire pericope points forward to Jesus' final command, which thereby becomes an emphatic climax. The reference to what must be rendered to God is the final element of this climactic command, a position which necessarily results in emphasis. Furthermore, the first half of Jesus' command is a direct answer to the question put to him and so is prepared by what precedes it. The second half, though following the same form and so integrated with the first half, has the additional value of surprise. It goes beyond the required yes or no answer, introducing something for which there is little preparation in the preceding dialogue. It also catches our attention because it involves a clever variation of the formulation in the first half. Furthermore, the very mention of this second claim upon man relativizes the importance of the first. We must now measure and compare the two claims, which prevents Caesar's claim from being absolute. The two claims, moreover, are clearly unequal. We know this not only from other parts of the Bible, which do not favor the supposition that a king's claims are equal to those of God, but also from this text itself. Because the first half of Jesus' reply is prepared by the dialogue which precedes, its meaning is also specified and limited by this setting. In reply to the discussion about the coin, "the things of Caesar" means, first of all, Caesar's coins. This phrase may, indeed, mean more than that, but it is on such coins that the text focuses the reader's attention. There is no similar narrowing of the reader's attention in the case of "the things of God." The lack of preparation for this phrase leaves it without limit, as is appropriate to the claims of God /125/. Finally, vss. 16-17 involve witty play with the question of who owns the coin. The image and inscription on the coin are taken as evidence that it is Caesar's. Why, then, should men worry about returning it to its owner? This is wit, not a serious argument, for in one sense the coin is Caesar's but in another sense it belongs to the man who rightfully possesses it and who must decide how it will be used. This witty reply not only gives an answer to the inquiry but also minimizes the importance of the inquirers' concern. Indeed, it would appear gallingly flippant to those worried by the tax issue, for Jesus responds to one of the most important political and religious problems of his day by treating it as if it were an obvious case of restoring another man's property. Jesus' wit, however, opens a space for a second concern which exceeds and embraces the first. The inquirers' concern is played down so that it may be absorbed into something greater. With a quick and clever variation of the same words, Jesus turns the attention of the hearers from the question of the tax to the question of God's claims upon his world. The hearers' concern with the tax, minimized in this witty way, is thus overshadowed by a greater concern. So the use of forceful language to redirect one's concern, found in an antithetical aphorism like Mark 7:15 (see pp. 89-94), occurs here also.

Jesus' answer breaks out of the hard lines of positions for and against cooperation with the Roman conquerors, which form the presupposition of the question by which the opponents hope to trap Jesus. In a political sense Jesus takes a "middle" position. Middle positions often have little chance in times of political extremism. However, the form of Jesus' words, and of the story in which they are transmitted, give them the force to challenge fixed positions and to live beyond the original historical situation so as to speak to other real or seeming conflicts between the claims of the state and of God. To be sure, this text has frequently been used to protect the Christian citizen from the claims of God by defining "the things of God" in a narrow sense and isolating them from concerns of the state. As we have seen, this is wrong for a number of reasons. It falsely assumes that vs. 17 is meant to be a clear rule of behavior which must refer to clearly separable realms. It neglects the fact that the final reference to God is formally the climactic element in the story and that, in contrast to the case with the "things of Caesar," the story suggests no limit to the "things of God." It fails to see that the inquirers' concern with the tax is wittily minimized so that God's claims may be the dominant concern even in relation to the state. These conclusions agree with the dominant view of the Bible as a whole, which makes clear that the God of whom it speaks is not one who limits himself to private religion and personal morality.

17. Mark 3:22-26. Satan Divided.

22   And the scribes who came down from Jerusalem were saying, "He is possessed by Beelzebul," and "By the prince of demons he casts out the demons." 23 And he called them to him, and said to them in parables, "How can Satan cast out Satan?
24   And if a kingdom is divided against itself,
        That kingdom cannot stand.
25   And if a household is divided against itself,
        That household will not be able to stand.
26   And if Satan has risen up against himself and has been divided,
        He cannot stand, but is coming to an end."

Our text is part of a longer section of polemical material dealing with the interpretation of Jesus' exorcisms. The parallel sections in Matthew and Luke begin by recounting a particular exorcism, which becomes the occasion for the following charge (cf. Matt 12:22-23, Luke 11:14). This is not found in Mark. Instead, the accusation of the scribes in Mark 3:22 is preceded by the statement of Jesus' relatives or friends that "he is beside himself." This suggests that Mark saw a connection between the two charges. Our text is followed in Mark by two further sayings directed to the same issue (vs. 27, vss. 28-30). The sudden introduction of the new image of binding a strong man in vs. 27 and the shift in thought and vocabulary in vss. 28-30 suggest that these sayings were formed separately from vss. 22-26. Their original independence is confirmed by the parallels in Matthew and Luke, for, following Q, they insert other material between the sayings about Satan divided and the strong man, and Luke's version of Mark 3:28-30 is found in an entirely different context. Since I have decided to limit myself to the simpler formal units in the Gospels, I will deal only with vss. 22-26.

Bultmann includes our text among the "controversy dialogues" (or "conflict sayings") (13-14). Like other controversy dialogues, it may have been used by the early church to defend its message against attacks. However, the remarkable thing is the kind of "defense" which is presented, one which relies upon words with imaginative force. The overall structure of the text, consisting of accusation and response, contributes to this, for it makes Jesus' words stand out in this situation of tension. In this text, moreover, Jesus' words take the accusation into themselves and use it in an unexpected way. Jesus' reply daringly adopts the perspective of the accusation itself. It is primarily this surprising twist which gives these words their special power. Thus the relation between accusation and answer is more intimate in this text than in some others /126/.

The significance of Jesus' answer is largely lost when its imaginative force is not appreciated. Several recent interpreters find vss. 24-26 less than convincing as an argument. Ernst Haenchen, pointing to "the weakness of this argumentation," feels that it bypasses the presuppositions of the opponents rather than encountering them. In the opponents' eyes the prince of demons might well allow Jesus to drive out demons in order to work an even greater evil among the men thereby deluded (146) /127/. However, Jesus' reply does, in fact, encounter his opponents' presuppositions, presuppositions which lie at a deeper level than those which Haenchen has in mind. Not only do the opponents assume that Satan may assert his evil power by driving out demons but they (like all of us) have a làrge rigid structure of presuppositions. These presuppositions prevent them from seeing Jesus as the decisive witness to the coming of God's kingdom. It is this structure of presuppositions that Jesus' reply attacks. Since it is intimately related to the feeling-filled vision of self and world in which each one of us has so great a stake, this structure is largely impervious to rational argument. Encountering the presuppositions of the opponents, then, requires something more than a discussion of Satanology. It requires the awakening of a counter-vision with sufficient imaginative force to crack the hard shell of this structure. This is what these words attempt through their surprising adoption of the perspective of the accusation, thereby presenting a view which the opponents can neither reject nor accept, which lodges in the midst of their presuppositions like an indigestible irritant.

The intent of these words is obscured when the interpreter assumes that they are merely an argument to show that the "opponents are talking nonsense" (Bultmann: 14) or are caught in a "self-contradiction" (Haenchen: 146). There is more to these words than this. To be sure, vs. 23b does suggest a contradiction in the opponents' accusation. It indicates that the accusation is questionable and supports this by suggesting that Satan would then be engaged in two contradictory actions. The Greek word order emphasizes the resultant tension by placing the two occurrences of the word "Satan" in immediate conjunction. It is a mistake, however, to allow vs. 23b to so dominate our interpretation of the passage that we regard vss. 24-26 as simply a more complex version of vs. 23b. It is doubtful that vs. 23b is an original part of the tradition /128/. It was evidently not found in the Q version of our text, for neither Matthew nor Luke have it /129/. Furthermore, the transition to vs. 24 is rather awkward. Even within Mark's text as it stands, this question is not strong enough to dominate the strongly patterned language and striking train of thought in vss. 24-26, so long as we examine these verses closely enough to discern their true significance. Vs. 23b serves, rather, as an opening wedge, an initial indication of the questionability of the firm convictions of the opponents. Vss. 24-26 do not simply continue this thought but deepen it, so that, whether or not one continues to assert that Jesus is casting out demons with Satan's power, one is forced to stand with Jesus and see what he sees.

The charge "By the prince of demons he casts out the demons" assumes that the demonic world is organized like a government under a ruler. This assumption is accepted into the reply /130/. The purpose of our text is not to give approval to a particular theory of the demonic world. At the end, the hearer emerges with no clear picture of such matters; indeed, he may find that his view of his own world is in shambles. This fall from certainty comes about through using the weight of the opponent's assertion against him. For this reason the assumption in the charge is not only picked up in the reply but reinforced through the threefold repetitive pattern which dominates vss. 24-26. These verses contain three conditional sentences with basically the same structure and vocabulary (though there are some variations in word order and verb tense). The pattern is clear when we note that the shifting nouns "kingdom," "house," and "Satan" have been inserted in turn in what is basically the same sentence /131/. We have encountered such threefold patterns before (see pp. 43-44, 130, 136, 161). In them the first two members establish a pattern which is then used postively or negatively in interpreting the third. They provide the filter through which we are to view the third instance. In this case they do so by calling to awareness the nature of structured social groups — the kingdom, the household (this is the meaning of οἰκία ["house"] in this text) — and also the threat which internal dissension poses to them. The pattern evokes the hearer's awareness of civil war, family bitterness, and their disastrous results. Thus the pattern reinforces the presupposition of the accusation that the demonic world is a structured society with its own government, but at the same time it reminds the hearer that such societies are prone to collapse through internal dissension. The reply of Jesus does not argue for the idea that the demonic world is a society with its own ruler. This is not necessary, for it is already contained in the accusation. Neither does it simply adopt that view without development, however. It reinforces it by the threefold pattern and deepens our awareness of the danger of dissension in such a society.

Not only the natural tendency of men to defend themselves but also the pattern of criticism and defense so common in the controversy dialogues lead us to expect that Jesus will reject the charge. Instead there is a surprising continuity between charge and reply. We are allowed to imagine that in Jesus' exorcisms Satan actually has risen up against Satan. This unexpected continuity between the charge and Jesus' own words nevertheless results in a disturbing challenge to the hearer's settled judgments about Jesus, his work, and the hearer's own situation.

The challenge is presented by taking up the charge and using it as the premise for Jesus' own "argument." The striking oddness of what is happening becomes fully clear when we realize that Jesus is using a false charge (from the viewpoint of early Gospel tradition) as the premise by which he reaches a *true* conclusion (also from the viewpoint of early Gospel tradition). The conclusion is seriously affirmed, and the speaker wishes us to accept it. Vss. 24-26 go an important step beyond vs. 23b. Rather than emphasizing the absurdity of the charge, Jesus in vss. 24-26 uses the division of Satan against himself as the premise from which he concludes that Satan "cannot stand, but is coming to an end" (vs. 26). In each of the three sentences in vss. 24-26, it is the conclusion, rather than the premise, which is the natural point of emphasis. Furthermore, vss. 24-25, which supply the pattern in light of which we are to judge the situation in vs. 26, lend plausibility to the conclusion in vs. 26, for the experiences of which they speak, civil war and family dissension, are quite credible. Is the emphasis on the collapse of kingdom, household, and Satan merely meant to underline the absurdity of asserting that Satan is divided? Such a view not only ignores the fact that kingdoms and families do perish through internal strife but also the fact that the conclusion in vs. 26 is not absurd from the viewpoint of the New Testament. The proclamation of the end of Satan's rule and freedom from his power is one of the ways in which the New Testament announces its good news. This is apparent in the saying which follows in vs. 27, for, in its present context, this saying must equate Jesus' exorcisms with the plundering of the strong man's house and the strong man can only be Satan. Thus vs. 27 proclaims that Satan has lost his power /132/. Although vs. 27 was originally a separate saying, the combination is significant here. Vs. 27 helps us to understand the conclusion in vs. 26 as proclamation by reinforcing its salvific sense. This help is necessary when vss. 24-26 become part of a book for Christian readers, who are often quicker to defend Jesus than to understand him. Jesus' original opponents could not so quickly reject the premise from which Jesus is arguing, for it reflects their own charge.

The necessity of reinforcing the conclusion in vs. 26, guarding against too quick a rejection of what is there affirmed, helps to account for the ways in which vs. 26 departs from the pattern established by vss. 24-25. Instead of one, there are two verbs in both the protasis and apodosis of vs. 26. The reference to Satan having "risen up" against himself adds vividness by picturing the situation as a rebellion, thus carrying further the imagery of vs. 24. The phrase "is coming to an end" /133/ is also significant. This phrase, found only in Mark's version of our text, appears at first glance to be an unnecessary addition by someone insensitive to literary art. While the rest of vs. 26 repeats or closely conforms to the field of imagery established by vss. 24-25, this final phrase introduces something new /134/. Although a ruler who has lost his power through rebellion may die, that result does not necessarily follow from what has been said. Thus there seems to be an outside force at work here, resulting in an idea which has its origin and justification not in the text's own little world but outside it. This shift threatens to shatter the world of images established by the text and lead us back to the world of literal meanings /135/. However, this slight suggestion of the literal has a significant function within our text, for it supports the conclusion in vs. 26 against the tendency to regard it too lightly. In order to shake the presuppositions of the hearer, the text must establish a balance between absurdity and seriousness. Against opponents this balance is supported by the fact that the charge taken up into Jesus' reply is seriously meant. However, when Jesus' words are read by Christians who reject such a charge out of hand, the text easily becomes simply a confirmation of what we already know: that we are right and the opponents wrong. Then the balance must be redressed by emphasizing the reality of the conclusion to which the charge leads. Perhaps even the Christian may wonder a bit that truth thus comes out of falsehood and that Jesus is so free as to accept this blasphemous charge long enough to build an imaginative bridge to his opponents. We see, then, that details of the text agree with our previous observation that the conclusion in vs. 26 is not absurd but a serious assertion /136/.

This imaginative bridge invites the hearer to cross over and see what the speaker sees. Such a bridge cannot be built in the public world of literal meanings, the world reduced to what all accept for purposes of interpersonal commerce, for this public world is itself being challenged. The speaker must disclose the truth by using words which, taken literally, are false, as happens in the case of metaphor. The words are successful insofar as they are able to induce an imaginative vision with sufficient power to undermine the obviousness of literal meanings. We have discovered a strange combination of falsehood and truth in our text, for a premise which (we feel) is false is used as the basis for a true assertion. Jesus' reply blends the vision of his opponents and his own vision by means of an argument of the form "if . . . then . . . ". The argumentative form is important here. It provides the cement for this bridge between two worlds. It is the commonly acknowledged strength of such arguments which holds together what most listeners would separate. Thus logic is being used in a strange way to attack what appears logical to the listener. The odd counterreasoning, which neither Jesus' opponents nor his supporters can accept, acts like gravel in the gears of our machine-like interpretations of the world. The machine comes to a halt. We do not know what to make of this. We must begin again to sort out the real from the unreal, for the pieces no longer fit together as they did. We must rethink our judgments concerning the significance of Jesus and the time that he brings.

This may be put in another way by noting that Jesus' reply has entrapped his opponents in a dilemma. They are faced with two alternatives, and each places them *with* Jesus, seeing what he sees, rather than over against him. They may stick to their accusation, but this means that Satan's kingdom is collapsing. This places them with Jesus, who is proclaiming the coming of God's kingdom, God's triumph over evil. Or they may retreat from their charge in confusion, admitting that it is false. But if Jesus' power is not demonic, must they not admit that it is divine? A dilemma, even if it is not just a trick, may be fairly superficial, so that a minor readjustment in our thought takes care of the matter, with no serious threat to our basic perspective on self and world. Other dilemmas, even if we can think of avenues of escape, may have the imaginative force to turn thought in a new direction, resulting in important shifts in understanding our situation and what it demands, and finally affecting our basic perspective on self and world. The dilemma in our text is formed for this purpose. It wishes to drive a wedge deeply into the foundations on which the opponents have built their world. It not only undercuts their specific charge but also their whole assessment of Jesus' exorcisms, so that they are faced again with the possibility that now is the time of the approach of God's kingdom, as Jesus has announced, requiring the type of response which Jesus has demanded. This dilemma reaches into the depth of personal existence, posing real dangers to the secure world of the past. To be sure, the hearer can still escape, for these forceful words can neither coerce the will nor solve all problems. They are a disturbing invitation to which the hearer in turn must respond.

The text is not only disturbing to Jesus' opponents but also to those who rush to Jesus' defense. While other New Testament texts regard one's judgment concerning Jesus as crucial, Jesus' answer here leaves open not only the question of his own rank but even the question of whether he is in collusion with Satan in order that, in one way or the other, the opponent may be helped to see the crumbling of Satan's power and the coming of God's kingdom. Here the Christian is faced with his own sort of quandary. Have we rightly located in our situation the crucial point of decision between faith and rejection? Are we mounting our defense of Jesus at the right point and in the right way? Should we seek equally daring ways of speaking across the gulf between believer and sceptic? In spite of the fact that our text is "dated," being based upon a specific accusation which is rooted in a world view different than ours, these questions may be fruitful and help us to uncover the continuing power of the text to suggest ways of pointing to what Jesus saw by speaking as he spoke. Doubtless this will also mean that we must decide whether we really can affirm with Jesus that Satan's power is coming to an end. It is not only the opponent who is faced with a difficult decision.

NOTES

/1/   For the latter view, see Paul Minear (133ff). Minear believes that the original nucleus of Matt 6:28-30 corresponded line by line to 6:26. This assumes that the original was characterized by strict symmetry, which is dubious.

/2/   So Luke, while many manuscripts of Matt add "or/and what you shall drink." However, there is significant manuscript evidence for the omission of this even in Matthew. Its later addition could have been caused by Matt 6:31.

/3/   "Life" ($\psi v \chi \acute{\eta}$) probably refers to the inner life-force, which, in what follows, is acknowledged to be quite dependent on food.

/4/   However, Luke's reference specifically to the ravens makes the language more forceful. God cares even for the ravens, who according to God's law are unclean. Cf. Lev 11:15, Deut 14:14. Luke's reference to the ravens also produces a pattern of alliteration: $\kappa \alpha \tau \alpha \nu o \acute{\eta} \sigma \alpha \tau \epsilon \ \tau o \grave{v} \varsigma \ \kappa \acute{o} \rho \alpha \kappa \alpha \varsigma$ . . . $\kappa \alpha \tau \alpha \nu o \acute{\eta} \sigma \alpha \tau \epsilon \ \tau \grave{\alpha} \ \kappa \rho \acute{\iota} \nu \alpha$ (noted by Wrege: 177).

/5/   The phrase   σήμερον . . . βαλλόμενον   has parallel structure in
Matthew. In Luke there is variation among the manuscripts as to word order, but the
best attested reading gives a chiastic structure to the phrase, placing σήμερον and
αὔριον in closest conjunction. Both structures emphasize the contrast between the two
situations and so the ephemeral nature of "grass."

/6/   This contrasts with the view of Paul Minear (138).

/7/   From Annie Dillard's remarkable meditations on nature we may add the
images of the tree with lights in it and the mockingbird's daring fall. Dillard rightly
affirms such gracious beauty in full awareness of the dark side of nature.

/8/   The following section substantially reproduces my article "The 'Focal
Instance' as a Form of New Testament Speech: A Study of Matthew 5:39b-42" (1970).
Reprinted from *The Journal of Religion* 50:4, 372-85, by permission of The University
of Chicago Press. C 1970 by The University of Chicago.

/9/   It is not entirely clear whether we should understand vs. 42 as two sayings
or as one saying doubled. The first half may refer to gifts to beggars (so in the RSV),
which would be slightly different than the loans mentioned in the second half.
However, the verb δίδωμι may be used of money given in trust (cf. Matt 25:15; Luke
19:13,15) as well as of outright gifts, and so both halves of the verse may refer to loans.
In either case the two halves of the verse refer to situations very similar to each other
but quite distinct from the preceding verses, and should be taken as one saying. Note
that the two halves of the verse are joined by a conjunction while the verse as a whole is
set off from the preceding by the omission of the conjunction. Compare the way in
which pairs of related words are marked off by asyndeton in Matt 24:38.

/10/   In Luke the adjectival participle is used throughout, the subjunctive of
prohibition is placed last in vs. 29b, and the length of the three sayings is even more
regular (if vs. 30 is counted as one saying). On rhythm in Luke 6:29-30 see above, pp.
47-48. This rhythm further supports the formal unity of the Lukan text.

/11/   It is important to carry the investigation of form beyond the level of
syntax. If we looked only at the syntax of these commands, they might be mistaken for
casuistic legal material. The argument which follows will show why this is wrong.

/12/   Vs. 42 is less specific, for it lacks the concrete detail in the preceding
sayings. What follows will apply most clearly to 5:39b-41.

/13/   Cf. e.g., Matt 5:44//Luke 6:27-28//Didache 1:3//Justin Mart., Apol. I,
15, 9; Matt 5:46-47//Luke 6:32-34//Ignatius to Polycarp 2:1//Justin Mart., Apol. I,
15, 9-10; Matt 7:1-2//Luke 6:37-38//I Clem. 13:2//Polycarp to Phil. 2:3; and the
variations in the tradition of the words we are discussing: Matt 5:39b-42//Luke 6:29-
30//Didache 1:4-5//Justin Mart., Apol. I, 15, 10 and I, 16, 1-2.

/14/   The higher fine prescribed in the Mishnah for a slap with the back of the hand suggests this (cf. Strack-Billerbeck 1:342). To be sure, the relevance of this is questionable, and some interpreters suggest that Matthew's reference to the right cheek merely reflects the tendency of the tradition to add details. However, this does not explain the fact that when such a detail is found in one gospel but not in the parallel, as in Matt 5:29-30, 39; Luke 6:6, 22:50, it always refers to the right, never the left. This seems to reflect a general assumption that the right is the more important side of the body, and so damage to it more serious, which supports the view that a blow on the right cheek is more extreme.

/15/   In Luke the order of the two garments is reversed, and the situation envisioned may be a robbery rather than a lawsuit.

/16/   Compare the case of Simon of Cyrene in Matt 27:32, where the same technical term is used.

/17/   William Beardslee (72) discusses the "intensification" of the proverb in the synoptic Gospels, resulting in a shift of function from identifying repeatable experience to "jolting the hearer . . . into a new judgment about his existence." We might speak of the focal instance as an instance or example intensified, with a similar shift in function. Any example may remain specific and yet be applicable to other analogous situations. This is also true of a case in case law. However, the focal instance differs from these in its extremeness, with the result that it challenges the basic goals and values by which men live. John Dominic Crossan (1975) develops a related point of view, suggesting that Matt 5:39b-41 is case law parody. This is an interesting idea, but I am not sure that the extremeness in this passage necessarily amounts to parody.

/18/   Like Matt 5:39b-42, 5:32 makes use of a participial construction and a conditional relative clause to describe the cases being considered. However, these are followed by present indicative verbs rather than imperatives or subjunctive of prohibition. For formal parallels to 5:32 in the wisdom literature see Klaus Berger (1970-71:28-30). In contrast, Berger judges 5:39, 41 to be closer to a legal form. Cf. 1970-71:27, n. 2. Berger considers only the syntax of the sentences, not the formal characteristics in which we are most interested. Even if his form critical judgments are correct, these other formal characteristics expose 5:32 to use as a legal rule and protect 5:39b-42 from such use, which indicates that the function of sayings cannot be judged only on the basis of a form critical analysis of syntax.

/19/   This idea of the focal instance as illuminator of the hearer's situation should be understood in the light of H. R. Niebuhr's discussion of the way in which we interpret ethical situations (cf. pp. 24-26 above). My reference to the "moral imagination" and "imaginative shock" is a particular application of Ray L. Hart's discussion of the imagination (cf. pp. 21-24 above).

/20/   Matt 5:25-26 was originally a parable (cf. Jeremias, 1963:43-44) but was probably understood by the author of Matthew as a focal instance.

/21/   The "hypocrites" are probably a particular group (the scribes and Pharisees and their successors) of whom Christians of the Evangelist's time already had a negative view. Our text uses this prejudice as a lever against another prejudice, the assumption that the followers of Jesus are in no danger of sharing in such hypocrisy. The negative view of the "hypocrites" makes the possibility of following their example rather than Jesus' radical commands all the more disturbing.

/22/   There is variation here, but a concern with antithetic parallelism is apparent from the fact that in two instances we find a ὅπως clause in the second half, corresponding to the ὅπως clause in the first half, and the other instance (vs. 6), which uses the phrase "to your Father who is in secret, " suggests not only the contrast between what is seen and what is secret but also between what holds for men and what holds for God. Note that in vs. 18 the ὅπως clause is lengthened in order to make the antithesis fully clear.

/23/   See Friedrich: 85-86. No solid evidence is provided for the use of trumpets by Jews in the giving of alms.

/24/   πλατεῖα refers to a wide road or street, in distinction from a narrow lane.

/25/   The times of prayer seem to have been related to the times of the sacrifices in the temple. Prayer at the "ninth hour," i.e., in the middle of the afternoon, is the best attested (see Holtzmann; cf. also Strack-Billerbeck 2:696-702). The Holtzmann article is more helpful in that it recognizes the need to discriminate between the practice when the temple service still existed and later rabbinic instructions.

/26/   It is possible that vss. 5-6 arose at a time when the early church was beginning to break with Jewish practice and that vs. 6 was meant literally even if it involved giving up the daily hours of prayer. Such a break with religious custom is seldom easy, however, and it is commanded only because of a radical view of the danger of having one's religious acts seen by men. The command in vs. 6 is extreme because it is based on this radical view and tries to shape behavior to it.

/27/   See Paul Minear (63). Concerning our text he says, "By attacking those desires [for social approval] at the point of their ultimate theological legitimation, Jesus' demand undermines the mythological sanctions which support all social structures."

/28/   Strictly speaking, vs. 3 should not be included here since there is a difference between hyperbole and the focal instance. However, the breaking down of the limits of literal language which I will stress in what follows applies not only to the focal instance but even more clearly to hyperbole, since in hyperbole the mind *cannot* rest in the literal meaning. Hence what follows will apply to vs. 3 as well as vss. 6 and 17.

/29/   Cf. Murray Krieger (1960:256): "The extreme . . . is both more pure and more inclusive — pure in the adulterations it rejects and inclusive in the range of less complete experiences it illuminates even as it passes them by."

/30/   On the "truth" of such language see further pp. 115-17 below.

/31/   On the open-ended series see pp. 69-70. The generalizing introduction in 6:1 seems to show an awareness of the broad implications of these commands, for it relates them to the whole area of doing "your righteousness." That this goes beyond acts of "piety" (the RSV translation) in any narrow sense is shown by the use of δικαιοσύνη as a comprehensive term for the realization of God's will in the life of the disciple in Matt 5:20 and 6:33. Georg Strecker (149-58) argues that the references to "righteousness" in 5:20, 6:1, and 6:33 are all redactional and are similar in meaning.

/32/   Cf. Northrop Frye (329): "A good deal of the strategy of teaching is rhetorical strategy, choosing words and images with great care in order to evoke the response: 'I never thought of it that way before,' or 'Now that you put it that way, I can see it.' What distinguishes, not simply the epigram, but profundity itself from platitude is very frequently rhetorical wit." Sten H. Stenson (ch. 3) gives an interesting discussion of wit in relation to religious language. While Stenson emphasizes that wit completely derails rational discourse and stands out of every world order, this does not seem to be entirely true of the texts we are examining, for they upset the old order by announcing a new, surprising order.

/33/   Gospel of Thomas 14 is close to Matt 15:11. In Vaticanus Mark 7:15 has been improved slightly to come closer to syntactic parallelism. Note also the structure of Mark 7:18, 20.

/34/   In the majority of the manuscripts this is balanced and reinforced by the saying "If anyone has ears to hear, let him hear" in vs. 16. This is probably not an original part of this passage, but it indicates that a major part of the manuscript tradition felt that such a saying was appropriate following vs. 15.

/35/   Vss. 14, 17-18a are probably the work of the Evangelist. Vincent Taylor (343-44) refers to some of the evidence.

/36/   ἄνθρωπος ("man") means a human being, not a male person. The question in vs. 2 reflects the Jewish legal situation in which the husband held the power of divorce. The answer in vs. 9 need not be limited to that situation.

/37/   Note that the saying speaks of separating what God has joined rather than of separating oneself from a person. Thus it moves beyond the question of vs. 2, speaking more generally as well as forcefully. This tendency of the saying to encompass as much as possible makes it doubtful that we should understand "separate" to refer strictly to divorce. The Greek verb is not the same as that used in vss. 2-4, 11-12 in referring to divorce, it occurs in sentences which have nothing to do with divorce, and it here takes a neuter object rather than the personal object we would expect with the meaning "divorce." Thus the saying points beyond a narrow concern with divorce, bringing to mind the many ways in which man and wife may be led apart. For a similar view, see Heinrich Greeven (381).

/38/   On the relation of the focal instance as illuminator to practical decisions in particular situations see pp. 74-76.

/39/   Cf. Bauer (94). The word is probably more forceful than the translation "lose." Cf. Ernst Lohmeyer (1959:171). Compare James 4:12, where it also stands in antithesis with σώζω , and Matt 10:28, where it also has ψυχή as object. In both cases we must translate "destroy". To be sure, the destruction in Mark 8:35 affects the subject himself and so is also his loss.

/40/   The reader should compare this with William Beardslee's interesting discussion of the "intensification" of the proverb in the synoptic Gospels (see p. 2 above).

/41/   It cannot be denied that within other parts of the New Testament they do so appear and that this saying was spoken within a context in which such a world view was accepted. Nor do I wish to imply that the systematic development of a religious world view through the use of such symbols as "God" and "heaven" is a meaningless task. However, it is wrong to understand the language which we are studying as simply the decorative expression of such a world view. Rather, it has a certain priority to and independence of the world view which may be drawn from it, and so may continue to speak when such a world view is called in question, providing a basis for new systematic formulations of Christian faith.

/42/   The last text is discussed on pp. 171-77. Klaus Berger (1972:576) notes the frequency of antithetical sentences in these Markan controversy dialogues.

/43/   Rudolf Bultmann (144) believes that the double form of the saying in Mark 10:43-44 is earlier than the single form in Mark 9:35. It is true that Mark 9:35 shows traces of the double form, but this may only indicate that the Evangelist was aware of the connection between the two passages of his Gospel. Bultmann's view does not account for the fact that we encounter the single saying in Matt 23:11 and Luke 9:48c, and that the doubling of the saying may well be part of the tendency toward expansion which is apparent in the addition of Mark 10:42-43a. Longer versions occur at Matt 20:25-28 and Luke 22:25-27. However, the passage in Matthew is clearly dependent on Mark 10:42-45. Luke's passage probably is also, for, in spite of considerable difference in wording, there is remarkable agreement in the basic structure of the two passages, as well as agreement in the choice of certain words.

/44/   The manuscripts differ in their placement of μέγας in vs. 43, but the most strongly attested reading places ἐν ὑμῖν last in the clause. This makes sense because of the contrast between vss. 42 and 43.

/45/   The connection to which I am pointing is supported by the word link μεγάλοι-μέγας between vss. 42 and 43.

/46/   Cf. Eduard Schweizer (223): "Vs. 45 is not only a doctrinally correct explanation of Jesus' pathway but also a justification of the previous statements. . . . Jesus' suffering is explained, but not in a way which makes it possible to take note of it or preach it in a purely intellectual manner. The explanation makes it possible to believe only if one pursues the life of a disciple in the kind of discipleship described in vss. 42–44." The significance of vs. 45 for the Christian life can also be illumined by H. R. Niebuhr's discussion of Christ as symbolic form and paradigm (1963:154ff. and 162ff.).

/47/   There is also a shift in tense, for the present tense of repeated action is used in the four imperatives, thereby calling to mind the many situations to which these commands are relevant. This is followed by the aorist subjunctive with οὐ μή (an emphatic construction), or, when this can no longer be used, by the future, for God's judgment is understood to be a single, decisive event.

/48/   Cf. Bauer *s.v.*, meaning 6b, though Bauer classifies this text under 6a.

/49/   Note Luke 6:36, where the reference to God is explicit. See also Strack-Billerbeck 1:443. The use of the passive in Luke 6:37-38 may be caused less by aversion to naming God than by concern for the force of the saying. The word play rests upon the verb. Because a noun subject is avoided, the emphasis on the verb is very clear, for it is the only important word in the clause.

/50/   B. Couroyer points out that similar phrases occur in loan contracts for grain as part of the stipulations for repayment. He cites pre-Christian papyri. In itself, then, the saying suggests an exact repayment. See also Strack-Billerbeck 1:444-45. Its function in Luke must be understood in relation to the sentence which precedes it.

/51/   The verb δώσουσιν ("they will give;" RSV: "will be put"), like the passive verbs in the preceding commands, refers indirectly to the action of God. Cf. Strack-Billerbeck 2:221.

/52/   This was brought to my attention by Robert Morgenthaler (38).

/53/   There does seem to be a difference between the law of talion as found in Exodus 21:23-25 and the texts with which Käsemann deals, for the former mentions a series of cases, establishing gradations of punishment through making the punishment correspond in each case to the offense. Albrecht Alt (341) regards this as characteristic of the Old Testament *Talionsformel.* In the "sentences of holy law," however, there seems to be little concern to make legal distinctions about the degree of punishment. There are no clear distinctions between being one of whom the Son of Man is ashamed (Mark 8:38), being denied before God (Matt 10:33), and not being forgiven (Matt 6:15), nor do these verses form parts of a series.

/54/   Some of the other examples of hyperbole in the synoptic Gospels also result from the desire for an extreme antithesis. Cf. Matt 6:2-3, 23:24.

/55/   It is possible, though not certain, that this contrast was already in use. Cf. Strack-Billerbeck 1:446. In the rabbinic passages cited, the beam in the eye is also used as an extreme metaphor, but it occurs as a defensive retort from one who has been criticized. In the Gospels the one who speaks in this way is not defending himself.

/56/   See Gospel of Thomas 26, where this pericope is found without the repetition in Matt 7:4. The version there also does not use question and command, and so the personal attack upon the hearer is considerably weaker than in Matthew and Luke.

/57/   Pierre Bonnard (97) sees a difficulty in vs. 5, for it seems to contradict vss. 1-4 by raising the possibility of removing the log and then being able to criticize another. However, vs. 5 does not undermine vss. 3-4. It calls for a radical redirection of attention. What was previously ignored must now have first claim on one's concern. Whether removing the log and turning one's attention to others is a real possibility or is spoken in irony, the fascinating speck in the brother's eye is now placed in the distance because our attention is directed to our own problem. Vs. 5 also subtly suggests that people with logs in their eyes may not see too well, so our brother's situation may look different when the log is removed.

/58/   Richard A. Edwards (see n.d.: 49-50) refers to these verses as examples of the "eschatological correlative." He also notes that "the impact of the correlative is its bringing together of the past, present and future." Through this correlative the future appearance of the Son of Man "can be anticipated, or its character can be anticipated, by a series of past or present events which will then demand action in the present" (55).

/59/   This asyndeton probably contributes to the forcefulness of these words. Cf. F. Blass and A. Debrunner (sec. 460): "Asyndeton and polysyndeton often, though by no means always, lend rhetorical emphasis: . . . asyndeton, by breaking up the series and introducing the items staccato fashion, produces a vivid and impassioned effect."

/60/   The prepositional phrase $\overset{\text{"}}{\alpha}\chi\rho\iota\ \overset{\text{~}}{\eta}s\ \overset{\text{'}}{\eta}\mu\acute{\epsilon}\rho\alpha s$ has a conjunctive function here, corresponding to   in the clauses which follow, and must be placed first for clarity of meaning. Thus the verb is placed as early in the clause as possible in each of the three clauses.

/61/   For those who do not know Greek, it should be pointed out that the Greek tenses not only convey time but also kind of action. The imperfect tense refers to continuous or repeated action ("They were eating, they were drinking," etc., though each English phrase corresponds to one word in Greek), while the aorist tense refers to punctiliar action, i.e., to action simply conceived as an event with no implication of continuity or repetition.

/62/   Dieter Lührmann (75-83) believes that the reference to Lot is an expansion under the influence of Jewish tradition in which the flood and the destruction of Sodom were regarded as outstanding examples of the punishment of godless men.

/63/   Apart from this passage Tyre and Sidon are mentioned in the New Testament only in the neutral sense of places to or from which someone travels. In contrast, Sodom serves as a type of evil and of God's judgment. Cf. Luke 17:29, Rom 9:29, 2 Pet 2:6, Jude 7, Rev 11:8.

/64/   Isa 23:1-18; Ezek 26 - 28; Gen 18:16 - 19:29; cf. Isa 1:9, 10.

/65/   According to Dieter Lührmann (64), our text "takes up the Old Testament form of the oracle to the nations (Völkerorakel) and turns it against Israel." Such a polemical reversal of the usual use of an established genre would add to the impact of these words.

/66/   The last phrase is especially forceful because of the use of the nominative personal pronoun, which is used only for emphasis.

/67/   Note that Gomorrah is not mentioned though the pair Sodom and Gomorrah is common. This is an indication of the sense of formal balance which governs the whole composition.

/68/   Or καταβιβασθήσῃ. The text is uncertain here, but the antithesis and rhyme are present in both readings.

/69/   This is the significance of the particle μή.

/70/   There is strong manuscript evidence for the omission of this saying in Matt 16:2-3.
/71/   I am referring to the long reading found in many manuscripts of Matthew whether this was an original part of Matthew or not.

/72/   The reference in vs. 56a to the earth as well as the sky (only the latter is found in Matt) may result from the desire to state man's ability as broadly as possible and so be another indication of the desire to strengthen the foil to vs. 56b.

/73/   Or πῶς οὐκ οἴδατε δοκιμάζειν. The latter is supported by impressive manuscripts, but the former is the more difficult reading since it departs from the parallelism.

/74/   For the modern reader the text's reference to predicting the weather may cause difficulty. We tend to see weather prediction as an affair of technical reason and the understanding of our time and what it requires as a much more complex decision in which the self is strongly involved. Thus what the text holds together, so that man's success in one and failure in the other appears odd, we regard as not comparable. In order to appreciate the force of the text, we need to understand weather prediction less as a technical activity than as an instance of man's constant concern to discover personal meaning ("Today I will get wet." "Today I will be hot.") within his perceptible world.

/75/   In Mark 10:30, Luke 18:30 this phrase is given a definite meaning by contrast with "the age to come." This contrast is absent from Luke 12:56.

/76/   In Luke the contrast between what is desired and what might be given is heightened by referring to a snake and a scorpion, which are not only useless for food but harmful, for the reference to a scorpion suggests that a poisonous snake may be in mind.

/77/   Cf. Matt 19:29//, 10:34-37//. There is strong manuscript support for the inclusion of "wife" in Matt 19:29, but the possible influence of Luke's parallel text makes this reading doubtful. So it may be only Luke who refers explicitly to leaving one's wife (cf. Luke 18:29, 14:26). However, it is clear that in most cases a disciple who left house and children would also be leaving his wife. Such separation could result either from the demands of the Christian mission or from the bitter strife which could arise in families when one member became Christian. For the latter situation see 1 Cor 7:12-16.

/78/   Ernst Lohmeyer (1956:283) also understands the passage against this background.

/79/   The exception must include followers of Jesus, for no one would expect non-Christians to follow Jesus' special teaching.

/80/   Nor to Jesus' statement in vs. 12. The conjunction "for" in vs. 12 indicates that it supports the assertion in vs. 11 rather than providing the content of "this word."

/81/   This interpretation is not excluded by the use of the term "eunuch." As we will see below, this is a metaphor in the third sentence of vs. 12, pointing to an incapacity for normal family life which arises because of the kingdom.

/82/   Paul applies the same language to sexual union with a harlot in 1 Cor 6:16.

/83/   Yebamoth 8.4. Cf. Strack-Billerbeck 1:806-07. Although this passage of the Mishnah uses a different phrase to refer to the congenital defect, the phrase "from the womb of the mother" was also frequently used by Jews to refer to a congenital state. Cf. Jacques Dupont: 194, n. 3.

/84/   Castration as a cultic act was practised by certain cults of Asia Minor. However, nothing in the text suggests this as relevant background. Instead, our text speaks of self-castration in the context of the classes of eunuchs recognized in Jewish law. Although eunuchs sometimes held important government positions in the ancient world, they were generally despised as a class. They were attacked for their bodily defect and the supposed lessening of character which accompanied it. On this see Georg Wissowa and Wilhelm Kroll: col. 453-54, and Josef Blinzler: 257, n. 11.

/85/   Deut 23:2 (Engl. 23:1) prohibits a eunuch from participating in the assembly of the Lord.From the prohibition of offering a castrated animal Siphra Lev 22:24 derives a general prohibition of castration (cf. Strack-Billerbeck 1:807). This prohibition of castration of man or beast is also found in Josephus, *Jewish Antiquities* 4:8, 40 (290-91), together with the instruction to shun eunuchs. Furthermore, the rabbis taught that it was the duty of every man to marry and have children, a teaching which they derived from the divine command in Gen 1:28. Cf. Strack-Billerbeck 2: 372-73. More favorable statements about the eunuch are found in Wis 3:14 and Philo, Quod Deterius Potiori Insidiari Soleat 176, as Klaus Berger (1972:573) points out. On Jewish attitudes see further Schneider, and Blinzler: 260.

/86/ On the impossibility of the literal sense see Blinzler (260-61).

/87/ Jacques Dupont rightly notes the connection between this saying and certain proverbs which establish an enumerative pattern and then introduce a surprising shift at the end. Cf. Prov 30:18-19, 33, and Dupont (191ff.). Dupont's remarks on the form of Matt 19:12 are perceptive. In discussing the three sentences he says, "It is clear that the first two are mentioned only to better assure the effect of surprise that the third must produce" (195), and later remarks, "The logion deliberately wishes to astonish" (196).

/88/ Among the synoptic Evangelists, this is clearest in the writings of Luke. Cf. e.g., Luke 1:79, 2:14, 19:38, Acts 10:36.

/89/ See Isa 3:25, 22:2, 51:19, 65:12; Jer 5:12, 14:12-13, 15-16, 18, etc.

/90/ The Thayer *Lexicon* (153) translates, "To cut into two parts, cleave asunder, dissever." T. A. Roberts (305) also notes the connection between μάχαιραν and διχάσαι . He refers to the use of the latter word in a physical sense in Aquila's translation of Lev 1:17 and Deut 14:6.

/91/ The Greek sentence consists basically of two nouns and their genitive modifiers. This allows the tension between the two nouns to emerge starkly. In contrast to the LXX, this sentence preserves the succinctness of the original Hebrew, departing from the most literal rendering of the Hebrew in doing so.

/92/ Compare the similar "I" sayings listed by Bultmann (152-53). In these sayings important facets of the essential meaning of Jesus' ministry are presented in brief form. An example is Mark 2:17: "I came not to call the righteous but sinners."

/93/ The latter word refers to the act of baptism but is comparatively bland.

/94/ The daughter-in-law (literally, "bride") is probably the bride of the son of the family, and so the mother and the mother-in-law are the same person (J. M. Creed: 179).

/95/ Toward the end of vs. 53 the rhythm seems to move slightly more slowly due to introduction of some articles and pronouns. However, the manuscripts vary considerably in these details. The small rhythmic units occur in pairs ("father against son and son against father"), but the second half of each pair is already a repetition of the first half in reverse order, so the smallest unit of the rhythmic pattern has two major stresses, falling on the two nouns.

/96/   Cf. Rom 16:13, 1 Cor 4:14-15, Phil 2:22, 1 Thes 2:11, 1 Tim 5:1-2, Phlm 10, John 19:26-27, and the frequent use of "brothers" as a way of addressing fellow Christians. Erich Klostermann (1926:118) lists some of the preceding passages. Acts 2:44-45, 4:32-37 indicate that the early church "had all things in common." The reference to "houses" and "fields" in Mark 10:30 does not necessarily presuppose such wide-spread redistribution of wealth as Acts suggests, but it must at least indicate a general willingness to share food and shelter when special needs arose.

/97/   Matthew and Luke agree in wording only insofar as they agree with Mark. (The reading "hundredfold" is most strongly attested in Matthew, in agreement with Mark rather than Luke.)

/98/   Matthew adds an explicit question about reward to his version of Mark 10:28. That this question is already implied in Mark is shown by the fact that Jesus' reply does concern the disciples' reward.

/99/   The two series differ only in the fact that the second uses the plural throughout, omits "fathers," and employs the conjunction "and" instead of "or."

/100/   It might seem possible to place a colon after "a hundredfold" and so understand the "hundredfold" to indicate the great value of both the reward "in this time" and "in the age to come," rather than indicating the number of houses, brothers, etc. However, "a hundredfold" is meant quantitatively and applies directly to houses, brothers, etc., as is shown by the fact that the list in vs. 30 is entirely in the plural, although this is not the case in vs. 29. The text is speaking not just of a great reward but of a great number of possessions and relatives. Note also that the second enumeration is connected by "and" rather than "or." The nature of the reward is not limited to what has been sacrificed. All this contributes to the forceful extravagance of this part of the saying.

/101/   An important characteristic of the "narrated world," according to Erhardt Güttgemanns (see 1972:31-32), is that it avoids direct dialogue between addresser and addressee (or speaker and hearer) and substitutes an indirect or mediated dialogue by means of the story. The communication process is maintained because addresser and addressee partially appear in the story, as well as existing outside it.

/102/   Luke 9:59-60 is different than the other scenes in that the request is preceded by Jesus' command, so that there are three parts to the conversation. Note that the parallel in Matt 8:21-22 has only the request and reply. This difference does not greatly affect the basic form, for the brevity of the scene is maintained and attention still focuses on the request and the reply.

/103/   "Son of Man" must refer here to Jesus. Otherwise Jesus' reply would not be relevant to the question of following him. Synoptic usage suggests that "Son of Man" is used here as a title of authority and honor, which increases the strangeness of the fact that such a one is denied what even animals and birds have.

/104/   Cf. C. F. Burney: 106, 132.

/105/   Furthermore, the initial letters of the last words of the lines form the pattern ε-κ-ε-κ. Whether this was consciously intended is uncertain.

/106/   Material relevant to understanding the importance for ancient Judaism of the duty of burying one's father is conveniently collected by Martin Hengel (1968:9ff.). He points to the central significance of the command to honor father and mother; the importance of service to the dead among the works of love in Jewish piety, so that it takes precedence over normal religious duties; the special regulations to insure that one who dies without relatives will be properly buried, carried to the point of removing the prohibition against defilement for the high priest and Nazirites; the widespread motif in ancient literature of the request for burial through one's own son; and the desecration caused by a failure to bury a dead man and conduct the funeral rites. The original sources may be found through Hengel's extensive references. Hengel concludes, "There is hardly a Jesus-logion which offends in a sharper way against law, piety, and mores together than Matt 8:22=Luke 9:60a" (16).

/107/   Hans G. Klemm rejects the view which I have just adopted because he believes that it weakens the text. I disagree. The tension of rejecting a duty of such importance remains as strong as ever. Furthermore, the meaning of Jesus' words is enriched. Jesus speaks of a possible, though offensive, way of handling the father's burial (Others can take care of the matter) and suggests that those who put family duties above discipleship (the choice which faces both the man in the story and the reader) may already be part of the "dead." Siegfried Schulz (439, n. 264) provides supporting references for the metaphorical sense of "dead."

/108/   When the qualities of the focal instance (extremeness and specificness) are the result of the narrative setting and not of Jesus' words alone, we may wish to speak of a "focal encounter" rather than a focal instance. A story is a focal encounter not because the scene is specific, which is true of stories in general, but only if the issue or problem addressed in the dialogue is a specific and extreme case, resulting in the specificity of explicit meaning and breadth of implicit meaning which characterizes the focal instance. On the focal instance see pp. 71-72.

/109/   The relevance of the call of Elisha in 1 Kgs 19:19-21 (cf. T. W. Manson, 1949:73) is doubtful. Elisha is called *away* from his plowing while plowing is here a metaphor for discipleship.

/110/   Note that vs. 61 repeats both "I will follow you" in vs. 57 and "let me first" in vs. 59 (with slight variation in word order).

/111/   The phrase is used of family or relatives in the Koine (cf. Bauer: 615).

/112/   Counting vs. 35, where the order is reversed and "sister" is added to "brother."

/113/   Cf. Ernst Lohmeyer, 1959:81: The external scene is important to the story because it is a realization of the meaning of Jesus' word.

/114/   Matthew substitutes "stretching out his hand," an equally dramatic gesture.

/115/   However, there is a shift from ἰδού to ἴδε, and the latter retains more of its original imperatival force. See E. J. Pryke: 418-19. Some manuscripts add "and your sisters" to vs. 32. However, the omission is more strongly attested. The later addition of these words may be due to the desire to balance vs. 35.

/116/   Rudolf Bultmann (29-30) believes that vs. 35 originally stood alone and that the content of this saying was later pictured in an "ideal scene" in vss. 31-34. He sees a discrepancy between vss. 34 and 35 because one cannot presuppose that those referred to in vs. 34 do the will of God. This sort of argument is the result of failing to think consistently in terms of his own insight that this is an ideal scene. If that is the case, one cannot interpret vs. 34 in light of the likely composition of such a crowd during Jesus' ministry but must ask what this crowd represents. This is made clear not only by vs. 35 but also by 4:10-11. Following one further scene in the Gospel, the Evangelist picks up the same phrase (οἱ περὶ αὐτόν, "those about him"), and this group is addressed as those to whom the mystery of the kingdom has been given. Thus the Evangelist understood both 3:34 and 35 to refer to followers of Jesus, the representatives of the church. Cf. Matt 12:49. There is reason for the scholar to use his scalpel only if there are parts of the text which do not fit the function of the finished text. Mark 3:31-35 is so thoroughly shaped to its rhetorical purpose that there is little ground for this.

/117/   J. D. Crossan (1973a) believes that Mark shows animosity toward the relatives of Jesus and that this, combined with his polemic against the disciples, reflects a struggle against the hegemony of the Jerusalem church. Werner H. Kelber (25-26, 53-54) expresses a similar view. It is possible that Mark 3:31-35 reflects such polemic either by Mark or at a pre-Markan stage. However, the connection of this text with Mark 10:28-30 indicates that this was not its only point of relevance in the life of the early church.

/118/   See the short form of this text in Justin Martyr, Apology I, 17, 2.

/119/   Reinhard Breymayer (41-42) cites views of Aristotle and modern linguists which suggest that unusual explicitness and redundance may be an indication of lying.

/120/   According to Günther Bornkamm (121), the introduction of the coin refers the opponents "to a decision which they have already made a long time ago. Gaily they conduct their business, unconcerned about the image and emblem of Caesar on these coins, so long as they can do business with them. Only when they come to pay their tax are their passions roused, and they feel called upon to make their 'profession of faith'." Whether this is a fair judgment is open to question. In any case, Mark's text seems unconcerned to make this point, for vs. 16 leaves the source of the coin indefinite rather than making clear that it was already in the possession of the questioners.

/121/   Reinhard Breymayer (23-40) assembles extensive notes on views of linguists and rhetoricians which may relate to the persuasive power of the coin in this story.

/122/   At least if we assume a Palestinian setting, as is commonly done. However, Martin Rist calls attention to the fact that our text would have a sharp and relevant message for the early church outside of Palestine in response to social pressure for worship of the emperor. Since the relation of the Christian to the state was a continuing problem, even Gentile Christians would be interested in Jesus' attitude toward the imperial tax. According to Rist, the reference to the coin's image and inscription would raise the problem of idolatrous worship. Faced with this concrete problem, the command also becomes concrete: Christians are instructed to pay their taxes but must refrain from giving to Caesar the worship which is due to God alone. Note that the emphasis on the second half of Jesus' answer makes good sense in this setting.

/123/   Therefore, L. Goppelt (184) accuses interpreters who assert that the first half of Jesus' reply is overshadowed by the second of failing to "do justice to the situation of Jesus in relation to Judaism."

/124/   This has been asserted by others, e.g., Günther Bornkamm (122), but it requires careful consideration of the form of our text for its full justification. Furthermore, this does not mean that "the entire problem of the state is . . . put in the margin" (Bornkamm: 123) but rather that we must not consider the claims of the state apart from the claims of God.

/125/   This is true even if "the things of God" refer to men, who bear God's image just as Caesar's coin bears its owner's image, for this does not narrow the scope of the duty man owes. This view of "the things of God" is adopted by G. Bornkamm (123) and is supported by Charles H. Giblin. Contrary to Giblin, I do not believe that this view is necessary to explain the meaning and importance of the final phrase of Jesus' answer.

/126/   This is true even though vss. 22-23a show signs of Markan editorial activity. Cf. Vincent Taylor: 238-39. There are actually two charges in vs. 22, and the answer is more closely related to the second than to the first. While there is no further reference to the "Beelzebul" of vs. 22b, vss. 24-26 are closely tied to 22c because they make use of the charge's assumption that the demonic world is like an organized society with a ruler.

/127/　　　　Eduard Schweizer (86) also asserts that "in terms of pure logic" this passage is "not thoroughly convincing."

/128/　　　　Cf. John Dominic Crossan (1973a:90-91). He argues that vs. 23b is the work of the Evangelist.

/129/　　　　Matthew's version, which is a conflation of Mark and Q, seems to incorporate it later in the passage, at 12:26a.

/130/　　　　This does not mean that this was assumed by all first century Jews. Foerster detects a difference in the relevant Jewish materials in this regard. In the Tannaitic material "the demons are not brought into any firm connection with Satan," while in some of the pseudepigrapha and Qumran scrolls they are "connected with, or subordinated to, Satan" or a similar demonic prince. Cf. *TDNT* 2:13,15; 7:156.

/131/　　　　On the reinforcing additions in vs. 26 see below. Note, however, that the basic vocabulary of vss. 24-25 ("against itself," "divided," "cannot stand") is carried over into vs. 26, where it places a particular interpretation on the matter at issue.

/132/　　　　Other passages which refer to the overcoming of Satan or the release of men from his power: Luke 10:17-19, John 12:31, Acts 10:38, 26:18, Rom 16:20, Rev 12:7-10, 20:1-3, 10. For Jewish references to the end of Satan or the power of evil see Foerster: *TDNT* 2:78, n. 43, and 7:156, n. 24.

/133/　　　　More literally,"has an end." "End" here refers to death. Cf. V. Taylor: 240.

/134/　　　　The expected contrast to "stand" would be "fall," but the final phrase of vs. 26 leaves this imagery behind. Cf. E. Lohmeyer (1959:79).

/135/　　　　Recall that, according to Murray Krieger, a work of literary art is an organic unity which prevents words from referring atomistically to the outside world. See above, pp. 14-17.

/136/　　　　Vs. 26 is also set off from vss. 24-25 by the shift from ἐάν and the subjunctive to εἰ and the indicative. In the New Testament the latter construction "is predominantly used with reference to a present or alleged reality." Cf. Blass-Debrunner, sect. 371-72. The uprising of Satan against himself may be understood as a reality alleged by the opponents, though untrue, but may also be understood to refer to what is really so. In either case, vs. 26 moves to a level of greater seriousness than vss. 24-25.

CONCLUSION AND PROSPECT

If the reader recognizes the value of the questions and concerns which permeate this essay, the primary purpose of my work has been accomplished. I believe that this value has been demonstrated in some detail through the preceding studies of texts. We should keep in mind, however, the partial nature of what has been accomplished. I have not attempted to include all the synoptic sayings. While forceful and imaginative language is not equally apparent in all of them, there are other sayings in which it is found, and they also may reward investigation of its function. Especially the sayings in brief narrative setting (the "apophthegms") need further study. This will require further attention to the nature and significance of narrative, which has only been touched upon in this essay. Eventually this should lead to study of both the brief stories in the Gospels and of the whole story of Jesus, which encompasses these stories and the sayings. Beyond these stories and sayings there are, of course, other types of Biblical texts in which imaginative language may be found /1/. So there is much unfinished business. Further study may also require modification of the context of understanding, the concerns and assumptions as to what is worth seeking, which we bring with us as we investigate the texts.

I would hope that some of the concerns and emphases of this essay will be preserved in further study. Among these emphases I mention a respect for the text as a unique unity (a unity which may exist at various levels, from individual pericope to Gospel to, perhaps, the Bible as a whole) which discloses its full meaning and value only through the interaction of its parts. I would also include the desire to understand how the text speaks to those deep human concerns which have traditionally found expression in religion.

In the study of stories /2/ we need to consider not only narrative structure (an important *part* of the task) but also the text-reader (or hearer) dimension of the event of narration. It is

201

important to investigate how a storyteller invites the hearer to interact with his story and how this may, on occasion, affect the hearer's perspective on self and world, the deep meanings by which he lives. Our study should focus not only on characters and actions (on a more abstract level, actants and functions) but also on scenes, statements, and narrative techniques which qualify the reader's attitudes and shape his sympathies /3/. Anything which adds evaluative and affective qualities to the story will be important in this regard. Understanding how the story is shaping our vision will make us aware that it is possible to see the event otherwise, helping us to preserve our freedom. But we may also with open eyes decide to acquiesce to the story's vision.

The story of Zacchaeus in Luke 19:1-10 provides an illustration. Zacchaeus is the primary actor in vss. 2-8. He is the seeker and the story narrates the outcome of his quest. However, vs. 10 shows that this is also the story of Jesus' seeking of the lost /4/. Since Zacchaeus is only a minor character in Luke, why is he placed in center stage in so much of this story? Evidently the narrator wants us to experience his problem and be sympathetic to his quest. The narrator arouses concern with Zacchaeus' problem and interest in the success or failure of his quest, which provides a counterbalance to the attitude of the crowd, the group which blocks and excludes Zacchaeus. This counterbalance is necessary because the "crowd" may be present in the reader, and so the reader's sympathies must be reshaped. The reader's sympathy is especially important in a story which understands salvation in terms of reaffirmation of Zacchaeus' rightful place in the people of the promise, the religious community (vs. 9), of which the reader is also probably a part. The reader must compare his own attitude with Jesus' decision to stay in Zacchaeus' house (the turning point of the story), for the question of whether the reader is willing to accept such a person as part of the community underlies the story.

Some of the important features of synoptic sayings are found in narrative form in the synoptic stories. We find repetitive patterns in individual stories and in larger narrative units. Strong contrast, especially between two characters in a story, is also frequent /5/.

Therefore some of the things previously said about pattern and tension (see above, pp. 39-58), and about other features of the synoptic sayings, may also be helpful in studying stories.

Although the quest for the historical Jesus will continue, there is also value in seeking to understand Jesus as a character in the Gospel story, irrespective of the historical accuracy of the events and words which it contains. This may involve studying the Jesus of one of the Gospels, but it is not the same as studying the Christology of the Gospel writer, if by that is meant his conscious affirmations about Jesus. What is assumed may be as important as what is consciously affirmed. Furthermore, one of the most important things about this Jesus will be the way in which he, through stories and sayings, is able to involve the reader imaginatively, challenge the assumptions of our ordinary world, and enable us to trust in a kingdom which authorizes us to see and act in new ways. Awareness of these dimensions of the Jesus story may change our understanding of its value and so reshape the way in which Christological questions are put.

There is a difference between the critical analysis of a text and the personal appropriation of that text by the reader. The two can interfere with one another. However, attention to forceful and imaginative language opens an approach to texts in which analysis and appropriation can be mutually supportive, as the preceding studies of texts indicate. Concern for the way in which a text wishes to be appropriated by the reader can lead to the analysis of important features of the text, and such analysis will often sharpen our awareness that the text does seek appropriation at a deep level. This helps to bring together aspects of the study of the Bible which have become separated, without undermining a properly critical stance (including the reader's right to say no) or the text's right to be heard as it presents its challenge.

NOTES

/1/   For a study of one such text see my article "The Magnificat as Poem."

/2/   On this subject see also my remarks on the significance of the narrative setting of sayings, pp. 152-57 above.

/3/   This will include the study of "description assertions" as well as the "action assertions" which carry the plot forward. William O. Hendricks (170-74) distinguishes between the two and insists that the former must be excised in order to make the underlying narrative structure of a story clear.

/4/   Here the distinction between "surface structure" and "deep structure" is useful, since the structure of the story may be analyzed in two ways, with either Zacchaeus or Jesus in the position of "subject." However, this does not imply that the "deep structure" is more important than the "surface structure." See above, pp. 31-36. On the meaning of the term "subject" in actantial analysis see Daniel Patte: 7-11.

/5/   Robert W. Funk (1974) shows the importance of this in the parables.

WORKS CONSULTED

Alt, Albrecht
1953   *Kleine Schriften zur Geschichte des Volkes Israel.* Vol. 1.
            München: C. H. Beck'sche Verlagsbuchhandlung.

Auden, W. H. and Louis Kronenberger, eds.
1966   *The Viking Book of Aphorisms.* New York: Viking.

Barthes, Roland
1970   "L'analyse structurale du récit à propos d'Actes X-XI."
            Recherches de science religieuse 58: 17-37.

Bauer, Walter
1957   *A Greek-English Lexicon of the New Testament.* Trans. &
            ed. William F. Arndt and F. Wilbur Gingrich. Chicago:
            University of Chicago.

Beardslee, William
1970   "Uses of the Proverb in the Synoptic Gospels." *Int* 24: 61-
            73.

Behm, J.
1967   See Kittel 4: 973-75.

Berger, Klaus
1970-71   "Zu den sogenannten Sätzen heiligen Rechts." *NTS* 17:
            10-40.

1972   *Die Gesetzesauslegung Jesu*, Teil I. Neukirchen-Vluyn:
            Neukirchener Verlag.

Black, Matthew
1967   *An Aramaic Approach to the Gospels and Acts.* 3rd ed.
            Oxford: Clarendon.

Blass, F. and A. Debrunner
1961   *A Greek Grammar of the New Testament and Other Early
            Christian Literature.* Trans. and rev. Robert W. Funk.
            Chicago: University of Chicago.

Blinzler, Josef
1957   " Εἰσὶν εὐνοῦχοι . Zur Auslegung von Mt 19:12." *ZNW*
            48: 254-70.

Bonnard, Pierre
1963   *L'évangile selon Saint Matthieu.* Neuchâtel: Delachaux &
            Niestlé.

206   Works Consulted

Bornkamm, Günther
1960   *Jesus of Nazareth.* Trans. Irene and Fraser McLuskey. New York: Harper & Row.

Breymayer, Reinhard
1972   "Zur Pragmatik des Bildes. Semiotische Beobachtungen zum Streitgespräch Mk 12, 13-17 . . ." *Linguistica Biblica* 13/14: 19-51.

Brooks, Cleanth
1947   *The Well Wrought Urn.* New York: Harcourt, Brace & World.

Bultmann, Rudolf
1963   *The History of the Synoptic Tradition.* Trans. John Marsh. New York: Harper & Row.

Burney, C. F.
1925   *The Poetry of Our Lord.* Oxford: Clarendon.

Buss, Martin J.
1969   *The Prophetic Word of Hosea.* Berlin: Verlag Töpelmann.

Chomsky, Noam
1957   *Syntactic Structures.* The Hague: Mouton.

1965   *Aspects of the Theory of Syntax.* Cambridge, Mass.: M.I.T.

1966   *Cartesian Linguistics.* New York: Harper & Row.

1970   "Deep Structure, Surface Structure, and Semantic Interpretation." Pp. 52-91 in *Studies in General and Oriental Linguistics, Presented to Shirô Hattori.* Ed. Roman Jakobson and Shigeo Kawamoto. Tokyo: TEC Co.

Colby, Benjamin N.
1970   "The Description of Narrative Structures." Pp. 177-92 in *Cognition: A Multiple View.* Ed. Paul L. Garvin. New York: Spartan Books.

Corbett, Edward P. J., ed.
1969   *Rhetorical Analyses of Literary Works.* New York: Oxford University .

Couroyer, B.
1970   "De la mesure dont vous mesurez il vous sera mesuré." *Revue Biblique* 77: 366-70.

Creed, J. M.
1930   *The Gospel According to St. Luke.* London: Macmillan.

Crossan, J. D.
1973a   "Mark and the Relatives of Jesus." *NT* 15: 81-113.

1973b   *In Parables.* New York: Harper & Row.

1975   "Jesus and Pacifism." Forthcoming in *No Famine in the Land: Studies in Honor of John L. McKenzie.* Eds. J. W. Flanagan and A. W. Robinson. Missoula, Mont.: Scholars Press.

Delorme, Jean
1972   "Luc V. 1-11: Analyse structurale et histoire de la rédaction." *NTS* 18: 331-50.

de Saussure, Ferdinand
1959   *Course in General Linguistics.* Eds. Charles Bally and Albert Sechehaye. Trans. Wade Baskin. New York: Philosophical Library.

Dibelius, Martin
1929   "Zur Formgeschichte der Evangelien." *ThR* N.F. 1:185-216.

N.D.   *From Tradition to Gospel.* Trans. B. L. Woolf. New York: Scribner's.

Dillard, Annie
1974   *Pilgrim at Tinker's Creek.* New York: Harper's Magazine Press.

Dupont, Jacques
1959   *Mariage et divorce dans l'évangile.* Bruges: Desclée de Brouwer.

Edwards, Richard A.
N.D.   *The Sign of Jonah.* Naperville: Allenson.

Foerster, Werner
1964a   See Kittel 2: 1-20.

208   Works Consulted

1964b   See Kittel 2: 72-73, 75-81.

1971   See Kittel 7: 151-63.

Friedrich, Gerhard
1971   See Kittel 7: 71-88.

Frye, Northrop
1967   *Anatomy of Criticism.* Copyright 1957. New York:
                   Atheneum.

Funk, Robert W.
1966   *Language, Hermeneutic, and Word of God.* New York:
                   Harper & Row.

1974   " Structure in the Narrative Parables of Jesus." *Semeia* 2:
                   51-73.

Gevirtz, Stanley
1963   *Patterns in the Early Poetry of Israel.* Chicago: University
                   of Chicago.

Giblin, Charles H.
1971   " 'The Things of God' in the Question Concerning Tribute
                   to Caesar. . . . " *CBQ* 33: 510-27.

Goppelt, L.
1964   "The Freedom to Pay the Imperial Tax (Mark 12, 17)."
                   Pp. 183-94 in *Studia Evangelica*, vol. II, 1. Ed. F. L.
                   Cross. Berlin: Akademie-Verlag.

Gottwald, N. K.
1962   "Poetry, Hebrew." *Interpreter's Dictionary of the Bible* 3:
                   829-38. Nashville: Abingdon.

Greeven, Heinrich
1968-69   "Ehe nach dem Neuen Testament." *NTS* 15:365-88.

Grundmann, Walter
1968   *Das Evangelium nach Matthäus.* Berlin: Evangelische
                   Verlagsanstalt.

Güttgemanns, Erhardt
1970   *Offene Fragen zur Formgeschichte des Evangeliums.*
                   München: Chr. Kaiser.

| 1971 | *Studia Linguistica Neotestamentica*. München: Chr. Kaiser. |

1972   "Linguistische Analyse von Mk 16, 1-8." *Linguistica Biblica* 11/12: 13-53.

Haenchen, Ernst
1966   *Der Weg Jesu*. Berlin: Töpelmann.

Hart, Ray L.
1968   *Unfinished Man and the Imagination*. New York: Herder and Herder.

Hendricks, William O.
1973   "Methodology of Narrative Structural Analysis." *Semiotica* 7: 163-84.

Hengel, Martin
1961   *Die Zeloten*. Leiden: E. J. Brill.

1968   *Nachfolge und Charisma*. Berlin: Töpelmann.

Hermanns, Fritz
1973   "Descriptions of Deep Structures are Translations into Artificial Languages." *Linguistics* 99: 71-77.

Holtzmann, O.
1911   "Die tägliche Gebetsstunden im Judentum und Urchristentum." *ZNW* 12: 90-107.

Jacobson, Richard
1974   "The Structuralists and the Bible." *Int* 28: 146-64.

Jakobson, Roman
1960   "Closing Statement: Linguistics and Poetics." Pp. 350-77 in *Style in Language*. Ed. Thomas A. Sebeok. Cambridge, Mass.: Technology Press of M.I.T.

Jauss, H. R.
1970   "Literary History as a Challenge to Literary Theory." *New Literary History* 2: 7-37.

Jeremias, Joachim
1963   *The Parables of Jesus*. Rev. ed. Trans. S. H. Hooke. New York: Scribner's.

1971   *New Testament Theology: The Proclamation of Jesus*. Trans. John Bowden. New York: Scribner's.

Käsemann, Ernst
    1969   "Sentences of Holy Law in the New Testament." Pp. 66-81
                in *New Testament Questions of Today*. Trans. W. J.
                Montague. Philadelphia: Fortress.

Kelber, Werner H.
    1974   *The Kingdom in Mark*. Philadelphia: Fortress.

Kittel, Gerhard and Gerhard Friedrich, eds.
    1964ff.   *Theological Dictionary of the New Testament*. Vols. 2, 4,
                7. Trans. and ed. Geoffrey W. Bromiley. Grand Rapids:
                Eerdmans.

Klein, Günter
    1964   "Die Prüfung der Zeit (Lukas 12, 54-56)." *ZThK* 61: 373-
                90.

Klemm, Hans G.
    1969-70   "Das Wort von der Selbstbestattung der Toten." *NTS* 16:
                60-75.

Klostermann, Erich
    1926   *Das Markusevangelium*. 2. Aufl. Tübingen, J. C. B.
                Mohr.

    1936   *Das Markusevangelium*. 3. Aufl. Tübingen: J. C. B.
                Mohr.

Koch, Klaus
    1969   *The Growth of the Biblical Tradition*. Trans. S. M.
                Cupitt. New York: Scribner's.

Kosmala, Hans
    1964   "Form and Structure in Ancient Hebrew Poetry." *VT* 14:
                423-45.

Krieger, Murray
    1960   *The Tragic Vision*. New York: Holt, Rinehart, and
                Winston.

    1963   *The New Apologists for Poetry*. Original copyright 1956.
                Bloomington: Indiana University.

    1964   *A Window to Criticism*. Princeton: Princeton University.

    1967   *The Play and Place of Criticism*. Baltimore: John
                Hopkins.

Lapointe, Roger
1971 "La valeur linguistique du Sitz im Leben." *Bib* 52: 469-87.

Lausberg, Heinrich
1960 *Handbuch der literarischen Rhetorik*. München: Max Hueber.

Levin, Samuel R.
1962 *Linguistic Structures in Poetry*. The Hague: Mouton.

Lohmeyer, Ernst
1956 *Das Evangelium des Matthäus*. Göttingen: Vandenhoeck and Ruprecht.

1959 *Das Evangelium des Markus*. 15. Aufl. Göttingen: Vandenhoeck and Ruprecht.

Lohr, Charles H.
1961 "Oral Techniques in the Gospel of Matthew." *CBQ* 23: 403-35.

Lührmann, Dieter
1969 *Die Redaktion der Logienquelle*. Neukirchen-Vluyn: Neukirchener Verlag.

Manson, T. W.
1949 *The Sayings of Jesus*. London: SCM.

1955 *The Teaching of Jesus*. 2nd ed. Cambridge: Cambridge University.

Marin, Louis
1970 "Essai d'analyse structurale d'Actes 10, 1-11, 18." *Recherches de science religieuse* 58:39-61.

Minear, Paul
1972 *Commands of Christ*. Nashville: Abingdon.

Morgenthaler, Robert
1948 *Die lukanische Geschichtsschreibung als Zeugnis*. 1. Teil. Zürich: Zwingli-Verlag.

Muilenburg, James
1953 "A Study in Hebrew Rhetoric: Repetition and Style." *VTSup* 1: 97-111. Leiden: E. J. Brill.

1969 "Form Criticism and Beyond." *JBL* 88: 1-18.

Works Consulted

Niebuhr, H. Richard
1941   *The Meaning of Revelation.* New York: Macmillan.

1963   *The Responsible Self.* New York: Harper & Row.

Olrik, Axel
1965   "Epic Laws of Folk Narrative." Pp. 129-41 in *The Study of Folklore.* Ed. Alan Dundes. Englewood Cliffs, N.J.: Prentice-Hall.

Ong, Walter J.
1971   *Rhetoric, Romance, and Technology.* Ithaca: Cornell University.

Patte, Daniel
1974   "An Analysis of Narrative Structure and the Good Samaritan." *Semeia* 2:1-26.

Preminger, Alex, ed.
1965   "Repetition." Pp. 699-701 in *Encyclopedia of Poetry and Poetics.* Princeton: Princeton University.

Propp, V.
1968   *Morphology of the Folktale.* 2nd ed. Trans. Laurence Scott. Austin: University of Texas.

Pryke, E. J.
1967-68   " IΔE and IΔOΥ ." *NTS* 14: 418-24.

Rengstorf, K. H.
1967   See Kittel 4: 414-15.

Richter, Wolfgang
1971   *Exegese als Literaturwissenschaft.* Göttingen: Vandenhoeck and Ruprecht.

Ricoeur, Paul
1967a   "New Developments in Phenomenology in France: The Phenomenology of Language." *Social Research* 34: 1-30.

1967b   *The Symbolism of Evil.* New York: Harper & Row.

1969a   "La structure, le mot, l'événement." Pp. 80-97 in *Le conflit des interprétations.* Paris: Éditions du Seuil.

1969b "The Problem 'of the Double-Sense as Hermeneutic Problem and as Semantic Problem." Pp. 63-79 in *Myths and Symbols: Studies in Honor of Mircea Eliade*. Eds. Joseph M. Kitagawa and Charles H. Long. Chicago: University of Chicago.

1970 "Qu'est-ce qu'un texte?: Expliquer et comprendre." Pp. 181-200 in *Hermeneutik und Dialektik*. Eds. Rüdiger Bubner, Konrad Cramer, Reiner Wiehl. Tübingen: J. C. B. Mohr.

Rist, Martin
1936 "Caesar or God (Mark 12:13-17)? A Study in Formgeschichte." *JRel* 16: 317-31.

Roberts, T. A.
1957-58 "Some Comments on Matthew x. 34-36 and Luke xii. 51-53," *Expository Times* 69: 304-06.

Schneider, Johannes
1964 See Kittel 2: 765-68.

Schürmann, Heinz
1958 "Die Sprache des Christus." *BZ* 2: 54-84.

Schulz, Siegfried
1972 *Q: Die Spruchquelle der Evangelisten*. Zürich: Theologischer Verlag.

Schweizer, Eduard
1970 *The Good News According to Mark*. Trans. Donald H. Madvig. Richmond, Va.: John Knox.

Spivey, Robert A.
1974 "Structuralism and Biblical Studies: The Uninvited Guest." *Int* 28: 133-45.

Stenson, Sten H.
1969 *Sense and Nonsense in Religion*. Nashville: Abingdon.

Strack, Hermann L. and Paul Billerbeck.
1922- *Kommentar zum Neuen Testament aus Talmud und Midrasch*. Vols. 1 and 2. München: C. H. Beck.

Strecker, Georg
  1962   *Der Weg der Gerechtigkeit*. Göttingen: Vandenhoeck &
                  Ruprecht.

Tannehill, Robert C.
  1970   "The 'Focal Instance' as a Form of New Testament
                  Speech: A Study of Matthew 5:39b-42." *JRel* 50: 372-85.

  1974   "The Magnificat as Poem." *JBL* 93: 263-75.

Taylor, Vincent
  1966   *The Gospel According to St. Mark*. 2nd ed. London:
                  Macmillan.

Thayer, Joseph H.
  1892   *A Greek-English Lexicon of the New Testament*. Trans.,
                  rev., and enlarged Joseph H. Thayer. New York: Harper
                  and Brothers.

Theissen, Gerd
  1973   "Wanderradikalismus: Literatursoziologische Aspekte
                  der Überlieferung von Worten Jesu im Urchristentum,"
                  ZThK 70: 245-71.

Via, Dan O., Jr.
  1967   *The Parables: Their Literary and Existential Dimension*.
                  Philadelphia: Fortress.

  1974   "A Structuralist Approach to Paul's Old Testament
                  Hermeneutic." *Int* 28: 201-20.

Weiss, Meir
  1961   "Wege der neuen Dichtungswissenschaft in ihrer
                  Anwendung auf die Psalmenforschung." *Bib* 42: 255-302.

Whalley, George
  1967   *Poetic Process*. First published 1953. Cleveland: World.

Wheelwright, Philip
  1962   *Metaphor and Reality*. Bloomington: Indiana University.

  1968   *The Burning Fountain*. Rev. ed. Bloomington: Indiana
                  University.

Wilder, Amos
  1971   *Early Christian Rhetoric: The Language of the Gospel*.
                  First published 1964. Cambridge, Mass.: Harvard
                  University.

Wissowa, Georg and Wilhelm Kroll, eds.
    1918   *Paulys Real-Encyclopädie der Classischen Altertums-wissenschaft* (Supplement 3). Stuttgart: J. B. Metzler'sche Buchhandlung.

Wittgenstein, Ludwig
    1968   *Philosophical Investigations*. Trans. G. E. M. Anscombe. 3rd ed. New York: Macmillan.

Wrege, Hans-Theo
    1968   *Die Überlieferungsgeschichte der Bergpredigt*. Tübingen: J. C. B. Mohr.

INDEX OF REFERENCES TO THE SYNOPTIC GOSPELS

217

INDEX OF SUBJECTS

219

220

114 n. 54-55, 126, 127, 136, 137, 138-
39, 140, 142, 150-51, 159, 162, 163,
163 n. 108, 164
family 59, 134, 135 n. 81, 138-39, 140,
141-47, 148, 150, 162, 162 n. 107, 164,
166-71. Cf. marriage.
feeling (emotion) 13, 41, 49, 51, 55,
143-44, 167, 179
field of care 31
focal encounter 163 n. 108, 164
focal instance 4, 53, 59, 67, 72-77, 72
n. 17, 75 n. 19, 77 n. 20, 86-87, 86 n.
28, 88, 96, 97 n. 38, 142, 163, 163 n.
108
force, imaginative 26-27, 28, 29, 45,
55, 88, 116, 117, 118, 119, 123-24,
137, 147, 152-53, 155, 156, 165, 170-
71, 178-79, 184
forcefulness 26-27, 41, 44, 51, 53, 63-
65, 64 n. 4, 67, 74, 80, 83-85, 88, 89,
92, 93, 94, 95, 96, 96 n. 37, 98 n. 39,
99, 100, 102, 103, 104, 105-7, 108, 108
n. 49, 110, 111-12, 113, 114-18, 119 n.
59, 120, 121, 122, 125-28, 126 n. 66,
131, 132, 132 n. 74, 133, 134, 136, 137,
138-39, 140, 141, 143, 144, 146, 150 n.
100, 151, 158, 160, 161, 162, 163, 165,
167, 169, 170, 176, 184
form and content 1, 3, 8, 8 n. 4, 9-10,
30, 40, 49 n. 12, 101
form and function 3, 6, 7-10, 26, 55,
56, 61, 66, 68, 71, 72 n. 17-18, 88, 92-
93, 94, 95, 96, 98, 117, 129, 133, 139,
144, 149, 152, 161, 169 n. 116, 170,
174, 184
form criticism 7-10, 72 n. 18
genre (literary type) 2, 4, 4 n. 1, 7-8, 9,
32, 125 n. 65
hermeneutics 23, 31, 35
historical authenticity 5, 5 n. 2, 203
historical study and text interpretation 5, 6-8, 9-10, 129, 132-33,
166, 169, 169 n. 116, 203. Cf.
interpretation (of texts).
holy law, sentences of 112-13, 113 n.
53
humor 151-52. 158-59, 162

hyperbole 8, 27, 52, 53, 76, 82-83, 85,
86 n. 28, 114, 114 n. 54, 116, 118
hypocrisy 27-28, 39, 79 n. 21, 85-86
idea 16, 27, 40, 94, 118-19, 123, 129
identification 156, 159
illuminator 26, 75-76, 75 n. 19, 97, 97
n. 38
image 22, 25-26, 27, 31 n. 7, 55, 62-67,
66 n. 7, 80, 82, 85, 104, 116, 118, 137,
141, 143, 145, 147, 178, 182
imagination 9, 21-28, 29, 45, 54, 66,
67, 73, 75 n. 19, 87, 88, 111, 116-17,
118, 127, 130, 132, 133, 137, 138-39,
143, 153, 156, 159, 165, 167, 181, 183,
203
imagination and the will 21-23
imagination, answering 23-24, 29,
30
imagination, moral 26, 74-76, 75 n.
19
imagination, role in constitution of
the self 21-24, 54, 55, 116-17
imagination, role in intention 23,
24, 54
imagination, role in memory 22-23,
24, 54, 66
Cf. force, imaginative; language,
imaginative.
imaginative shock 22, 23, 53, 54, 74-
75, 75 n. 19, 86, 103
incongruity 151-52, 158
indirectness 56, 69, 71-72, 73, 74, 77,
80, 87, 95, 100-1, 105, 118, 121, 124,
156, 156 n. 101, 159, 163, 164, 169,
170-71
information (in a text) 6-7, 40, 41, 44,
55, 108, 110, 115, 117, 121, 123, 128,
129, 147, 166
interaction 14, 15, 16, 21, 29, 33, 41,
42, 44, 55, 59, 61, 62, 67, 80, 89, 173,
201, 202
interplay (of saying and setting) 152-
54, 158, 165, 178
interpretation (of situations, of one's
world) 8-9, 25-26, 27, 54-55, 75 n.
19, 87, 131-32, 132 n. 74, 183-84
interpretation (of texts) 7, 9-10, 11,

INDEX OF MODERN AUTHORS

65084